AF072529

THE DAY
MICHAEL COLLINS
WAS SHOT

This edition published 2022
by Poolbeg Press Ltd
123 Grange Hill, Baldoyle
Dublin 13, Ireland
E-mail: poolbeg@poolbeg.com

© Meda Ryan 1989

The moral right of the author has been asserted.

Copyright for typesetting, layout, design © Poolbeg Press Ltd

A catalogue record for this book is available from the British Library.

ISBN 978 1 78199-726-0

All rights reserved. No part of this publication may be reproduced ortransmitted in any form or by any means, electronic or mechanical,including photography, recording, or any information storage or retrieval system, without permission in writing from the publisher. The book is sold subject to the condition that it shall not, by way of trade or otherwise, be lent, resold or otherwise circulated without the publisher's prior consent in any form of binding or cover other than that in which it is published and without a similar condition, including this condition, being imposed on the subsequent purchaser.

Cover design by Poolbeg Press

Maps drawn by Curly Cahalane

Printed and bound in the UK using 100% renewable electricity at CPI Group (UK) Ltd

www.poolbeg.com

THE DAY MICHAEL COLLINS WAS SHOT

MEDA RYAN

POOLBEG

About the author

Meda Ryan, historian and author, has participated in radio and television documentaries such as *Scéal Tom Barry* (the latter included in a box set entitled *The Road to Irish Freedom 1916–1923)*. She read the movie script of *The Wind That Shakes the Barley* for scriptwriter Paul Laverty and director Ken Loach, and offered concrete suggestions. During the screening, she was in constant touch with Ken Loach. She also advised scriptwriter and director Neil Pearson on his highly successful play *Guerilla Days in Ireland* (based on Tom Barry's early life).

For much of her work she has used Primary research interviews with participants. She has had articles published in a wide variety of history magazines and journals, and national and local newspapers.

Her published books include *The Day Michael Collins Was Shot* (Poolbeg Press); *Tom Barry: IRA Freedom Fighter* (Mercier Press); *Liam Lynch: The Real Chief* (Mercier Press); *Michael Collins and the Women Who Spied for Ireland* (Mercier Press); *16 LIVES: Thomas Kent* (The O'Brien Press) and others.

When a good chess-player has lost a game and is fully persuaded that the fault was his own, he sets aside the blunders he may have committed during the progress of the game to examine what mistake he made at the beginning, of which his adversary took advantage to compass his defeat. The game of war – a much more elaborate matter – is influenced by the conditions under which it is carried out, and, far from being within the power of one single will, it is the outcome of the friction and shock of all the thousand wills and passions which are brought into play.

Leo Tolstoy, *War and Peace*

For Donal

Contents

Acknowledgements xi

Preface to the First edition 1989 (with update) xvii

THE LEAD-UP
Part I – October 1890 to June 1922 1

Part II – June to August 1922 23

Chapters 1–16 39-254

Postscript 255

Appendix I
Letter from the Provisional Government
at 8.40 pm on 14-7-1922 263

Appendix II
Military Censorship General Instructions – July 1922 265

Appendix III
Peace Proposals – 19th August 1922 267

Appendix IV
W/T Office Portobello – 16th August 1922 269

Appendix V
O'Donoghue's Statement 270

Notes.. 274

Bibliography... 329

Index.. 339

Illustrations
Photographs between..94-95

Maps between..222-223

Acknowledgements

As I look through my notebook of names and addresses, I notice with sadness that many of those who willingly gave information are no longer with us. But without their generosity of spirit there would be no book.

A sincere word of gratitude is due to Jim Kearney and Neilus Flynn who sowed the initial seeds for my research, and were indirectly responsible for this book. I am deeply indebted to Dómhnall Mac Giolla Phóil who went out of his way to locate people for me, and who, with his wife Mary, listened to my problems while I worked on the manuscript. I am also indebted to Eily Hales McCarthy (Tom Hales' daughter) and her husband Gus, who gave me continuous encouragement.

Michael Collins (nephew of General Michael Collins) trusted me with his uncle's original notebooks. Ned Barrett gave me affidavits which he had acquired over the years because of his personal interest in events relating to Michael Collins. I thank both sincerely.

Without the help of Dr. Leo Ahern, Dr. Gerald Ahern, Dr. Christy Kelly, Dr. Michael O'Riordan, Dr. Daniel Coghlan, the late Canon Joe Ahern and a representative of Dr. Cagney, this book would be incomplete.

I am indebted to the kindness of Raymond (Ray) Smith and Jim Nicoll, both of Independent Newspapers, who unreservedly gave me information and guided me towards Jock (John) McPeak's solicitor and the McPeak family. (The latest information available to me confirms that Jock McPeak spelled his name thus and not "McPeake" as many historians have believed. *Document in Cathal Brugha Military Barracks*.)

I am deeply grateful for the assistance and courtesy of the staff in the Archives Department of University College Dublin, and to that department for the use of material; also to the Mulcahy Trust for access to and permission to quote from the papers of Richard Mulcahy; to Kieran Burke and Tom McCarthy, Cork City Library, both of whom speedily responded to my queries; to Brid Frawley of the University of Limerick (N.I.H.E.) Library, who devoted some of her spare time to doing research for me; to Commandant Peter Young, Military Archivist, Cathal Brugha Barracks, Dublin, who was so efficient in his responses to my queries, and to his assistant Sergeant Joe White; to the late Lieutenant Colonel Joseph Foley, Plunkett Barracks; to Commandant David Collins and Lieutenant Tom Boyce, Cathal Brugha Barracks; to the staff at Collins Barracks Dublin; to Brigadier General Kevin Nunan, Lieutenant Colonel Gerry Mulrooney, Captain O'Connor, Pat Lynch and the staff at the Curragh Military Barracks who explained the various types of arms and ammunition to me, who took me on a trip in the *Sliabh na mBan* armoured car and

∽ ACKNOWLEDGMENTS ∽

who showed me around the premises; to Oliver Snoddy of the National Museum, Dublin, who was extremely helpful with all my queries; to Noel Crowley and Mary Moroney, Ennis County Library; to the Library Staff at Mary Immaculate College, Limerick; to the library staff of the *Irish Independent*, the *Irish Times*, the *Irish Press* and the *Cork Examiner*; to the staff of the *Sunday Press*, the *Sunday Independent*, the *Clare Champion*, the *Limerick Leader* and the *Southern Star*; to the staff of Shanakiel Hospital, Cork, and to the Ordnance Survey Office.

The responsive attitude of so many whom I interviewed over the years is deeply appreciated: Daniel Corcoran, Cormac McCarthaigh, Peg Cleary, Tommy Dineen, Dan Cahalane, Conchur Ó Muíneacháin, Ned Galvin, Paddy Lynch, Con Murphy, Michael Murphy, Paddy Desmond, May Twomey, Jim Carmody, Dr. Paddy O'Sullivan, John L. O'Sullivan, Seán Byrne, Mary C. Duggan, Jerh. Galvin, Jack Mahony, Kathleen Donovan O'Driscoll, Kate O'Mahony, John Byrne, Hazel P. Smyth (B&I), Seamus O'Donovan, Brother John Nolan, Finbarr Murphy, Kathleen McCarthy, Agnes Kiely, John Joe O'Sullivan, Rev. Canon Seán Piggott, Nuala Cuddy, Seán Collins-Powell, Michael Collins-Powell, Liam Collins and Cathal O'Shannon; also the late Emmet Dalton, Ernest Blythe, Seán MacBride, Todd Andrews, Bill Powell, Timmy Sullivan, Madge Hales Murphy, Michael Brennan, Joe Dolan, Judge Fionán Lynch, Frank Aiken, Dan Bryan, Tom Kelleher, Pat Buttimer, Billy Barry, Jim Woulfe, Riobárd Langford, Siobhán Lankford, Lena Corcoran, Pake Sheehan, David Neligan, Pádraig Ó Maidín, Seán Hyde, Timmy Kelleher, Mick Sullivan, Liam Deasy, Tom Barry, Charlie Foley,

ACKNOWLEDGMENTS

Jerh. Collins, Michael O'Brien, Dan Sando (Sandow) O'Donovan, Kathy Hayes, Jack Murray, Jerh. McCarthy, Anna Mulqueen, Tom Murray, Charlie O'Shea, Tom Taylor, Denis Lordan, Con Slattery, Bill McKenna, Máire Comerford, General M.J. Costello, John J.O'Connell, James Cahalane, Maurice Collins, Pat Murray, Jim Murray, Tim Allen, Jim Doyle, Nancy McCarthy, Maggie Sheehan, Charlie Brown, Patrick Mahony, Dan O'Callaghan, Jim Riordan, Jack Lane, John Joe Lyons who was most helpful in locating people and places, Professor Lucy Duggan, Mary O'Neill Walsh, Anastasia Ryan, Loretto Hannon and Pat Hannon; also Brian Murphy, Niall Meehan and Jack Lane for their on-going support, and Rizwan Sardar for his help with computer technology.

Grateful thanks is also due to Catriona Ryan, Archives Department of the *Nenagh Guardian* who located newspapers from files; also to the staff at the National Library, especially Berni Metcalfe, Maria O'Shea, Nora Thornton and James Harte who kindly did some research for me, and were most co-operative in locating documents and manuscripts; Lisa Dolan of the Military Archives was most helpful in locating documents in the Pension files; also the National Museum, the Public Records Office, the British Library Board Newspaper, to RTÉ Archives and the Registrars of Deaths in Cork, Ennis and Dublin, and especially the help of Deirdre Griffin.

Curly Cahalane, Architect, was a tremendous help in measuring on location and drawing to scale the maps that accompany this book.

Grateful thanks to Seán Kelleher, Nellie Shannon (Timmy

ACKNOWLEDGMENTS

Sullivan's sister) and the Hales family, Knocknacurra, who gave me photos from their private collections.

Dr. T. Ryle Dwyer read the manuscript in the early stages of the work and I am sincerely grateful for his helpful suggestions.

I would also like to record my thanks to Philip MacDermott and Jo O'Donoghue formerly of Poolbeg Press.

I want to thank the many people who gave me hospitality during the course of my research, and also those who gave me information and assistance but did not wish to be named. Thanks is also due to the many who could not help directly but who took the trouble to write or telephone, explaining where information could be obtained.

I am sincerely grateful to Poolbeg Press, and especially for the continuous help and encouragement of Paula Campbell (Publisher). Sincere thanks to Kieran Devlin (Managing Director) and David Prendergast (Production Manager) for his meticulous attention to detail. Editor Gaye Shortland did tremendous work on the manuscript. I found her extremely thorough and encouraging; she did trojan work as we went over details in order to obtain correctness in so far as was possible.

A special word of gratitude is due to my family, especially Gary, Ita and Zelda, who were most helpful while I researched and wrote the manuscript; furthermore, they did some research for me. Also to relatives and friends for their patience throughout my research and writing.

Any omission in this acknowledgement has not been deliberate, as the assistance of all has been gratefully appreciated.

Preface to First Edition 1989
(with update)

Michael Collins was shot dead in an ambush on 22nd August 1922, and in the years since then conflicting stories have been told about how he met his death. Growing up approximately 10 miles from Béal na mBláth where the ambush took place, I was well aware from an early age of the existence of these differing stories and of the passions they were capable of arousing – but it was not until 1973, when I was researching for a book on guerilla warfare in West Cork, that I became engrossed in the circumstances and the manner of Michael Collins' death.

While I was researching the War of Independence and the Civil War periods in West Cork the names of members of the Hales family of Knocknacurra, Bandon, were regularly mentioned to me. Robert Hales Senior had been a man of determined Fenian opinions and his family had been amongst the first organisers of the Volunteers in West Cork. Three of his sons, Bob, Bill and Seán, fought in the crucial Crossbarry ambush on 19 March 1921 while another son Tom had been serving a jail sentence for Republican activities. Madge, a daughter, was at the same time a dispatch carrier for Michael Collins and liaised with yet another brother, Dónal, an IRA supporter and journalist who was living in Italy.

PREFACE

Seán Hales had been in Frongoch prison with Michael Collins after the Rising of 1916. In January 1919, Collins had helped the family with the formation of the Cork 3rd Brigade at Kilnadur, Dunmanway; by this time he had become a frequent visitor to their home. But it was a friendship that was torn in the bitter divisions that followed the signing of the Treaty. Tom Hales, Michael Collins' best friend, took the anti-Treaty side on his release from jail in December 1921 and in May 1922 Madge tried to pull de Valera from a platform in Bandon, accusing him of having tricked Collins. But the Civil War divisions were most marked on the day that Michael Collins was shot: Seán Hales, Commander of the pro-Treaty forces in West Cork, was one of the last people in Bandon to whom Michael Collins spoke before taking his fatal journey along the road where Tom Hales, his brother, was amongst the Republicans who lay in ambush positions throughout the day.

When Seán Hales was shot dead a little over three months later, on 7 December 1922, it was alleged that he was killed because he was investigating the death of Michael Collins. (Stories abound as to why Hales was shot.)

In the course of my research for the book on guerilla warfare in West Cork, I called on Neilus Flynn. During the interview he informed me that Collins had visited the Hales brothers in his house. (After the Hales' house was burned to the ground by the Black and Tans, some members of the guerilla forces stayed with the Flynns.)

This interview led to questions on Collins' death, and Neilus Flynn confessed to knowing "a Republican" who had participated in the Béal na mBláth ambush. Flynn wasn't sure if this man would grant an interview. "I'll let you know, next time you call," he said.

That man, who after some persuasion agreed to give his version of the story, was Jim Kearney. I was hooked. I had to continue investigating the death of Michael Collins and abandon my original intention of writing a book on guerilla activities in West Cork.

All the publications I encountered further fuelled the speculation as to how Collins met his death, rather than solving the mystery:

Piaras Béaslaí, *Michael Collins and the Making of a New Ireland* (1926): "There are circumstances in connection with the death of Michael Collins which have never been fully cleared up."

Rex Taylor, *Michael Collins* (1958): "Rumour and speculation are to a great extent the aids to the conversation, and the once-yearly ceremony at Béal na mBláth (the place of his death) undoubtedly reopens the topic."

Eoin Neeson, *The Civil War in Ireland* (1989): "Even today, notwithstanding the spate of recent biographical studies in newspaper articles and in book form, the facts relating to the ambush have not yet been fully gathered, evaluated and made public."

Margery Forester, *Michael Collins – The Lost Leader* (1971): "The shot that found him was almost certainly a ricochet, possibly off the armoured car."

F.S.L. Lyons, *Ireland Since the Famine* (1971): "Collins perished in an ambush laid by Irregulars, shot through the back of the head on what can only be described as a characteristically reckless expedition in which no ordinary Commander-in-Chief would have involved himself. But Collins was no ordinary man."

John M. Feehan, *The Shooting of Michael Collins – Murder or Accident?* (1981): "Michael Collins was killed in circumstances open to many different interpretations."

This is just a sample of some authors' treatment of the subject.

Because initially most of my research consisted of interviews, I accumulated numerous recordings and transcripts as I found I had to return many times to key people to clarify points. I encountered many conflicting stories, some of them bizarre. For instance, in a letter to the *Cork Examiner*, 14 September 1927, the Very Rev. P. Treacy, P.P. stated that he agreed with the tenor of a speech delivered by Canon Cahalane who said: "The day Michael Collins was killed, where was de Valera? Ask the people of Béal na mBlath and they will tell you ... The night before the murder, he slept in the immediate neighbourhood."

The numerous innuendos which apportioned "blame" to so many people further demanded that the truth be explored, and exposed.

After I had sent several letters and made telephone calls to Emmet Dalton, he finally agreed to grant me an interview. (Afterwards he co-operated with Cathal O'Shannon on a programme on his own life for RTÉ.) One interview led to another, and I was extremely fortunate in finding Billy Barry (Republican) who was involved with Jock McPeak (National

Forces until he changed sides) in stealing the *Sliabh na mBan* armoured car from Bandon National headquarters in December 1922 and handing it over to the Republicans. This led to my meeting Jim Woulfe, the driver of the armoured car in the Collins' convoy on the day Collins was shot. Woulfe travelled with me on the route from Limerick to Cork, and to West Cork and back to Béal na mBláth. Timmy (Tim) Kelleher, Collins' guide from Macroom to Bandon on that eventful morning, was my passenger on another occasion. Both journeys were made with a recorder running as we travelled. This combination gave me an understanding of Collins' last journey, and the many stops and detours which the convoy was forced to take.

Raymond (Ray) Smith of Independent Newspapers put me in touch with Jim Nicoll, in the London branch of the *Irish Independent*. These men had co-operated in writing a series of four articles in the *Irish Independent* on 18–21, May 1971, based on interviews given by Jock McPeak. Jim Nicholl put me in touch with McPeak's solicitor, who in turn told me where McPeak's wife lived; by this time, McPeak, who had spent the years following his activities in Ireland living under an assumed name, had died in England. (I had hoped to help to fulfil Billy Barry's lifelong wish of a reunion with McPeak.)

A chance encounter at a historical conference brought me in touch with Dr. Daniel Coghlan of Crosshaven. He recommended that I see Dr. Gerald Ahern who had been a doctor in Shanakiel Hospital, where Michael Collins' body had been taken after his death. This opened another area. Dr. Gerald Ahern supplied me with documents and letters that he had obtained from Diarmuid Brennan who had spent years working on a book about Michael Collins. (I spoke to Diarmuid Brennan's sister, Mrs O'Brien.) Dr. Gerald also gave me names, addresses and personal letters which enabled me to get in touch with the doctors (mainly living in various parts of England) who had examined Michael Collins' body.

Meanwhile, I familiarised myself with the stones, the gaps and the ditches at Béal na mBláth. I almost haunted the place. Apart from the obvious advantage of helping me to know what those whom I interviewed were talking about, this also enabled me to gauge the credibility of individual stories.

Word of my research travelled: many times when I returned to my parents' home near Bandon, my father or some member of my family had acquired the name of a person who had requested that I call. And so my list grew.

Varied would be the best word to describe the incidents I encountered during my research – from finding myself lost on dark nights on country roads, to travelling around the Curragh army grounds in the *Sliabh na mBan*. But, forever etched in my memory are the tears in old men's eyes, men who fought either with or against Michael Collins during the Civil War – tears of affection, of grief, and of love of a leader.

Sadly, a substantial number of men and women whom I interviewed for this book are no longer with us; however, I am happy that one of the survivors of the ambush, Jim Kearney, is still hale and hearty. [Jim died on 23rd December, 1995, after my writing this preface to the original publication of this book.] Though he had kept his story from the public for many decades, he said in the course of an interview with me, in 1976, "A country, I hold, that is ashamed of its past has no future."

Many of Michael Collins' friends who took the anti-Treaty side believed that he would not have been pro-Treaty but for his involvement in the Treaty negotiations. Certainly, he felt "the split" more deeply than most. However, his personal writings are infused with hope for unity. Glad that "the foreign Power was withdrawn, the fight with the English enemy was ended", it was his belief that the duty of the Irish people was "to preserve the freedom" which they had won, because he maintained "the only way in which individual views could be rightly put forward by patriotic Irishmen was by peaceful argument and appeal". He asked, "Can we not concentrate and unite, not on the negative, but on the positive task of making a real Ireland distinct from Britain – a nation of our own?" He was convinced that there was only so much he or any leader could do, because "leaders are but individuals and individuals are imperfect, liable to error and weakness. The strength of the nation will be the strength of the whole people."

Many biographies of Michael Collins have been written, so I decided to concentrate on his final days. In the brief outline of his life in the Lead-Up (Part I and Part II), I have made specific reference to two controversial incidents: his alleged involvement in the killing of Sir Henry Wilson and his

∽ PREFACE ∾

appointment as Commander-in-Chief of the army of the Provisional Government.

The multitude of tasks which Collins undertook, especially following his appointment as Commander-in-Chief, would fill volumes. I have chosen only samples from his correspondence to demonstrate the complexity of his responsibilities and the circumstances that led to his death.

The affidavits which were given to me by Dr. Ned Barrett, together with Collins' correspondence in the Mulcahy Papers, other papers and other sources, plus the interviews which I had with Emmet Dalton and Ernest Blythe, have all helped to place in perspective Collins' dilemma in early August. During this period he was caught between working to end the Civil War, and trying to formulate a contingency plan for the six counties.

Historian T. Ryle Dwyer has a recording of an interview given by Michael Collins' sister, Hannie, who had completed arrangements for a holiday in Ireland in August 1922. On the morning of 23 August, 1922, she arrived at work in the Kensington branch of the London Post Office. As she was about to enter her office she was stopped, taken into the superintendent's room and told that there was a rumour her brother had been killed the previous night. She was not surprised; during the night she had a premonition around the time he was killed. "I know how unhappy he had been for so long," she said. At the moment of death "the load went ... from his mind, so it went from mine".

Because my information about the ambush has been

compiled mainly from a vast number of interviews, I have not put individual reference notes in that section; I have given the names of the main contributors and listed the others in the acknowledgement pages. Many people gave me details of what happened as they saw it, only on condition that I would not manipulate their story to suit any particular slant. This I hope I have not done, as I endeavoured to be fair to both the pro- and anti-Treaty sides of the conflict, and considered all the details supplied. The pieces of the jigsaw of events were sometimes hard to find and, even after finding them, often hard to place. Michael Collins became a legend in his own lifetime; because he was killed in the prime of life, that legend grew. The course which the Civil War took after his death, with the execution of prisoners, led people to speculate that if Michael Collins and Seán Hales had lived, the conduct of the war would not have sunk to such a low ebb.

Over forty-three years after Collins' death, in April 1966, Comdt. General Tom Barry (anti-Treaty) stood at Michael Collins' birthplace before an estimated 15,000 people to unveil a monument erected to the memory of the Commander-in-Chief. During his oration, Barry said, "Let us leave it that each of us, like I did myself, believed in the correctness of our choice. I concede that those who were on the opposite side believed that their decision was the right one too." Dr. Ned Barrett, who was responsible for bringing "the two sides" together on that day, could never understand why, during his youth in what he maintained was "a very Republican family", two pictures hung side by side in the living room – "one of

PREFACE

de Valera and the other of Michael Collins". Such was the esteem of the Irish people for Collins.

One of the many surprising discoveries I made while researching the book was that Michael Collins' death has never been registered. This I found out when I tried to acquire a copy of his death certificate, to check the cause of his death.

Now, at last, his death can be registered. Michael Collins was shot dead at Béal na mBláth on 22 August 1922. The mystery of how he was shot is solved in this book, which should finally set the historical record straight.

Meda Ryan
January 1989

Apart from some minor updates, the above preface is as I wrote it in January 1989.

The book was launched in the Imperial Hotel, Cork, on 22 August 1989. That date fell on a Tuesday. So, it was on the exact date and day 67 years previously that Michael Collins had left that premises at 6.10 am according to his diary, and that evening his body was brought back outside the premises.

At the launch that evening John L. O'Sullivan, pro-Treaty Forces, was present. He was one of the last people, with Major General Seán Hales, Column Commander of Government Forces in West Cork, and a few others who had

∽ PREFACE ∽

spoken to Michael Collins prior to leaving Lee's Hotel, Bandon, and heading towards Cork via Béal na mBláth.

Also present was Jim Kearney, engineer, one of the principal participants in the ambush, which was organised by Liam Deasy, G.O.C. Southern Division, and Tom Hales, Comdt. 3rd Brigade anti-Treaty Forces (Seán Hales' brother). These two men met for the first time. It was an emotional meeting. The evening was a memorable one.

Jim Cluskey in *The West Cork News* 25/8/1989, under the large heading **THE TRUCE** wrote:

Two men who had fought in bitterly opposing sides in the Civil War shook hands in Cork's Imperial Hotel last Tuesday – 67 years to the day after the death of Michael Collins. "It was a moment in history that can never be recaptured," according to author Meda Ryan. The coincidence of 67 years to the day was continued into the speeches. The time at which O'Sullivan and Kearney addressed the attendance was as close as made no difference to the time in which the ambush took place. Ms. Ryan commented: "One thing that came out clearly from their speeches was that they both went out to fight as soldiers and they both believed that what they were doing at the time was right."

Tuesday night was replete with coincidences. Because it was in that hotel that Michael Collins slept on the night before his death and to the steps of which he was brought after his death. Meda Ryan commented: "John L. O'Sullivan concluded his speech, with tears in his eyes, as he said: "Michael Collins, wherever you are, Ireland will never forget you.""

PREFACE

Following the publication of the book, there were numerous letters to newspapers, many of them saying that Jim Kearney was not an ambush participant. Also, over the years, writers have denied that he was there and said they could not find any proof that he was. Yet from my research I believe he was one of the principal men (a trained engineer) engaged in the ambush, especially at the later stages when the actual ambush took place, as opposed to the prepared ambush where he and the men waited for the anticipated convoy throughout the day.

Due to this denial, I found it necessary to write a special chapter on Jim Kearney for this edition, using many of his letters and others to newspapers. I have as far as possible allowed the letters and statements to "speak for themselves". Initially, following publication, I was reluctant to write letters to the newspapers to defend his claim, but found that some replies I had to make in letters to newspapers involved such a move.

Over the years I had intended to revisit my initial research due to some inaccuracies, especially on the actual ambush. Also, the map though correctly drawn had people and vehicles in places where they were during the ambush while others were listed in places prior to or at the beginning of the actual ambush. Consequently the main map was misleading.

PREFACE

Therefore, I returned to my original recordings, notes, and transcripts, plus other material, which involved an amount of painstaking work. I also asked Curly Cahalane to redo the maps, taking account of the primary research done on site with ambush participants. We put a tremendous amount of work into inserting what the participant told both of us on the site. We worked on these together.

In the years following my interviews with participants in the ambush, John M. Feehan, Mercier Press (my then publisher) commissioned me to write a short biography of Tom Barry: *The Tom Barry Story*, published 1982. I also researched and wrote *Liam Lynch: The Real Chief*, published by Mercier Press in 1986. While researching and working on these books, I had an opportunity to meet with many of the people who either had participated or had connections to my 'working' book on Collins. My list of friends, contacts and primary sources grew.

Initially, following research, I wrote a draft of a biography of Michael Collins, and within that was '*The Day Michael Collins Was Shot*', but then I realised that story was swamped. Therefore, I decided to concentrate on that, and worked on it more thoroughly, and did much further research, including more interviews with participants.

When I returned to my research for this book, I discovered that I had a vast amount of correspondence in my files on Collins, including responses to my questionnaires. Many decided they would be happy to speak with me personally.

I found correspondence between Dr. Gerald Ahern and his friend Diarmuid Brennan who had done an immense amount of research for a book on which the doctor was working. There was also a vast amount of correspondence with other doctors who examined Collins' body. Dr. Christy Kelly had taken several photos of the body and he had given those to Dr. Gerald. Dr. Gerald had also taken many himself, including of the armoured car. These, as well as other photos, were in his album.

Diarmuid Brennan, in one letter to Dr. Gerald (18/1/1971) said that he could "see '**THE HOODED TERROR**' clearly written in large print on the *Sliabh na mBan* armoured car. He details the capture of it by "the diehards" where after a search the "Government forces found it in a hay shed". It appears that part of the original car has not been found. Therefore, the "clearly written" print has never been located. Whether it is held as a souvenir by somebody or has rotted is unknown.

Dr. Leo Ahern (Major General) who was Dr. Gerald's brother, and Dr. Christy Kelly were the doctors who examined Collins' body in Shanakiel Hospital. The photos of that, which were in Dr. Gerald's album, were given to Diarmuid Brennan.

In a letter from Dr. Gerald (30/11/1974), referring to a letter I had sent him (15/6/1971), he wrote: "Diarmuid Brennan had written a book on Michael Collins. He began his research work in 1969 and had completed the book in 1972, and in 1973 it was in the hands of the publishers. He came to see me three or four times as I had much information. He was to call on me at Christmas, I think, but died suddenly ... The publishers held the publication up on account of a possibility of libel." He mentions relatives and all the "legal complications" and adds "I never got back my photograph book".

Dr. Gerald gave me access to his letters from Diarmuid Brennan, and suggested that if he was of any help to come and "see me and cross-examine me and I will do anything I can that may be of assistance, but please let me have the letters back".

We corresponded and I called to speak to him, at his home in Cork at the time, on many occasions. Later he went to live in England where his brother Dr. Leo lived. I returned the originals of Diarmuid Brennan's letters to him. Due to the loss of Dr. Gerald's photo album, we see only *the one photo* of Michael Collins' body with bandaged head laid out with the soldier-bodyguards, the lighted candles and the large mounted crucifix. This photo was taken by Dr. Christy Kelly. The original is missing.

I wish to state that I find much sadness when I read about all these wonderful people whom I interviewed. I had travelled to different parts of Ireland and to England. This was time-consuming, with early train journeys and late ones also and much driving, but interesting and I believe worthwhile.

In the intervening years since the publication of my book, many other books have been published on the death of

PREFACE

Michael Collins, some based on speculation. There are also new biographies. I discovered that his death had not been registered when writing and publishing my initial book which was 67 years after his death. I have now discovered that it still has not yet been registered, though it is 100 years ago this year. The anniversary is on 22 August 2022. His death should now be registered, as the mystery of how he met his death is solved in this book.

The Lead-Up

Part I – October 1890 to June 1922

Michael Collins was born on 16 October 1890 at Woodfield near Sam's Cross outside Clonakilty, County Cork. His father was seventy-five years old and his mother forty years younger when Michael, the youngest of eight children, was born.

He grew up to be a strong, active child and, as the years progressed, it was discovered that he was intelligent, quick-witted, quick-tempered and that he enjoyed active sport. Early in life, the brown-haired lad was made aware that he would have to find his own place in the world, that there was no money for him on the farm, but that every pair of hands was necessary for farm-work. This became more acute when his father died, just as Michael reached his sixth year.

At Lissavaird, two miles from his home, he attended school under the influential eye of Denis Lyons, a man moulded in the Fenian nationalist tradition, which he passed on to his pupils. Michael was an avid reader. He not only read but studied the writings of Thomas Davis whose works influenced his later perception of Ireland's future. By this time he was "head of his class" in Clonakilty school where John

Crowley was preparing him for the British Civil Service Examination. During the weekdays he stayed with his married eldest sister Margaret (O'Driscoll) and the weekends found him cycling home to Woodfield. Though he had an aptitude for figures, he much preferred the outdoor life, playing hurling and football and competing at running.

At the age of fifteen he passed the Post Office entrance examination and in July 1906 he said goodbye to his sick mother and left Woodfield for a position as a temporary boy clerk in the West Kensington Post Office, London, where his sister Hannie had been working for some years.

For the next nine and a half years he lived with Hannie in a flat over a shop at 5 Netherwood Road, West Kensington. Hannie took him to the homes of her English friends so that he would understand the people among whom he lived, and also understand their way of life.

Six months after he had left home, his mother, who had not been well for some time, died. Because of job pressures and the cost involved, neither he nor Hannie was able to return for the funeral.

He soon joined the Gaelic Athletic Association (GAA) in London and played, usually, at midfield. Though not a skilled player, he was dedicated and fair though his hot temper often caused him to clash all too quickly with his companions. (He was on the winning team that played a Scottish team in Liverpool in 1914.) He became secretary to the GAA's Geraldine Club in 1908 and held the post until 1915. This brought him in contact with the London Irish and introduced him to the Gaelic League classes where Irish language and Irish customs were promoted. Here he explored the stories of the Fenians (1858) who were dedicated to secure the Independence of Ireland and the establishment of an Irish Republic through physical force.

In November 1909 he was "sworn in" as a member of the Secret Society of the Irish Republican Brotherhood (IRB)[1] in Barnsbury Hall Islington, having been introduced to the Brotherhood by fellow Corkman, Sam Maguire.[2] (A leading member of the IRB, Jeremiah O'Donovan Rossa, had been born "only across the fields" from Michael's Woodfield home.)

In this organisation in London, Michael found common ground with fellow countrymen with whom he enjoyed all sports, running and jumping. He got boundless pleasure from wrestling and tussling and he became dedicated to the Irish "national cause".

During his annual holidays he stayed with his brother Johnny and Johnny's wife Kathy at home in Woodfield. He would often be found in some neighbour's kitchen discussing the progress of the IRB and the GAA. During those long summer evenings of his two weeks' holidays, he once again renewed his friendship with Bob Hales, a world champion runner, and the other Hales brothers Seán, Tom and Bill. Not having been endowed with a singing voice, Michael could be relied on to recite his customary poem, "Kelly and Burke and Shea"[3] as he stood his "full height beside the kitchen dresser" during the evening after the harvest had been threshed. And when Jeremiah McCarthy, the local musician, played the barn-dance tune on his accordion, Michael gave full vent to his vigour as he whirled with one of the local girls around the kitchen.[4]

Back in London, he visited the theatre regularly and took a keen interest in painting. During these years he would sometimes be found in the company of the Irish painter, Sir John Lavery and his good-looking wife, Lady Hazel, having been introduced to them in 1913 by Crompton Llewylen Davies. Hazel, born in America of Irish ancestry, liked Ireland and "took a deep interest in Irish affairs".[5] Through his friendship with Crompton Llewylen Davies and his wife Moira (O'Connor), Michael had become part of the "London Society Scene". Crompton Llewylen Davies was Lloyd George's solicitor at the time, and Solicitor General to the British Post Office, where previously Michael had been working in the accounts department. During this period he gleaned knowledge of Lloyd George's temperament upon which, years later, he was able to draw.

Michael, being a good conversationalist and a high-spirited young man, was often invited to parties held in that circle,[6] where art, painting, and literature were discussed, and where he developed a strong friendship with Sir James Barrie, author of *Peter Pan*. Influenced by his circle of friends, he read the works of Dickens, H.G. Wells, Scott and George Bernard Shaw; he even confided copied extracts from Shaw's *The Man of Destiny* to his wallet.

The underlining of a passage in Whitman's *Leaves of Grass* reflects his philosophy at the time:

I exist as I am, that is enough,
If no other in the world be aware I sit content,
And if each and all be aware I sit content.

In 1910 Michael had changed employment from the Post Office to the stockbroking firm of Horne & Co in Moorgate, and shortly afterwards to a Labour Exchange in Whitehall where he earned £70 a year. "The trade I know best is the financial trade, but from study and observation I have acquired a wider knowledge of social and economic conditions and have specially studied the building trade and unskilled labour."[7] As he became competent at typewriting, a further period found him working in the London office of the Guarantee Trust Company of New York.

Early in 1914, he wrote in a personal notebook: "However happy I happen to be in a particular job, the thought is always with me that my future is otherwise than among the facts and figures of money. Yet I do not dream of greater things ... only the thought is always there."[8]

Perhaps it was this thought that sparked off the idea of enrolling as an Irish Volunteer in No. 1 Company, London, on 25 April 1914. He was then 24 years of age. Forthwith he began his weekly contributions towards the purchase of a rifle. His drilling with the company took place in a German gymnasium at King's Cross and, as with all his activities, he endeavoured to give of his best.

August of that year saw the outbreak of the Great War. Talk of conscription began. And in England many Irish, when faced with this prospect, began to return home. By this time Michael had been promoted to the position of treasurer of the IRB for London and the South of England.

Towards the end of the year, he had considered joining his brother Patrick in Chicago, but first decided to take a short trip to Dublin. Through the IRB, he contacted Tom Clarke and Seán Mac Diarmada. After his first meeting with them, he had decided on his future. His return to London was brief.

On 15 January 1916, he left his sister's flat in Kensington (after the British Government had introduced a certain compulsory military service) and journeyed back to Ireland. Back in Dublin, he found employment with Craig, Gardner & Co. Accountants. Here he became friendly with Joe McGrath, who was later to become his "right-hand" intelligence man. In the evenings he became heavily involved in the work of the IRB and the Volunteers where, at Larkfield Manor training camp in Kimmage, he perfected his shot in preparation for the Rising which took place in Dublin on Easter Monday 1916.

Staff Captain Michael Collins served as aide-de-camp to Joseph Plunkett, one of the leaders of the Rising. He was near the front rank of the group that seized the GPO. When the exhausted Plunkett, who was ill, went upstairs to rest during the fighting, Collins took his turn at the operations table in the main office. Despite the confusion, he efficiently plotted positions in other parts of the city on a map and kept the Commanding Officers informed about reports brought in by Cumann na mBan, then acting as women's auxiliary of the Irish Volunteers.

While in charge of the instrument room below the parapeted roof of the GPO, the section of the building that got the greatest shelling from British artillery, he found the heat from the flames intense. Yet, showing no fear, he struggled through flames, and constantly praised the men under his command for their gallantry. Under sniping and gunfire the men held the building until Saturday afternoon when various parts of it were ablaze.

Collins was among the weary men who had to throw down their guns and were led to the lawn of the Rotunda Hospital. There he spent that night with the group under military guard. The following morning the prisoners, cold and miserable, were marched under heavy military escort to Richmond Barracks.

A light-hearted and humorous young man, Collins went into the Rising as if to satisfy his restless spirit and savour his first experience of war. He enjoyed the prestige of soldering: he was cool and efficient. He had set himself a challenge and was determined to achieve honour. Soon he learned that war was no game, that he would have to accept defeat and humiliation and witness suffering. His character was being shaped by the bitter experience of the Rising and by his arrest. Some of his fellow Volunteers would, over the weeks ahead, face the firing squad,[9] while he and others would be imprisoned.

He was one of 238 men shipped from Dublin docks to the detention barracks at Stafford on 1 May 1916, and listed as "Irish Prisoner 48F."[10] Three weeks of solitary confinement were followed by the prisoners being allowed to see each other briefly in the exercise yard. The end of June found him in one of the British internment camps in Frongoch, North Wales. Here two important factors structured his future. First, he formed friendships with men of similar ideas and ideals. Secondly, he advanced his study of the Irish language and English literature. His friendships, his knowledge, his determination, and his ability to think clearly – all these contributed to his leadership qualities and earned him the nickname "The Big Fellow".

Fellow Corkman Seán Hales, who became his greatest friend, was to play an important part in Collins' life during the Civil War. An athlete and sportsman, he was often found wrestling with Collins. The two strong-willed men could be found tussling with each other in the exercise yard, with neither giving in, until exhaustion would demand that they call it quits.

Collins was among the untried prisoners who were released unconditionally in December 1916. He was happy to return to Clonakilty and he walked the last few miles to Woodfield. When he went in the door on Christmas night, he found his family and neighbours "waking" his grandmother whom he loved, and who had died the previous night. Over the following three weeks he sampled the feelings of the people in his native locality and compared these with his own. He discovered that since the Rising and the executions, local volunteer bodies, who had been meeting at centres throughout West Cork, had become more determined to achieve their objective by physical force.

Back in Dublin in January 1917, he found lodgings at 44 Mountjoy Street, which was to be his base over the next few years. His appointment as secretary and accountant of the Amalgamated National Aid Association and Volunteer Dependants' Fund earned him a wage of £2/10s a week. Working at 10 Exchequer Street, he gained important experience which was helpful in his IRB activities later. According to Joe McGrath he was extremely methodical: "a ball of fire, very quick on the uptake, rarely if ever missing a point and a good listener where learning the job was concerned."

His capacity for work impressed all who came in contact with him. Being extremely methodical but quick-tempered, he would sometimes have little patience with those who did not see his point of view. He liked to joke and sometimes swore with a variety of expletives followed by a loud burst of laughter.

At this stage it was becoming clear that he had decided to devote his life to the nationalist cause. With the aid of Ned Broy, an employee of Dublin Castle, Collins began to build a highly professional and successful intelligence network which was eventually to crack the British espionage system in Ireland. In February 1917 he was co-opted to the Supreme Council of the IRB, and with Sam Maguire he made periodic trips to London to organise a system of gun-running. Shortly after the death of his friend, Thomas Ashe[11] (who died in Mountjoy Gaol after being "force-fed"), Collins was appointed secretary of the Supreme Council of the IRB and thus a member of the three-man standing Executive.

In April 1918 Collins was arrested and sent to Sligo Gaol for making a speech in which he told the people to resist the conscription which the British Government intended to enforce on the Irish people. He was one of the first to jump bail and go on the run, a decision which was to become policy for the movement. (He successfully evaded capture for the duration of the War of Independence.)

In the 1918 general election he was returned as Sinn Féin member for South Cork and took his seat in January 1919. He was appointed Minister of Home Affairs and later, as Minister of Finance, was responsible for organising a successful National loan. He continued to be an active member of the IRB Executive, and in mid-1919 he became President of the Supreme Council, a post which he held until his death.[12]

By now Volunteers were being trained throughout the country and ambushes, raids and arrests were taking place – what was later called the War of Independence.

The British intelligence structure was efficient and powerful with vast resources and a reputation for invincibility, yet within a few years Collins had broken it. He created his own spectacular system which monitored British military planning. His men sorted mail in post offices throughout the county; they were porters in hotels, ticket collectors in railway stations, workers in factories, dockers in ports and warders in prisons. In the Post Office, Collins' cousin Nancy O'Brien arranged for decoded messages to be sent to him. In important military centres around the country he had men and women who supplied information. Many ordinary people were the eyes and ears that aided Collins' network. Furthermore, he tabulated material received from four key men who infiltrated G-Division (plainclothes detective division) of Dublin Castle (Joe Kavanagh, James MacNamara, Ned Broy and Dave Neligan). In the second half of 1919, when the war against the British intensified, Collins structured a special "Squad" made up of twelve men who were given the task of eliminating key members of British Intelligence.

In early October 1920 a special group of British officers with Secret Service training (under Col. Sir Arthur Winter) arrived in Ireland, hoping to crack Collins' network. They mingled with some of the G-men in the Castle, but mainly they posed as businessmen, and were dubbed "The Cairo Gang" – not because they had anything to do with Cairo (as has always been believed) but because they frequented a pub known as The Cairo.[13]

Through Collins' intelligence system, detailed information was obtained about them, and in a simultaneous attack on their homes, digs and guesthouse accommodation, in a pre-dawn raid on 21 November 1920, the Squad shot dead eleven British Intelligence agents.[14] This provoked a reprisal: British forces invaded Croke Park that afternoon while a football match between Tipperary and Dublin was in progress, firing indiscriminately on the players and the crowd. Twelve people died, including a woman and two children, and sixty were wounded.

Collins, meanwhile, rode around Dublin on an rusty old

bicycle. He attended meetings in various pubs and venues, often avoiding capture by seconds. Once, when his office was being raided, he heard men coming to his door so he handed his revolver to his secretary. He went to the window but discovered there was no down-pipe, so he gathered up a bundle of papers, bustled past the men at the door, went up one flight of stairs and out through the skylight.

Many instances have been recorded where Collins narrowly avoided being captured. Twice on Christmas Eve 1920 he evaded the police. Early in the night, he had asked for a private room in the Gresham Hotel for a meeting with some of his men, but none was available. As the men made their way to the main dining room they were stopped by a group of Auxiliaries. Collins, though caught with an Ordnance Survey map in his pocket, bluffed his way out, went with his companions to Vaughan's Hotel (one of his regular haunts) and had only just left that premises when the place was raided.

During this period while de Valera was in America collecting funds, Collins was a regular visitor to the de Valera family home in Greystones, lending moral support to de Valera's wife, Sinéad.

While on the run he stayed in a hotel in Granard, County Longford, owned by the Kiernan family. He became friendly with the attractive Kitty Kiernan and soon a romance developed. In times of separation she wrote to him constantly, and he responded often, sometimes with brief notes. Their prolific letter-writing during the short period of their association can be found in a book entitled *In Great Haste*. edited by Leon Ó Broin (Pub: St. Martin's Press), and in *Michael Collins and the Women Who Spied For Ireland*, by Meda Ryan (Pub: Mercier Press).

In Collins' native West Cork during this period, the guerilla campaign had been notably successful under the leadership of such men as Tom Barry and Liam Deasy. In mid-May 1921, Collins decided that he would like to discuss the campaign with Tom Barry, Commander of the 3rd West Cork Flying Column. (Tom Hales, Collins' close friend, had been instrumental in the setting-up of a volunteer force in various districts of Cork No 3 Brigade. This active-service force was termed a Flying Column and would be rapidly trained to participate in ambushes and raids. Hales was arrested on 27 July 1920; a few months later Tom Barry became commander of this newly formed column, and achieved success in ambushes such as Kilmichael, Crossbarry, Rosscarbery, and others.) When they met, Barry informed Collins that more arms and ammunition were urgently needed in order to step up the campaign so that the British government would be pressurised into a surrender situation. Dónal Hales, a journalist in Italy,[15] with whom Collins was in constant contact, was in the process of securing a shipment of armaments which was to land near Union Hall in West Cork. Though a big planning operation was undertaken by the IRA in West Cork in preparation for the armament, this shipment did not materalise. And, by mid-1921, events seemed to be closing in on Collins. Dave Neligan was the only "inside" intelligence man left in the Castle and he told Collins "things are getting hot". Furthermore, a bid to rescue the jailed Seán MacEoin, leader of the Longford Flying Column, failed. Almost in despair, Collins wrote: "Cork will be fighting alone."[16]

Lynch's membership of the Supreme Council of the IRB was the coordinating link between Collins, president of that council, and other leading members – Richard Mulcahy and Eoin O'Duffy. Liam Lynch was Comdt. Cork No 1 Brigade. Liam Deasy was Comdt. No. 3 Brigade and Seán Moylan was Comdt. No 2 Brigade.

Pleading for arms by the three Cork Brigades was useless. Collins and GHQ were powerless. Collins told de Valera "unless the boys get arms and ammunition, it's all over". He decided to make one more effort and sent Madge Hales over to her brother Dónal in Italy; she was to report back to Collins on the position.[17]

It had reached the stage where further resistance was proving increasingly difficult for Collins. Cracks had begun to appear in his intelligence system and he began to doubt whether the Volunteers could hold out for very much longer as an effective force.[18] Madge Hales arrived back from Italy in June 1921 and informed Collins that only half a boatload of armaments could be obtained, and other difficulties meant that the anticipated arms shipment to Ireland was postponed again.[19]

There was talk that a truce was imminent, and on 11 July a truce was announced which was welcomed not alone by Collins but by all of the IRA.

In Collins' native county the three Cork Brigades hoped

it would be a short truce and that a fresh supply of ammunition would soon make it possible for them to renew the fight. However, these men who were not consulted felt they should have been, especially because Collins had shown his appreciation of their intensive fighting.[19] It appears that seeds of discontent were sown at this period which were to spring to life later.

Collins was aware of the failure to obtain munitions and how this very serious shortage hampered the fight, "because men, no matter how determined they may be, or how courageous, cannot fight with their bare hands".[20] Yet, he did not inform any of the brigades of the difficulties he had encountered in the acquisition of the Italian arms shipment and so the information remained within GHQ. This was a mistake on Collins' part which later was to create many enemies for him.

By this time de Valera made it known that he was prepared to talk to Lloyd George and subsequently received an invitation to London.

Following intensive Dáil debates, it was decided that Collins should be among the five-man delegation led by Arthur Griffith, which would travel to London to negotiate treaty settlement terms. Collins was reluctant to accept this responsibility. He maintained that by remaining at home he would be in a stronger position to influence Republicans towards a compromise settlement, which all felt sure would be the outcome. But de Valera argued that Collins was vital to the delegation.[21]

Speaking in the Dáil, Collins said, "To me the task is a

loathsome one. If I go, I go in the spirit of a soldier who acts against his judgement at the orders of a superior officer."[22] But de Valera could not be dissuaded and, when Cathal Brugha and Austin Stack refused to go, Collins accepted the responsibility. "I had no choice," he said. "I had to go."[23]

On Saturday, 8 October 1921, before his departure for London, he became unofficially engaged to his girlfriend Kitty Kiernan. In a letter to her he wrote of "an arrangement" they had. They would keep in touch, they would write to each other, and he would be home periodically. The first meeting of the delegation took place in London on 11 October 1921. Throughout the period of negotiations, he wrote to Kitty regularly. Mostly it was just a few lines, letting her know how he felt about the progress of the negotiations and some personal words. He telegraphed her to visit him. With her sister she made the trip to London in late October.

One day Michael asked Kathleen Napoli McKenna, one of the secretaries, to accompany the Kiernan sisters on a shopping expedition. They each were to select a gift for which he would pay. Kitty selected a smart woollen dress. Kathleen McKenna said, "Mick, who was very much in love with Kitty, was a proud man as he left Cadogan Gardens with one of the sisters on each arm". (Their engagement was not officially announced until after the Treaty ratification.)

Collins was an able negotiator. During one of the committee meetings in the London debates, Churchill was arguing some carefully prepared points while the Irish delegation remained silent.

"Have you any answer to these?" Collins scribbled on a note to Emmet Dalton.

"No," came Dalton's reply.

Having listened a while longer, Collins suddenly became exasperated and slammed his fist on the table. "For Christ's sake, come to the point!"

Churchill sat speechless. While he still had a stunned expression Collins erupted into an infectious laugh which Churchill, in spite of himself, soon joined, thereby dissipating much of the force of his carefully prepared case.[24]

On the afternoon of 5 December 1921, Lloyd George held up two envelopes, saying: "Here are the alternative letters which I have prepared ... we must have your answer by 10 pm tonight. You can have until then, but no longer, to decide whether you will give peace or war to your country."[25]

When the delegation withdrew, "Michael Collins rose, looking as though he was going to shoot someone. I have never seen so much pain and suffering in restraint," wrote Winston Churchill.

Late that evening Collins visited his friends Sir John and Lady Hazel Lavery at 5 Cromwell Place. He was extremely angry that pressure was being brought to bear on him, because he disagreed with aspects of the Treaty. Sir John failed to dissuade him when he "lost his temper". But eventually "after hours of persuasion" Hazel succeeded in calming him. Then "She took him to Downing Street in her car that last evening, and he gave in," Sir John wrote.[26]

Collins was reluctant to embroil Ireland in a further war.

He knew more than any member of the delegation how his efforts to obtain further arms had failed. He was aware, as he wrote afterwards, that the alternative to the Treaty "sooner or later" was war, and aware also that "what we fought for at any particular time was the greatest measure of freedom obtainable at that time ..."

At 2.20 on the morning of 6 December, both sides signed the "Articles of Agreement for a Treaty between Great Britain and Ireland". The first and basic section stated that Ireland would have the same constitutional status in the British Empire as Canada, Australia, of New Zealand and South Africa "with a Parliament having powers to make laws for the peace, order and good government of Ireland and an Executive responsible to that Parliament, and shall be styled and known as the Irish Free State".

Afterwards, Birkenhead said, "I may have signed my political death warrant tonight."

Collins replied, "I may have signed my actual death warrant."[23]

After signing the Treaty, Collins went back to the Laverys' home where he was able to relax after a difficult day's bargaining. Then he returned to his lodgings in the early hours of the morning and went to bed. Though he regarded the Treaty as "the first real step for Ireland", deep down he was aware that many of his friends both in the Volunteers and in the Dáil would not accept his explanation.

He could not rest so he got up and in a letter to his friend, John O'Kane, asked: "Will anyone be satisfied at the bargain?" He could visualise the disturbance that was about to erupt.

He was writing his obituary because, as he told O'Kane, "a bullet might just have done the job five years ago".[29]

It was a disturbed Collins who returned to Ireland to face the Dáil questioning.

He never hid the fact that he disliked politics and was much more at ease while working on intelligence and soldiering. "To be a politician one needs to keep tongue in cheek for all of the day and most of the night; one needs to have the ability to say one thing and mean another; one needs to be abnormally successful at the art of twisting the truth," he wrote. "Can you wonder that I think and think, yet never manage to achieve peace of mind? It is more than possible that one's words will be taken out of context, twisted, warped, shaped into a lie, and be flung back into my teeth."[30]

Back in the Dáil in Dublin, after some intense discussion and often bitter remarks, the Treaty motion was carried by seven votes on 7 January 1922.[31] Subsequently, de Valera resigned as President of the Republic and Arthur Griffith was elected in his place. Griffith appointed a cabinet which included Collins as Minister of Finance. The ratification of the Treaty opened the way for the foundation of a Provisional Government which assembled on 14 January. Michael Collins was elected Chairman.

Political confusion reigned as Griffith and his temporary government endeavoured to complete the business of the Second Dáil and Collins and his Provisional Government proceeded to take over power in the area encompassing the Twenty-Six Counties as constituted by the 1920 Government of Ireland Act. Control of the Six (northern) Counties rested with Stormont.

As army barracks were being evacuated by the British military they were being replaced by either pro- or anti-Treaty men depending on the area or the circumstances. Military men who declared for acceptance of the Treaty were armed, uniformed and paid by the Provisional Government, thus fanning the nucleus of the "National" army (later the Free State Army), with headquarters at Beggar's Bush. Anti-Treaty men like Liam Lynch, Rory O'Connor, Tom Barry and others regarded this as a betrayal of Mulcahy's undertaking that the IRA would be maintained as the Army of the Republic. The seeds of a military struggle were being sown.

An air of hostility began to emerge throughout the country as anti-Treatyites began to make their presence felt. Despite the Dáil cabinet's prohibition, an army convention was held on 26 March with the intention of renewing the army's allegiance to the Republic. The result of this convention was a split in the army. An Executive and an Army Council with Liam Lynch as Chief of Staff were formed. This meant there were two armies in the country, one loyal to the Provisional government and the other to the Republican Executive. On 14 April, Rory O'Connor seized the Four Courts as headquarters despite Liam Lynch's opposition to the move. This act was seen by Churchill as a major act of defiance against the Provisional Government. Collins and Richard Mulcahy (Minister of Defence) were reluctant to act against former comrades, and did everything possible to avoid open confrontation.

Ironically, Collins and Lynch continued to work together in sending arms to the North. At this stage, they wanted to help Northern Catholics who were the victims of pogroms. Because it was vital that guns sent to the North should not be traced back to the Provisional Government, Collins insisted that the Executive men (anti-Treatyites) should supply an agreed number of rifles towards "the Northern operation". Beggar's Bush (Army of the Provisional Government) then replaced these with an equal number of British-supplied weapons. Both the Republican Executive and Beggar's Bush co-operated in supplying men for an offensive which began in Belfast on 18 May 1922. Even after the army split, both sides (Lynch and Collins to the fore) had a common policy which they continued to operate jointly, though two separate army commands had been structured.[32] This shows that Collins was prepared to work with his opponents to undermine one aspect of the Treaty, while supporting the Treaty in public. He was well aware of the ambiguity of this situation.

During the early months of 1922, IRB conferences continued to be held in an effort to save the organisation from splitting on the Treaty issue. Though Collins and Lynch were the principal protagonists on the opposing sides, each respected the other's apparent immovable position; there was a sense of brotherhood born out of their intimate association during the War of Independence. However, as President of the Supreme Council, Collins succeeded in getting the organisation to accept the Treaty. This led inevitably to further conflict.

At a Republican Executive convention held on 18 June,

Tom Barry proposed that instead of further discussion on army reunification, the convention should give an ultimatum to the British Government to withdraw their troops within seventy-two hours.[33] He wanted to renew the war with Britain and hoped that this would unite the army. When Lynch, Deasy and Moylan disagreed, a split occurred on the issue. Joseph McKelvey was voted to replace Lynch as Chief-of-Staff of the Executive. Tom Barry, Rory O'Connor and Liam Mellows left the meeting.

An election was held in June 1922 and, despite the existence of a Pact between de Valera and Collins to rule out confrontation between Treatyites and anti-Treatyites, the vote turned out to be an expression of the people's views on the Treaty. The election results announced on 24 June showed that out of one hundred and twenty-eight seats, fifty-eight pro-Treaty candidates were elected and thirty-five anti-Treaty – plus thirty-five others. Collins was later accused of sabotaging the pact.

Events were gaining momentum. The political atmosphere created by the Treaty division was now cemented by the failure of the Pact, and the collapse of the attempt at army reunification.

The Lead-Up

Part II – June to August 1922

In London, Reginald Dunne and Joseph O'Sullivan of the IRA's London battalion assassinated Field Marshall Sir Henry Wilson, Military Adviser to the Six County Administration, on 22 June 1922. Dunne and O'Sullivan were arrested.

The British ministers incorrectly blamed the Four Courts garrison for the killing, believing that they had ordered the assassination. Rory O'Connor made a public statement that he had nothing to do with the killing. "If we had, we would admit it." It has been alleged that Collins ordered or consented to the killing, yet this has never been established. He had given an order for the assassination in pre-Treaty days and it has been suggested that this was never cancelled. But Joe Dolan of Collins' old intelligence group said that Collins instructed Sam Maguire, O/C Britain during the Anglo-Irish War, to carry out the execution. Maguire, he said, carried out the order by asking "Dunne O/C London to do the job". Margery Forester in *The Lost Leader* states: "Collins was not a man who absent-mindedly left execution orders unrevoked. It is infinitely more probable that, far from doing so, he renewed the order to Dunne shortly before it was carried out when the Belfast pogroms were at their height."[1]

It is true that, angered by the frequent and futile murders of Catholics in the North, Collins insisted that it was the duty of the British Government and particularly that of Wilson (whom he mistrusted) to restore order in the North of Ireland. By now he believed northern events were moving towards a state of conflict in which the south would become involved, thus wrecking the Treaty and his "stepping-stone" policy.

However, Collins agreed with Griffith's assessment of the killing of Wilson that "It is a fundamental principle of civilised government that the assassination of a political opponent cannot be justified or condoned".

Regardless of whether or not Collins had any knowledge of, or any involvement in, Wilson's death, he took full responsibility for the lives of Dunne and O'Sullivan. He sent Tom Cullen to London to see if they could be freed or if there were any escape possibilities. All of Collins' plans to rescue the two men were futile, having proved impracticable, even his bizarre scheme to have a distinguished British person taken and held as a hostage.[2]

When the London Government placed blame for the killing on the anti-Treaty forces in the Four Courts, Collins searched for a way out of the dilemma. "He paced the floor, hurried out to see Tim Healy about legal counsel for their trial, and brushed aside other pressing business even from close colleagues with the curt rejoinder that Dunne and O'Sullivan were more important."[3]

Ernest Blythe was present when Griffith and Collins jointly formulated a statement of condemnation for the press. Watching and listening to the two men, Blythe formed the impression "that though Collins was as disturbed as Griffith was, he had more information about it than his senior colleague ... But that does not mean that he was involved. The London branch [IRB] could have decided ... perhaps they had their own motives" for killing Wilson.[4]

Despite publicly condemning the assassination, Collins' "dualism" had him privately seeking rescue methods. The event led to emergency cabinet meetings being held in London. Though the British could not prove any connection between the shooting of Wilson and the IRA in the Four Courts, suspicion was deep because documents were found on Dunne and O'Sullivan which referred to an IRA scheme and the need for organisation in London.[5]

Mentally, Collins was in a state of torture. Blythe remembers him being irritable while he searched for a "loophole". He gave the impression that "he didn't want his former colleagues who were in the Four Courts to be blamed in the wrong, even though they were fast becoming his military enemies".[6]

Despite all Collins' efforts to free the men, Dunne and O'Sullivan were tried at the Old Bailey on 18 July, 1922, found guilty and sentenced to death.[7] Nevertheless, as the days moved on Collins was still troubled. Mr McDonnell of London sent him a "note of the evidence at the appeal" and arising from this Collins wrote to Cosgrave: "I am of the opinion that we must now make an official representation that mercy be extended to these men. Please let me know what is being done in the matter."[8]

Collins' letter was discussed at a Provisional Government meeting "and it was decided that official representations should be made to the British Government on behalf of these men". [9]

The Law Officer prepared another appeal which was unsuccessful. The law took its course.

Despite Collins' allegiance to his colleagues in the Provisional Government and the honouring of the Treaty signature, he was up to this period engaged in a dualist approach, especially in his activities relating to the Northern operation. His method was to placate both of the divisions which resulted from the army split. Moreover, he continued his membership of the IRB (secret organisation) together with Lynch. Reginald Dunne was also a member of this organisation. Dunne had not actively either opposed or supported the implementation of the Treaty, but like Sam Maguire he was great friends with Collins since their London IRB days. So whether the assassination of Wilson, which was planned by the London IRB network, was carried out under Collins' orders, or taken on by Dunne to win favour with Collins or in the hope of uniting the army to a common purpose is a debatable point.

Collins' attempt to seek a reprieve for Dunne and O'Sullivan does not necessarily mean that he had ordered the killing of Wilson; his concern might only have meant that he wanted to secure his friends' freedom. Moreover, he was, during this period, still communicating with the anti-Treatyites.

Dunne's anger expressed to Bill Aherne the week before the killing does not bear out the allegation that Collins had given the order to assassinate Wilson. Bill Aherne (an anti-Treaty supporter) told Ulick O'Connor that he met Reggie Dunne in Dublin a week before the affair and "he remembered clearly how angry Dunne was that Collins would not allow him proceed with the killing".[10]

Furthermore, Collins spoke to Emmet Dalton during a visit to Portobello Barracks a few days after the shooting of Wilson about a modus operandi in connection with Dunne and O'Sullivan. The possibility of organising an escape was discussed. These men were Collins' friends. According to Dalton, Collins was angry that the London IRA had taken an irresponsible attitude "at this time" – this was a day or two prior to the decision to shell the Four Courts. "Collins had enough of problems around this period; he was hoping that army reunification was still a possibility," said Dalton. "Therefore, I do not believe that Collins ordered the shooting of Wilson at this time ... Any orders prior to the Truce were revoked when the Truce was declared."[11]

Whoever ordered or decided on the shooting of Sir Henry Wilson, the event brought matters swiftly to a head.

On the day Wilson was shot Lloyd George wrote to Collins "to inform" him "that documents have been found upon the murderers" which "reveal the existence of a definite conspiracy against the peace and order of this country". Other information revealed "that active preparations are on foot among the irregular elements of the IRA to resume attacks upon the lives and property of British subjects both in England and in Ulster". Lloyd George was no longer prepared to permit Rory O'Connor "to remain with his followers and his arsenal in open rebellion in the heart of Dublin, in possession of the Courts of Justice ... " On behalf of "His Majesty's Government" he felt "entitled" to ask Collins to "formally" bring "to an end" this "state of things".

Furthermore, he was prepared to place at Collins' disposal "the necessary pieces of artillery which may be required".[12]

Whatever Collins' involvement in the death of Wilson, he took full responsibility and yielded to British pressure. On 24 June, Macready, still in command of the remnant of British forces in Dublin, received orders to attack the Four Courts the following day.[13] While he was preparing to carry out orders the British Cabinet altered its decision, and in agreement with Macready cancelled its instructions. Instead, Churchill, speaking in the House of Commons on 26 June, gave the Provisional Government an ultimatum. Unless they brought the occupation of the Four Courts to a speedy end, the Treaty would be regarded as having been violated and so "full liberty of action" would be resumed.

The other issue that made the storming of the Four Courts inevitable was the holding (as hostage) of pro-Treaty Deputy Chief-of-Staff, J.J. (Ginger) O'Connell by Executive Forces. He was held in order to secure the release of Leo Henderson who had been arrested by Provisional Government troops whilst on the point of commandeering transport for the removal of supplies to the North – a project on which both sides (Collins' men/Lynch's men) were still nominally cooperating. Collins' dualism had to stop.

"It was decided" by him and by the Provisional Government at an emergency meeting that "notices should be served on the armed men in illegal occupation of the Four Courts and Fowles Hall that night, ordering them to evacuate the buildings, and to surrender up all arms and property". Should they refuse to comply with this order then Collins was determined that "the necessary military action would be taken at once".[14]

Blythe believed that in agreeing to lay siege to the anti-Treaty forces in the Four Courts, Collins hoped that those inside would surrender and, as a consequence, the lives of Dunne and O'Sullivan who were awaiting execution could be saved.[15]

Liam Lynch visited the Four Courts on the night of 27 June. Here the split in the Republican garrison was healed and Lynch resumed his position as Chief-of-Staff. Ernest Blythe said that the cabinet members believed "the Republicans were still split when we laid siege to the Four Courts. Collins estimated that because Lynch was not with them, our task would be easy."[16]

On Wednesday 28 June, an ultimatum delivered to the Four Courts garrison to surrender before 4 am yielded no response. At 4.07 am two eighteen-pounder guns borrowed from the British Army opened fire on the building and so the Civil War officially began. By Friday, 30 June, the Republican garrison had surrendered unconditionally. Churchill was pleased and sent a congratulatory telegram to Collins.

The day of reckoning had arrived for Collins. He would now have to be prepared to fight openly against his friends. Lynch, Deasy and a number of the Republican Executive, who were in the Clarence Hotel across the river from the Four Courts when the attack opened, issued a hurried proclamation calling on the Republican army to resume the fight for the Republic. They made their way south, where the area south of a line stretching from Waterford to Limerick was to be held by the Republicans. Oscar Traynor took command in Dublin, where, during that week sporadic skirmishes caused much destruction.

At a meeting of the Provisional Government on 1 July, Collins announced that Richard Mulcahy, Minister of Defence, had transferred to Portobello Barracks, and had taken over command, and that Collins himself would act as Minister of Defence for the present. Also, "the Minister of Labour Mr Joe McGrath had taken up duties in the same barracks".[17]

On 3 July, at a Government meeting, it was decided that "the Army should be increased by a Volunteer Force, up to an extra 20,000 men levied throughout the country, to serve for a period of six months," at an estimated cost of £3,000,000.[18]

Problems were mounting for Collins. Demanding decisions had to be made daily.

During early July, anti-Treaty forces constantly clashed with Government forces, and it looked as though the Government, the Treaty and all that Collins had worked for were swiftly being eroded. Sporadic fighting had begun to spread throughout various parts of the country and, as most of the military barracks and the main cities and towns were in the hands of Republican forces, it was time to act. Matters discussed at Government meetings concerned military decisions rather than political issues. Collins needed to get a grip on the problems. He would go back to soldiering and take command. He wrote to W.T. Cosgrave, pointing out the priority required for military matters, suggesting that the government should issue "a sort of official instruction" on the formation of a War Council and appoint him as Commander-in-Chief.[19] So, at a Government meeting on Wednesday 12 July, Collins "announced that he had arranged to take up duty as Commander-in-Chief of the army and would not be able to act in his ministerial capacity until further notice, and that Messrs. O'Higgins, McGrath and Fionán Lynch had also been appointed to military posts".

At this meeting W.T. Cosgrave, Minister of Local Government, "was appointed to act as chairman of the Provisional Government and as Minister of Finance in the absence of Mr. Collins on military duties". There was agreement "that Parliament should be prorogued for a further fortnight, to meet on Saturday 29th instant, and that an official proclamation should be issued to that effect".[20]

A further meeting held later in the day dealt with the establishment of the Civic Guards and the proroguing of parliament, before moving on to discussion on the military situation. The Civil War was raging so this was the important matter. Collins was clearly commander of the military situation since the morning meeting. At this meeting three men were appointed to form a War Council: "Michael Collins – General Commander-in-Chief; Richard Mulcahy – General Chief of Staff and Minister of Defence. Eoin O'Duffy – General in Command South-Western Division."[21]

In recent years it has been alleged that Michael Collins was ousted from his position as Chairman of the Provisional Government and given the job as Commander-in-Chief of the Army in order to reduce his political power. But the note in his diary on the 12 July does not support this argument.

"At Gov. meeting this evening Council of War appointed, M.C. C in C; R.J.M. M.D. & C of S; G.O.D. South W. Command."[22]

This is an abbreviated version by Collins, recording the meeting and using the word "appointed".

From Collins' correspondence in this period, it is obvious that his principal aim was to get the country back to stability. As soon as he got into his office in Portobello Barracks, he set about organising the army,[23] organising reconnaissance[24] to monitor the activities of the anti-Treaty forces, and organising his "Immediate Objective"[25] of sending officers with men into each area. He wanted details of arms captured or surrendered,[26] he commanded that garrisons be strengthened,[27] he ordered commanders to take towns and to move on with their men,[28] he wanted lists of vehicles taken over from the British,[29] and ships should be prepared for the transportation of troops by sea.[30] Clearly, from the day he took over he fulfilled the role of General Commanding-in-Chief (title conferred on him)[31] for the Army of the Provisional Government.

The official letter sent to Collins and signed by members

of the Provisional Government stated: "You have been entrusted with the Supreme Command of the National Army and with General Mulcahy and General O'Duffy you have been constituted a War Council to direct the military operations now in progress ..."[32] (See Appendix I)

The *Irish Times* carried a leading article on Collins' appointment as Commander-in-Chief, regarding it as "a wise move ... everything must be done that is essential to deal with the heavy task that lies before the National force in the South and portions of the West".[33]

So, temporarily relieved of ministerial duties, Collins moved into quarters at Portobello Barracks. He disliked wasting time, as his notebook conveys. On this his first day in the barrack quarters, he wrote, "Spent the morning rather wastefully owing to delay B. of Works in fitting up rooms for working in".[34] In many of his letters he addressed Cosgrave as "Acting Chairman" or "Acting Minister of Finance" depending on the contents. Cosgrave wrote to Collins as "Commander-in-Chief" or "General Commanding-in-Chief" depending on the letter. On a few occasions Collins signed himself under the style of "Chairman"[35] and still regarded himself as such; however, his task at this period was to safeguard the stability of the country.

The administration of the National Army was a substantial responsibility. It would take time to organise the distribution of payment, food supplies and clothing to scattered groups of soldiers constantly on the move. Tirelessly, Collins worked into the night hours at his Portobello desk, as the letters and his notes show.[36] His notebook of those July days bears witness to the urgency with which he tackled most tasks and the number of items that crowded upon him. There were prison accommodation, medical service, engineering, press data, intelligence lists and a multitude of other concerns.

Clearly Collins was back on familiar ground, endeavouring to put behind him the arena of politics and concentrate all his energies on the military aspect. When Churchill wrote concerning political matters, Collins responded, "Since I have been entrusted with supreme command of the National Army, I have scarcely a moment for any business other than the urgent business of restoring peace and settled conditions to the country."[37]

Collins was concerned that the situation for Catholics in the North of Ireland was deteriorating and felt that the restoration of order was vital. Consequently, he said in a letter to Churchill that "were it not for my new obligations and commitments I would be devoting all available time and energy towards its solution".[38]

He sought and obtained support from the Government to make certain "political" decisions,[39] and he allotted to Dalton the task of recruiting men from the Legion of Irish Ex-Servicemen.[40]

Collins maintained that the majority of the Irish people accepted the Treaty. It was agonising for him that "the good fighting men from Cork" were his "opponents" but he hoped that without the support of the people they would "soon realise they have no hope"[41] because in this Civil War men "have died and are suffering for the very same principle that we fought the British for ..."[42]

He left the lines of communication open and was willing to talk to mediators, yet his primary objective was to get Republican-held areas under Provisional Government control and to stop the seizure of money from banks[43] and other revenue sources, thus suffocating the opposition before they could gain a secure foothold.

Having received reports that intensive organisation was being undertaken by the anti-Treaty leaders and reports also that they were gaining support in County Cork, Collins felt this could only be counteracted by co-ordinating the National troops and using the tactics of "a sudden swoop".

The sadness of Civil War is felt most when life-long friends become bitter enemies or when brothers and neighbours take opposite sides; indeed, Collins found the heartbreak of friends deciding to take the opposing viewpoint a piercing reality. This was brought clearly home to him when his friend Harry Boland was shot by Government forces while being taken prisoner on the night of 30 July; it marked a moment of truth.

In a letter to his girlfriend Kitty Kiernan, he mentioned seeing a small crowd outside St Vincent's Hospital: "My mind went in to his lying dead there and I thought of the times together ... Although the gap of 8 or 9 months was not forgotten – of course no one can ever forget it – I only thought of him with the friendship of the days of 1918 and 1919."[44]

Yet for Collins, duty came first. He asked the Director of Intelligence to place a guard on St. Vincent's Hospital and "to make a report on the exact condition of Mr. Harry Boland" and to find out "whether he has been operated on and what the doctors think of his condition ".[45] However, when Boland died, Collins gave the names of people who were "at the Inquest" to the Director of Intelligence because "they all made speeches about murder" and he wanted them to be watched.[46]

A couple of days later he asked Acting Major General Tobin to "detail a few men with some sort of a party to attend the Curragh races to see whether any of the Irregulars we want, attend. If there are any of them they could be put into the Curragh Camp temporarily."[47]

His former friends were now enemies and should be spied on. Correspondence that he received from Sir Alfred Cope told him that "Mr. Childers" had "made an attempt to get away to USA on the *Carmenia* from here yesterday, 6 August, 1922". With this information, Collins suggested to the Director of Intelligence that the best idea would be "that he should be arrested as a stowaway".[48] Such was the bitter twist required to win this Civil War, and the painful reality for Collins. But, by the first week in August, he had decided there would be no compromise; his opponents had no intention of yielding and this brought forth his true determination.[49]

"In the south, the immediate military problem that confronts us," he wrote, "is not so much the military defeat of the Irregulars in that area as the establishing of our Forces in certain principal points in the area, with a view to shaking the domination held over the ordinary people by the Irregulars."[50]

John L. O'Sullivan remembers Collins being in high spirits when he discussed a method of taking the West Cork towns. It was agreed that Major General Seán Hales, Column

Commander of Government Forces in West Cork, and John L. would set out by boat from Dublin with a number of men and land in the south. They eventually landed in Union Hall. Local men joined them and by the time they got to Skibbereen, they had about 150 extra men. The numbers increased as they moved along eastwards; they took Rosscarbery, Clonakilty, and Courtmacsherry. "There was some fighting along the way." They then headed towards Kinsale and took the town though with much difficulty and fighting as part of the overall strategy. In the same period, a massive invasion of Cork City was planned. Dalton set out by boat with a number of men, prepared to capture the city.

Collins had engaged his sister, Mary Collins-Powell, to liaise between himself and Emmet Dalton in Cork. She organised a volunteer force to help her brother. Collins was prepared to allow his sister to take the risk required in a Civil War, because he was "anxious for a speedy conclusion".

Dr. Gerald Ahern was a young qualified doctor who lived near Shanakiel Hospital where he worked. At the time, he sailed a yacht called *The Gull*, a twelve-ton boat owned by H.P.F. Donegan, Solicitor. Early in August 1922, Harry Donegan approached Dr. Gerald and asked him to take a woman to Rosslare: Mary Collins-Powell. Donegan himself and Fr. Dónal Murphy-O'Connor would sail with them. "We left on a Friday, and as the wind was against us we were unable to get to Rosslare, but after five days we pulled in at Kilmore Quay. As Waterford was in Government hands, it was easier to arrange transport from there to Dublin. Donegan got a taxi to Rosslare and from there it was arranged that Mary Collins-Powell would travel by train to Dublin. She had details of arrangements about the landing in Cork, and was to inform her brother, Michael Collins, that there were up to 500 men ready to join him in Cork but they were lying low due to lack of arms. Also she was in touch with neutral men in the county who would be intermediaries in future talks which might arise between Michael Collins and leaders of the opposing forces."[51]

While Mary Collins-Powell travelled to Dublin, Dr. Gerald with Harry Donegan and Fr. Donal Murphy-O'Connor returned to Crosshaven with *The Gull* and upon arrival were arrested by anti-Treaty men. They were locked in a shed with armed men on guard. Some days later when the pro-Treaty forces took Cork their guards abandoned them.[52]

"We have shown our determination to uphold the people's rights," Collins wrote. "It is at this moment merely a question of time to complete the clearing of those people. We want to avoid any possible unnecessary destruction and loss of life."[53]

In the south, with strong key men, Collins' military tactics were bearing fruit. By 10 August, Dalton and his men were making steady progress in Cork, but were hampered due to a shortage of men; Dalton requested Collins to send 300 more[53] and, when they were not arriving, Dalton pleaded, "I simply must get reinforcements immediately. I am at a standstill."[54]

Immediately Collins organised the transportation of reinforcements by boat and decided he would embark on an army-inspection tour of the south, taking in Limerick and Kerry. If all went well, he would proceed to Cork.

Chapter 1

GENERAL MICHAEL COLLINS, COMMANDER-IN-CHIEF OF THE IRISH ARMY, WAS KILLED IN AN AMBUSH BY IRREGULARS AT BÉAL NA MBLÁTH, BETWEEN MACROOM AND BANDON, ON LAST NIGHT (TUESDAY). TOWARDS THE CLOSE OF THE ENGAGEMENT, WHICH LASTED CLOSE UPON AN HOUR, THE COMMANDER-IN-CHIEF WAS WOUNDED IN THE HEAD.

This notice appeared in large print on the front page of the *Irish Times* and the *Irish Independent* on Wednesday, 23 August 1922, in a period when Ireland was being torn apart by a bloody civil war.

Michael Collins' body lay guarded by four soldiers in Room 121 of Shanakiel Hospital in Cork City. The crown and poll of his head were encased in bandages. His fingers were entwined around a crucifix.

He was clad in the better-fitting uniform he had got and worn for the first time ten days previously, at the funeral of his friend and colleague, Arthur Griffith.[1] In a chair to the right, his greatcoat was casually thrown. An officer came into the room, went to the other side of the iron-framed bed, and placed on the locker a blood-streaked cap, also Collins' Sam Browne belt and detached holster.[2]

At this early hour a hushed stillness pervaded the room as the officer left. Three large candles burned at each side of the bed; shadows flickered behind the closed curtains. Soldiers stood in silence;[3] their task was to guard the body of a man who for the best part of six years had cheated death while he fought for the freedom of Ireland; a man who had believed he wouldn't die in his own county of Cork. Yet, on Saturday, 19 August 1922, the day before his County Cork visit, he seemed to have had an intuition that the die was cast.

Outside, arrangements were being made for the removal of the body to St. Vincent's Hospital, Dublin. Later it would go to the City Hall for the lying in state. The main road to Dublin was impassable at various points: blocked as part of the Republican strategy, barricaded by fallen trees, trenches, and blown-up bridges. Consequently, arrangements were being made for the removal of the cortege by the steamer SS *Classic* which had arrived at Cork Harbour from Fishguard earlier that day.

The Irish people now mourned the death of a hero, a leader and a man of principles: the laughing boy from Clonakilty, County Cork, who became a soldier, who helped organise the Irish Republican Army into a fighting force, who cracked the British intelligence network in Ireland, who became a wanted man as the British Government placed a reward on his head, who was a negotiator and one of the signatories in the Articles of Agreement for a Treaty between

Great Britain and Ireland, who later became Chairman of the Provisional Government and Minister of Finance, who formed a War Council and became Commander-in-Chief of the Army during a bitter civil war.

Dr. Leo Ahern, Gerald Ahern's brother, was one of the doctors who carried out the medical examination following Michael Collins' admission to hospital, and had certified him dead.

Yet, one hundred years later his death has not been officially registered.

Over twenty miles away the early morning sun shone over Béal na mBláth valley. The mist which had shrouded the ambuscade on the previous evening had lifted.

It was 6 am. West of Béal na mBláth, three Republicans, Jim Kearney, Timmy Sullivan and Tom Hales, were in Jim Murray's field beyond the dwelling house and farmyard. Jim Kearney, on the instructions of Tom Hales, had got a shovel from Jim Murray and was digging a hole beside a tree.

Earlier, Kearney. Sullivan and a local man had found an officer's cap at the scene of the previous night's ambush. The cap, which had a large bullet hole to the right of the back stitching, was blood-stained and contained a quantity of human matter.

The men brought it to Tom Hales who was billeted in Murray's house. Hales took the cap. "This is human flesh, and must be buried," he said.

As the men now stood close to the sycamore tree, Hales, with the aid of a penknife, carefully levered off the front brass badge and yellow felt diamond. "A souvenir of a friend," he said sadly, and put it in his back pocket. He handed the cap to Kearney, who had dug a hole approximately a foot and a half deep. Kearney paused momentarily. "The penknife!" he said, stretching out his hand to Hales. With the shovel resting against his body, he severed the front strap from the officer's cap and put it in his pocket, but didn't speak.

Having completed the burial, Hales blessed himself; his two companions did likewise. Hales hesitated with bowed head. He had memories of his former friendship with Collins.

Hales was one of the founder members of the West Cork Volunteers. With Collins presiding, Cork No.3 Brigade was formed at a meeting in Kilnadur, Dunmanway, on 5 January, 1919, and Tom Hales was elected Commandant. Tom Hales had been arrested by the British in June 1920, severely tortured and imprisoned in Pentonville Gaol. While Collins was in London during the Treaty negotiations, he visited Hales on a few occasions. After the signing of the Treaty by Collins and the other plenipotentaries in December 1921, Hales was released. Though his brother Seán Hales backed Collins in the implementation of the Treaty, Tom took the anti-Treaty side. Afterwards Collins said, "More than any man, I would have valued his support."

As the men stood beside the buried cap, Tom Hales recalled his last conversation with Collins in London when Collins said, "Sure we're all Republicans."

Hales responded, "Whatever you do, settle the thing."

"I can't. There's no alternative," said Collins.

"I'd find an alternative," said Hales.

"What's the alternative?" Collins asked.

"Death!" said Hales. "I'd die first."

Hales told the men that morning, "Mick meant as much to me as any of my brothers, and I thought a lot of my brothers."[4]

He was unaware that on the previous day, while he and his Republican comrades lay in wait for Collins' convoy, Collins had said to Emmet Dalton, his escort in the touring car, "It's too bad he is on the other side now. Because he is a damn good soldier," and added pensively, "I don't suppose I will be ambushed in my own county." It is ironic that on that day also, Seán Hales, Tom's brother, was the last soldier to whom Collins spoke before leaving Bandon for Béal na mBláth, less than an hour before he met his death.

The three men who paused beside the spot where Collins' cap was now buried were unaware that their action was going to become part of a mystery that would not be solved for over sixty years; nor could they have anticipated that the cap would be one of the principal pieces of evidence in establishing how Michael Collins was shot.

Kearney handed Collins' revolver, which the men had found in the ambush location, to Hales, and told him of the motorbike that the outrider had abandoned on the roadside.

Chapter 2

Michael Collins rose to prominence during the War of Independence when as Director of Intelligence and of Republican activities he earned the loyalty of his friends and evoked the enmity of his British opponents. Having played a vital part in the Treaty negotiations and put his signature to the Articles of Agreement for a Treaty, he was determined thereafter to uphold his decision.

As Chairman of the Provisional Government he struggled, along with his former comrades, to reunite the army in the twilight months that led to a civil war. During this period, difficulties arose for him as he tried to reconcile the divergences between the military and the political elements within the cabinet. The situation often led to a dualistic approach by Collins when on the one hand he tried to remain loyal to the Treaty, and on the other he cooperated with the anti-Treaty men, especially in matters regarding the North of Ireland. This cooperation between Michael Collins and Liam Lynch is interesting, and shows how far both men, though with opposing views on the Treaty, were prepared to work to unite the country and create a 32-county Ireland.[1]

By early July the anti-Treaty forces were in command of large areas of the country so the Provisional Government had to make a stand. Collins was thus willing to accept the challenge of his "appointment as Commander-in-Chief of the National Forces".[2]

On 12 July, temporarily relieved of his duties as Chairman of the Provisional Government and Minister of Finance (posts to which he intended returning when the war was over), he donned his military uniform and moved into quarters at Portobello Barracks.[3]

The prestige of soldiering appealed to him: he had several photographs taken of himself in uniform and he liked the idea that "men should be ready for inspection by the Commander-in-Chief. Every man who could be spared should be on parade." He wrote memos suggesting how members of the National Army should present themselves.[4] Inefficiency disturbed him. Only a small proportion of the soldiers were men who had fought in the War of Independence. Some were young recruits while others were Irish soldiers who had fought in the British Army. Collins saw it as his responsibility to make them into a respectable "National Army".

Collins was a man who liked to joke provided the joke as not on him.[5] He was intolerant of the shortcomings of others – loyal to a certain point, but at that point he was prepared to bend the rules to suit a particular situation. He was an extremely sharp man at evaluating situations and people and a very methodical planner. These qualities became evident once he took over as "Supreme Commander" of the National Army. He coined the title "Irregulars" for the opposing forces (a label which was detested by them), insisted that newspaper reporting should substitute this title for the word "Republicans" and ordered that "descriptions of a military operation must not be published while the operation is still uncompleted".[6] (See also Appendix II)

Tireless, he pushed himself to the limits. He had set himself a task of building up a true Irish state, one based on the culture which "showed itself" most strongly along the western seaboard. "South and West and Northwest," he wrote. "To those places the social side of anglicisation was never able very easily to penetrate ... It is only in such places that one gets a glimpse of what Ireland may become again."[7] Being convinced that there was only so much he or any leader could do, because "leaders are but individuals and individuals are imperfect, liable to error and weakness", he believed that the future rested in the people's hands. "The strength of the nation will be the strength of the spirit of the whole people."[8]

There were times when he seemed to have a premonition of death. He would become morose, express a fatalistic view to a friend, but would just as quickly snap back into joviality. It was as if he didn't want to ponder on the negative.

In his new role as Commander-in-Chief, he threw himself fully into the task. Michael Hayes, a colleague, said of him: "He had shown he could work with others and with Richard Mulcahy he had always found co-operation easy, though in some ways they were different types of men. They shared a capacity for hard work, determined character and a total devotion to duty."[9]

By the second week in August, it was time for him to move

into the country to review the military posts. But first he would meet members of the 2nd and 3rd Northern Divisions. At the meeting in the Officers' Mess, Portobello Barracks, the Government and the Army were represented by Michael Collins, with Richard Mulcahy presiding, according to Thomas Kelly, a member of the 2nd Northern division who was present. "The position of the six counties was examined fully and carefully. Many and varied views were expressed, some quite heatedly, but the only statement of importance was the final summation and decision of Michael Collins," who said, "with this Civil War on my hands, I cannot give you men the help I wish to give and mean to give. I now propose to call off hostilities in the North and to use the political arm against Craig so long as it is of use. If that fails, the Treaty can go to hell and we will all start again."[10]

By this time Collins believed that the anti-Treaty forces "were beaten as an open force". He was "definitely on the idea of having some arrangements that would save the faces of the anti-Treatyites and enable them to stop fighting but the onus was on them to stop".[11] With this in mind, he would take a trip to the country and talk to his own men on location. So, on Saturday, 12 August, he "left Portobello barracks at 4 am exactly"[12] on an inspection tour. He would visit Kerry and cross the border into County Cork.

During his first official stop at Maryborough Gaol (now Portlaoise Prison), his eye, sharpened by years of practising intelligence work, fell on the grey colour that went right to the top of the prison wall. This, he felt, would facilitate prisoners who were trying to escape. After he left "a strip at the top of the wall was whitewashed". It was no pleasure to him to find that prisoners had decided to engage in throwing utensils at him as he walked through the ground floor – these were his own people!

The convoy drove to Limerick and while Collins was there he sent a message to Mulcahy asking him to send "tenders, spare parts and some Lewis guns" immediately because the Army were "moving forward against hostile positions".[13] Also he said he "must know" what "communications with Cork City" were like.[14] Mulcahy confirmed that communication with Cork was "only by boat and wireless". He had wired Dalton to communicate with Collins, because Dalton had reported on 12 August that Cork was "entirely in his hands".[15] Following this good news, Collins moved on to army centres at Patrickswell, Adare, Rathkeale, Newcastlewest and Abbeyfeale. At each venue he noted various activities which required attention and "any orders given were given with instructions to report" to O'Duffy when orders were completed.[16]

When Collins visited Coolbunion House in Castleconnell he became extremely angry at the lax attitude of the men. Sentries were not on duty at the various entrances: "The actual approach to the entrance of the house was filthy in the extreme." In a long letter to O'Duffy after his return, he summed up the situation by saying, "The whole appearance of the men and surroundings was unbecoming of army men."[17]

During this journey, Collins and his men encountered a number of problems: the Lancia went on fire at Naas and only started with difficulty and the Crossley Tender ran out of petrol near Roscrea. According to Collins' letter, "both the Tender and Lancia would have been left on the road were it not for a supply of aviation spirit, which was being taken at the request of the Air Service to Limerick". They had problems with a spare wheel, and during the journey in Kerry the armoured car supplied from Limerick got "ditched" – "due to an incompetent driver". Being a man who disliked slovenliness, he wanted to know, "Who exactly was responsible for passing the fleet as fit in every way?" because, "In the whole journey nothing happened that could not have been avoided by care, attention and ordinary foresight."[18]

He had intended travelling from Kerry to Cork, but on reaching Tralee late that night he received news that Arthur Griffith had died. Though Griffith had been unwell for some time, his death came as a shock to Collins who maintained that "he had sounder political judgement than any of us".[19]

Early the following morning, 13 August, Collins returned to Dublin for the funeral. This meant the postponement of the County Cork military barracks' inspection.

There was an air of confidence about Collins and the military men by this time. The *Irish Independent* reported on 16 August that "The National Army are advancing with no one to say them nay ... Of the thousands of irregulars who occupied Cork County a month ago there is no trace."[20] Regular supplies were now leaving Dublin for Cork by sea,[21] and Mallow, which was considered a gateway to Cork City, was now in the hands of the Government forces. "The war in its first stage may be considered to be over," The *Irish Independent* reported. "True that in Macroom a few irregulars still are to be found who may confound expectations by making some resistance. "[22]

Meanwhile, aerial reconnaissance of the vast southern region was undertaken by Commandant Russell, pilot, and Captain Bill Stapleton.[23]

On Wednesday morning, 16 August, Collins telephoned Cosgrave[24] before calling on Sir John and Lady Hazel Lavery who had arrived in Dublin on 12 August and were staying at Salthill Hotel, Monkstown, County Dublin. He then met members of the Provisional Government and together they went to Arthur Griffith's funeral Mass at 10.30 am. This was followed by the processional march to Glasnevin cemetery.[25]

As he walked through the Dublin streets behind the coffin, he stoically bore the loss of his dear friend and counsellor. On the same morning he got word that Dunne and O'Sullivan had been hanged (on 10 August) in Wandsworth Prison, London, for the shooting of Sir Henry Wilson. O'Sullivan had written a letter to his mother in which he listed a number of people to whom he wished to be remembered. Included in the list was the name of "Micky Collins". The same Collins had tried unsuccessfully to obtain a reprieve for the two men.

A bystander remarked on Collins' grim expression as he walked behind the coffin at the head of his staff. "Ireland's problems hang heavily on his shoulders."[26]

In a graveside tribute to Arthur Griffith, Collins said, "He always knew what Irish Nationality meant, just as Davis knew it. He never confused it with English Nationality. Some of our present day political leaders have done this under the guidance of English minds ... In memory of Arthur Griffith let us resolve now to give fresh play to the impulse of unity, to join together one and all in continuing his constructive work, in building up the country which he loved."[27]

Silently he moved back and stood, head bowed, beside the grave of his friend. His work was not yet concluded. His tour of inspection of southern counties had to be completed. With most of the major towns and cities in the hands of Government forces, it looked to him as if the Civil War would soon be over. The slow processional march to Glasnevin carried a certain amount of strain. Relieved that that part was over, he sighed: "I hope nobody takes it into his head to die for another twelve months."[28]

That evening Collins went back to the barracks where he wrote a considerable number of letters.[29] At 8 o'clock he went to the Laverys' where Hazel hosted a pleasant evening meal. He was pleased to be with friends after the ordeal of the earlier part of the day. At half past ten he left for Baldonnell to pick up "air service reports".[30]

On Thursday morning, 17 August, Collins received a letter from Eoin O'Duffy in Limerick stating that a Mr. Hayes had brought a letter to O'Duffy requesting Commandant General Hannigan to issue to Dan Breen, Republican guerrilla fighter, "a safe conduct" pass to see Collins. O'Duffy told Hayes that the matter would be considered; he would not issue a safe conduct to Dublin without first knowing whether Collins "would receive Dan Breen or not". O'Duffy said: "I respectfully suggest that you refuse to see him." (Dan Breen and Seán Treacy, with Seamus Robinson and local volunteers, had mobilised to capture gelignite from the military on the way to Soloheadbeg quarry, Co. Tipperary, on January 21, 1919. Eight ambushers waited in bushes. Two RIC men were killed. This day marked the opening of the War of Independence.)

In this letter O'Duffy explained how much territory was now held by the National forces. With Dalton in the Cork area and Prout in Waterford "with all three ... working in cooperation for a week which would bring us up to the 25th August, we might then be in a position to negotiate with advantage." Therefore, he expressed his view of the "importance of holding fast," as it was his belief that "the Labour element and Red Flaggers are at the back of all moves towards 'Peace', not for the sake of the country, but in their own interests ... This is why I suggest to you not to see Breen or any of the others ..."[31]

Collins, who consistently liked to confide his ideas to paper, jotted down some notes: "It may be well to keep open some avenue or avenues to peace. Advantages of making a public offer giving them an opportunity of (a) going home without their arms. (b) Behaving decently in support of the administration, and in acceptance of the People's verdict – we don't wish for any surrender of their principles ... "[32] These notes suggest that Collins did not want to close any door that might lead to peace.

Collins decided that he would resume his review of the forces in the south, see the situation for himself, and speak to the officers "on the ground". Immediately he sent a message to O'Duffy: "Am anxious to know progress towards Millstreet. Expect to see you linked up with Dalton everywhere within twenty-four hours. See you about ten o'clock on Saturday."[33]

His mind was made up. At this juncture he was not sure how far south he would go, but he was going south.

The following morning, Friday 18 August, he walked into the office of Joe McGrath, his intelligence officer, and announced his intention of travelling south. McGrath protested, pointing out the danger. But Collins was determined that he was not "going to run from his own Corkmen", and told McGrath to get a convoy organised.

McGrath later wrote all his objections in red ink in a letter which he intended putting on Collins' desk. But on reflection he decided that when Collins gave an order he wanted it implemented without argument.

A wire message arrived from Dalton in Cork, saying that "terms" had been communicated to him "by a Committee of prominent citizens of Cork". During a week's truce "facilities are to be afforded to the Republican military and political leaders to hold a meeting to discuss the making of peace".[34] Certain guidelines concerning arms, ammunitions and political prisoners, were listed.[35]

Collins responded by wire: "Will you say by cipher who the prominent citizens responsible for the offer are? Have the Irregular Leaders, political and military agreed to the offer and is it made on their behalf? Government offer published in the Press 5th June, and conveyed to the People's Rights Association, Cork, stands ... "[36] (See also Appendix III)

In his habitual manner he wrote in his notebook: "Every constitutional way is open to them" (the anti-Treaty forces) "to win the people to their side and we will meet them in every way if only they will obey the people's will and accept the authority of Government and of the people. That alone is our concern." Therefore "any further blood is on their shoulders. The onus placed unmistakably on their shoulders, the public must be kept aware of what we are upholding and of our willingness to avoid and prevent further loss."[37]

That morning, Saturday 19 August 1922, Hazel Lavery telephoned Elizabeth, Countess of Fingall because a number of important people had been invited to dinner at Kilteragh House in Foxrock, residence of Sir Horace Plunkett. She asked her friend, "Do you think Sir Horace would like me to bring Michael Collins over to supper tonight?" The Countess said she felt Horace would be delighted as George Bernard Shaw was also invited and both were "interested in the idea of meeting the rebel leader".[38]

That same morning in Portobello Barracks Michael Collins

was not feeling well. As he sat down to breakfast beside Richard Mulcahy he was "writhing with pain from a cold all through his body; and yet he was facing his day's work for that Saturday, and facing his Sunday's journey".[39]

In his Portobello office while he attended to some preliminaries, he received the telephone call from Lady Hazel Lavery. Shortly afterwards he left the barracks and went to his friends, the Leigh Doyles, in Greystones. With Kevin O'Higgins and others he had been a regular visitor to the Leigh Doyles' home. On this occasion he asked them "to take care of" his fiancée Kitty, who was staying at the Grand Hotel.

Recently he had a picture taken of himself in uniform. He gave them a copy; he would sign it when he returned from Cork. Now he was in a hurry.[40]

Back in his office, he dealt with a vast amount of correspondence. There were also last-minute decisions regarding his next day's journey. Throughout the day he wrote reports on the Engineering Services and ammunition and various allied items in connection with "Aerodrome-Air Communication".[41] He also wrote a tremendous number of letters. Though not in his usual top form, he wrote letters to the Director of Munitions,[42] the Director of Purchases,[43] the Director of Publicity,[44] the Director of Recruiting,[45] and to each of the commands in central barracks throughout the country. He required "Strength return and Nominal roll of all ranks,"[46] to be compiled "up to and including Thursday 24th inst 12 o'clock midnight" and this should include "every officer and other rank ... even if only on duty there for a few hours".[47] As

Commander-in-Chief, Collins required full statistics of the men under his control in order "to coordinate activities" and also to supply the cabinet with details for the next meeting of the Dáil.

Later in the evening, having checked with Joe McGrath that everything was in order for the morning, he was ready to relax for a few hours with friends. According to Sir John Lavery, Hazel was anxious that Horace Plunkett and Collins should meet. He said she took Collins to dinner at Kilteragh House the same evening without him. He added, "I was a little anxious, but for some reason did not go".[48]

Collins signed his name in Irish in the visitor's book at Kilteragh House. (This Irish version, *Mícheál Ó Coileáin*, was his usual signature.) He was not feeling well that night and because he was quieter than usual he did not impress Countess Elizabeth: "Not at all an eloquent man, and my recollection of the dinner is that it was very quiet, and almost dull."[49]

The writer, George Bernard Shaw, met him that night "for the first and last time". He said he was "very glad" he did. "I rejoice in his memory ..."[50]

The guests, who included W. T. Cosgrave, left early because, in the words of Sir John Lavery, "Michael Collins said he had to be in Cork next day. A car with an escort followed them." The guests went "for a drive in the mountains",[51] and while returning to the Salthill Hotel where Lady Lavery was staying, they were ambushed; "a half a dozen shots were poured into the car." On their arrival at the hotel, Sir John examined the car with an electric torch: "It seemed a miracle that no one was hurt, for there were six people in the car, sitting close together." Collins' slight illness caused him to make light of the ambush; he was complaining of a pain in his side and thought it might be "his appendix".

Sir John eventually persuaded him to accept his hot-water bottle. Collins, placing it under his tunic, smilingly said that "the pain was gone". With a "God bless you both" he jumped into his car ... dashing off into the night. That was the last time Sir John and Lady Lavery saw Michael Collins alive.[52]

When he reached Portobello Barracks, he told a colleague Joe O'Reilly how badly he had been feeling. O'Reilly made a hot drink with oranges and took it to Collins in bed. "God, that's grand!" said Collins. These words of gratitude encouraged O'Reilly who on impulse bent down to tuck him in for the night. Collins, not used to such personal touches, gathered his strength and shouted, *"Go to hell and leave me alone!"*[53]

Chapter 3

Michael Collins' last journey began on Sunday 20 August 1922.

At 5.15 am the unpainted wooden door of his room in the annexe at Portobello Barracks was opened. The Commander-in-Chief of the Army of the Provisional Government, dressed in his uniform, boots and gaiters, carried his officer's cap in his left hand with his gun-hand swinging loosely as he went down the steps and across the grounds for his breakfast. A few weeks previously he would have tripped the steps lightly, but this morning he walked. The big man looked tired and drawn as he made his way to the officers' dining room. Soldiers stood back and saluted as he passed.

Fionán Lynch, about to join him for breakfast, asked how he felt. "It's that damn cold!" Collins responded. As Lynch handed him a cup of tea, he remarked that he was feeling "lousy yesterday but wasn't quite as bad this morning". He had this "desperate pain" in his side the previous night but that was now gone.[1] A faint smile crossed his face when he said, "It must have been the oranges that did the job," as he related how Joe O'Reilly had brought him the hot orange drink in bed.

Now, he put his customary two spoons of sugar in his tea[2] and, while stirring it, began to tell Fionán Lynch about the near escape he'd had the previous night returning from Horace

Plunkett's dinner party. "The end can sometimes be so near," he remarked. He ate just one slice of bread, finished breakfast and got up. He wanted a few words with Joe McGrath, Director of Intelligence, before he set out on his journey. He mounted the stairs and went into McGrath's room.

"You're a fool to go!" McGrath told his superior officer.

But Collins was adamant. "Whatever happens to me, my own fellow countrymen won't kill me."

Walking beside Joe McGrath, he went down the cement steps, then put on his military greatcoat and went into the yard. The loud hum of the armoured car greeted him. The men who were to travel in the Crossley Tender awaited the vehicle, Reg. Number 01 8818, driven by Captain Jimmy Conroy. The original driver assigned to this job, Private Lyons, had been sent to Wellington barracks[3] where another tender was at the ready in case tender 01-8818 was not "up to" the journey,[4] because Captain Jimmy Conroy had said that it "was not pulling well" the previous day. Tender 01-8818 was now being serviced.

O'Reilly, who had given Collins the orange drink the previous night, woke suddenly, and on impulse rushed to the window. Collins was standing outside on the steps. "He wore a small green kit-bag over his back, his head was bent in gloomy meditation and, thinking himself unobserved, he let himself fall slack in the loneliness and silence of the summer morning."[5]

The distinctive sound of the Crossley Tender startled Collins. He saluted it and made his way to the Leyland Eight touring car.

Joe Sweeney rushed out the barrack door and said to Collins

that he had only just heard of his intention to travel south.

"Wait until things are more settled. You could get killed."

"No one is going to shoot me in my own country," Collins said.

Driver M.B Corry sat behind the wheel of the Leyland Eight. Collins, about to embark on his final journey through the country, mounted the Leyland and, in his efficient manner, took out his spiral notebook and jotted down, "Started 15 minutes late – Valve-spring broken in Fiat."[6]

The convoy set out from Portobello Barracks at 6.15. am. The Crossley Tender carried twelve men, including driver Captain Jimmy Conroy and relief driver Sergeant Cooney. Among the men were two machine-gunners to operate the Lewis-gun, plus seven riflemen including Captain Seán Edmonds, Captain Peter Conlon, and the man in command of the escort, Commandant Seán (Paddy) O'Connell. Captain Joe Dolan would join at Limerick.

Next in line was the Leyland Eight touring car carrying Collins and Fionán Lynch, with Corry and Quinn as drivers.

Bringing up the rear of the convoy was the Rolls Royce Armoured Car, Reg. number ARR 2, known as *Sliabh na mBan* (or anglicised *Slievenamon*, meaning "Mountain of the Women"), which was to play an important part in subsequent events. This was driven by Private Jim Woulfe, with co-driver Private Jimmy "Wiggy" Fortune. Seated in the back was Private Wally Coote, and Lieutenant Gough. Machine-gunner Private John (Jock) McPeak was in charge of the revolving-turret Vickers water-cooled gun.

It had been late on Saturday afternoon that most of the crew were informed of their forthcoming journey. Jim Woulfe had been Seán Hales' driver during the early stages of the Civil War.[7] Jimmy McGowen, the usual driver of the *Sliabh na mBan*, was sick, so Jim Woolfe was asked by Captain David Coates to take McGowen's place at the wheel.

Collins, having noted the problems with the tender, wrote in his personal notebook, "Is there a manifest of cars?"[8] He spoke to Fionán Lynch about the problems which he had encountered during his journey to Limerick and Kerry the previous week, when the convoy had had several mishaps and eventually had to get a replacement tender. He was "annoyed" because the "difficulties which had arisen on that occasion could have been avoided" if due care had been taken.[9]

The convoy headed through the side streets of Dublin. Though it was Sunday morning, this complement of men couldn't risk going to Mass or Church Service. Church bells chimed in the early morning. Through the outskirts of the city the convoy drove on its way towards the first stop at Curragh Barracks. Once out on the country road, Collins relaxed, according to his travelling companion, Fionán Lynch. "Both hands rested on his thighs," he said. He talked to Lynch, saying that while he had grown accustomed to city life, "deep in his veins there was always this love for the country". Despite his heavy cold, he was in "reasonably good spirits", with occasional "bursts of high spirits". But it angered him when they "encountered destruction caused by Irregulars ".[10]

The August sun and the sight of the open fields and bogs

appeared to revitalise him. He told Lynch that he hoped he would be able to get to Cork City and further; his true wish was "to visit his old home place and his relatives and friends in West Cork".

As they headed into the town of Portlaoise, there were ponytraps of Sunday worshippers leaving the town. Sometimes those on foot stopped and looked after them; others paid no attention. In the open yard of the Curragh, Collins dismounted and went to the O/C's office where they discussed the condition of the army stationed there. The gaol was overcrowded with prisoners. Collins said that some of them would shortly be transferred to Gormanstown camp which was in the process of being rewired and made more secure in order to hold extra prisoners. (Provisions were also being made for Gormanstown camp to hold some prisoners from Kilmainham.)

Collins took a brief walk around. Outside in the open yard he paused momentarily, took his notebook and pencil from his top pocket and noted "Prisoners for removal of say 200. Cipher to Dublin."[11]

After a further brief chat the two officers saluted and parted. Collins got back into the Leyland and the convoy journeyed towards Roscrea, reaching the it after 9 am. After a brief inspection by Collins, some words with the O/C and with Tom Waters, Intelligence Officer, the full convoy sat down to breakfast.

Seated in the Leyland once more, Collins remarked to Lynch that he was feeling much better. There would be no further stops until they reached Limerick. This territory was in the hands of Government forces, so there were no roadblocks or obstructions.

At Limerick Barracks the party were received by the G.O.C. Southern Command, General Eoin O'Duffy.[12] There was a private joke, a brief laugh as General O'Duffy remarked to his superior officer that it wasn't West Cork bacon they would have for lunch, but the best Limerick bacon and Limerick cabbage.

After the meal Collins took out his memo book and jotted down a few items discussed during their conversation: "... to wire for two doctors," one for hygiene and the other for examination of recruits. "Two strong fellows" were to report to General O'Duffy the next day.[13]

On the way into Limerick, Collins had noticed that the bridge at Annacotty was down. He ordered that it should "be rendered safe for traffic" immediately.[14]

At 2.35 pm he drafted a letter to Mulcahy, to inform Diarmuid Hegarty that the new forms for the army "must include many more particulars, among them authorisation to pay dependants' money to some definite person".[15]

There were many items which he and O'Duffy had to discuss. He had wired O'Duffy on 15 August in connection with matters which he had noticed during his previous tour south towards Kerry prior to Griffith's death. O'Duffy was now able to inform Collins that his orders had been carried out.

In his personal notebook Collins wrote: "Army men at Patrickswell depot be moved to the local school and overbridge made traffic-worthy; Lieutenant Drumm in Adare to consolidate his men in one position; trees that block roads near Croom to be removed; Sergeant Lambert to consolidate all his men in the police barracks ..." while a party of local volunteers under Lieutenant Kerley were to join forces with Commandant Keane's section.

Collins believed the Civil War was almost over; he didn't want any rancour, he said. The two men discussed the suggestion that Lieutenant Colonel Frank Thornton should make contact with Dan Breen. Father Dick McCarthy, a Limerick priest, was anxious to arrange a meeting between Breen and Collins and had suggested an old meeting place – Hickey's of Glenville.[16] Collins decided to consider the suggestion; he was always willing to keep his lines of communication open, but was in no rush, and certainly O'Duffy was against any compromise or meeting, at least for the present. Collins wasn't travelling on a peacemaking mission, according to Ernest Blythe to the author, though he was as always trying to think of an arrangement that would save the faces of the anti-Treatyites and enable them to stop fighting.[17]

Michael Brennan, Commander of troops in the Clare and East Limerick region, was in Limerick Barracks while the peace issue was being discussed. "It wasn't that he had any intention of offering a compromise, or giving any concessions," he said, but, because "he was very attached to Corkmen, like Lynch and Deasy, it was with reluctance he fought them".[18]

Frank Thornton left Limerick before Collins' own departure. As he travelled south of Clonmel that day, his convoy was ambushed at Ninemilehouse. Thornton was severely wounded and all the other members of his convoy were killed.

While in Limerick, Collins asked Tipperary soldier Jerry Ryan to send fifty of his best fighters to West Cork, because he was determined to end the conflict. (The Tipperary reinforcements were to travel by boat from Limerick to Bantry.)

At 4.05 pm he noted: "Tell QMG [Quarter Master General] that an ambulance is required here and that it should be sent with the doctors who were asked for in my earlier wire." Also, that "O'Duffy wants specially one hundred revolvers."[19] In addition he wanted to know when the Civic Guards would be ready to come to Limerick. "These must be regarded as members of the Army under the special conditions of their enlistment and are capable of being used for all duties."[20] He discussed with O'Duffy the training of Civic Guards which was at that time being undertaken at the Curragh.[21] A division of these would be allotted to Limerick.[22]

Following a review of the prisoners, Collins realised that there was much overcrowding in "conditions which endangered their health", also that "defence" was bad. He told Mulcahy in a wire that it was "essential" the "first removal" should be from Limerick where "there are four hundred and seventy" prisoners.[23]

After he had completed his business in Limerick, it was agreed that Eoin O'Duffy and an accompanying convoy would travel with the group to Mallow. Also, a motorcycle with rider Lieut. Smith would head Collins' convoy, and Captain Joe Dolan who was joining the convoy would travel in the tender.

According to Collins' personal diary, the convoy left Limerick at 5 pm.[24] They drove out the dusty roads towards

Kilmallock for a brief inspection. The clouds still hid the sun as they resumed their journey along the Limerick/Cork border and headed towards Charleville, then on to Buttevant. They arrived at Mallow shortly after 7.30 pm.[25]

From there O'Duffy branched off, visited Kanturk, Millstreet and went on to Rathmore, Killarney "and other areas under his command". (He was ambushed on three occasions during this tour.) [26]

The anti-Treaty forces, for their own protection, left roads mined and damaged bridges as they evacuated areas. It angered Collins to find such destruction. The destruction of the Awbeg Bridge meant that the Cork/Dublin railway line was out of action; it was for this reason that Collins' sister was unable to travel by train and pass on important information.

Collins spoke with Commandant Flood at the Mallow military post in the Royal Hotel and asked him to get word to Charleville in connection with "making good a passage over the Awbeg" river.[27] He jotted down in his notebook a reminder that when he got to Cork City he should see that "Engineering help" would be sent "to Mallow re Blackwater".[28] Archdeacon Corbett, along with the Bishop of Cloyne, Dr. Roche, happened to be in the hotel talking to Commandant Flood about the broken-down Mallow Bridge when Collins arrived. The Archdeacon asked when the bridge would be repaired.

"Give me a chance," Collins protested, and promised to have workmen there within a month.

"How is the struggle going?" the Archdeacon enquired.

To this, he got the brief answer that things were going well enough and that Collins hoped for a speedy reconciliation. Then Collins wheeled around and walked away.

"The poor man is in a hurry to meet his death," came the Archdeacon's prophetic remark.[29]

The main Cork/Mallow Road was blocked by fallen trees and, in addition, there was the fear that it would be mined. Therefore John O'Connell, a local man with knowledge of the by-roads, volunteered as an escort.

Continuing on the journey, the convoy jolted its way by the mountain route, an arduous task on the rudimentary road, especially with the cumbersome *Sliabh na mBan*. In Monee, the convoy halted at Dan O'Keeffe's farmhouse to check the overheated radiator of the Leyland and to replenish the radiators of the vehicles with water; this allowed some of the soldiers in the tender to take a breather. Shortly afterwards they resumed the journey and headed towards Whitechurch where a gathering had assembled at the crossroads. The driver of the touring car became nervous and was on the point of pulling up when Collins shouted, *"Drive on, you fool! Don't you see it's only the usual Sunday evening crossroads dancing?"*

It was almost dark when the convoy headed through Blackpool and into Cork City. Passers-by were alerted as it stuttered down the South Mall in the stillness of the night. The military headquarters at the Imperial Hotel were well lit. And just as the personnel at the barracks along the way were taken by surprise, so was Emmet Dalton, Commander of the Cork region. Dalton knew that he was due a visit from Collins, but he wasn't sure of the date. He was just wording a wire replying to Collins' wire in connection with 'peace proposals' suggested by 'prominent citizens of Cork'. (See Appendix III)

Collins stepped from the Leyland and strode into the hotel. He found two sentries seated side by side in the lobby with heads bowed in sleep. Irritated at the spectacle, he seized them both, in dashing style banged their heads together and walked on.

News of Collins' arrival in Cork soon spread and shortly a cheering crowd gathered around the hotel. Because Collins was a type of folk hero, they wanted to catch a glimpse of him. Inside he met some of his old friends, and a chance meeting with his sister Mary Collins-Powell somehow replenished his vigour. Mary was about to leave the hotel, having spent some time in conversation with Emmet Dalton, when her brother walked in the door. The two had a brief chat and planned a further meeting for the morning. His nephew, Seán Collins-Powell, drank a cup of tea with him and upon discovering that his uncle was taking a trip to the country the following day, asked if he could join him, but was quickly told that they both had their own jobs. "You see after your own work, and I'll do mine," was Collins' response.

Emmet Dalton discussed the military position and also the peace moves. He was of the opinion that the National forces were in a stronger position than at any time previously. "I could not see any reason why we should compromise. This, also, was Collins' belief."[30]

Collins was consistently forthright in either praise or chastisement; on this occasion he complimented Dalton and his officers on their successful campaign. Since the capture of Cork on 12 August there didn't appear to be any military opposition. Anti-Treaty forces had fled to rural pockets, such as areas north of Newcestown and around Ballyvourney. On the Cork–Bandon Road, they had felled trees and blown up the bridges at both Ballinhassig and Innishannon in accordance with the strategy of guerilla warfare, which was, as they saw it, their only hope of retaining control of certain areas.

It was now past midnight. Most of the men had gone to bed, some to quarters in the Victoria Hotel. Collins was feeling much better. Some of his old energy had returned and, with Dalton, he made plans for the morning and said that he looked forward with renewed optimism to an end to the strife. There was vigour in his step as he mounted the stairs of the Imperial Hotel and walked towards the bedroom which he was to share with Joe Dolan.

He plonked himself on the end of the bed, pulled off his boots and hurled them outside the door. *"If you wake first, call me!"* he shouted across to Joe who had the sheet pulled halfway up his face. Then there was a loud bang as Collins took a flying leap into bed.

Chapter 4

At five minutes to six in the morning Collins hurried down the stairs. He had decided that Monday 21 August 1922 was to be packed with activity. After breakfast he sat with Emmet Dalton at the mahogany table in the long room, planning the day's schedule.

The two men had been friends since the War of Independence when Dalton had undertaken daring tasks. They had been in London together during the Treaty negotiations, and now they were helping one another to end hostilities. Dalton, a slimly built, active man with British Army experience, was the anchorman in Cork. Since he, fellow-officers and men had taken the city, it was discovered that there were matters of finance requiring immediate attention so that the wheels of the Provisional Government could get into full motion.

But first there had to be a tour of inspection of military posts in the city. It annoyed Collins that discipline was lax at one of the depots and he let his annoyance be known to the officer in charge. It wasn't, he said, because the city was in the hands of Government forces that they should allow disorder to creep into the force; as Commander-in-Chief he would see to it that the country would have a strong disciplined "National Army".[1]

He visited his sister Mary and spent some time talking

privately to her. "She had been in contact with him over the previous few weeks, mainly because she was organising a volunteer unit to assist my forces," said Emmet Dalton. This was confirmed in correspondence from Diarmuid Brennan to Dr. Gerald Ahern which said that she had organised troops with the help of "H.P. Donegan and D. Murphy-O'Connor". The troops were travelling on *The Gull* under Captain Kelly, around the coast to land in Cork Harbour. Diarmuid Brennan describes this feat as "one of most spectacular moments" in history with "Collins' sister involved".[2]

Among the subjects Michael Collins and his sister also discussed was the organisation of the new Civic Guard Force and the Customs and Excise service. Because Patrick Powell, Mary's husband, was a Customs and Excise official, he had inside information about "irregularities that were taking place". Republicans were diverting Customs and Excise funds that rightly should have gone to the Provisional Government and were using them for their own purposes. Later in the morning, Collins was able to act on this information when he called to the Customs and Excise offices in Cork.

At 9.30 am, Collins sent a wire to William Hogan at Portobello Barracks: "Ask Cosgrave wire at once who used take charge of letting places like Moor Park, Kilworth, also representative Home Affairs must be sent here regarding ordinary prisoners, courts, justices."[3] Here he appears in his ministerial rather than military role, trying to prevent anti-Treaty misappropriation of rental income, and concerned about the courts and the judicial system.

In order to expedite the Provisional Government's military campaign in Cork, he sent a message to "tell [Commandant] Russell that Fermoy suitable for landing. Ask him if he could fly over West Cork area as follows: Macroom to Ballyvourney to Inchigeelagh, Bandon to Dunmanway." He was "most anxious to have these places reconnoitred".[4]

Collins and Dalton then went to meet the proprietor of the *Cork Examiner*, Tom Crosbie, at 10.30 am.[5] Collins wanted to discuss with him the general army position on publicity, also "the writing up of the situation" on the "People's Rights" viewpoint (a neutral group that worked for reconciliation) and "peace offers" which were being promoted.[6]

The anti-Treaty forces had blown up the printing works of the *Cork Examiner* before retreating from the city.[7] Frank Gallagher had been writing anti-Treaty propaganda during their take-over. Before retreating, "they caused eighty thousand pounds worth of damage to property," according to Mr. Crosbie, because "since the beginning of August the *Cork Examiner* had taken a firm stand in favour of the Provisional Government."[8] Later that day Mr. Crosbie would travel to London to try to buy printing presses.[9]

At 11 am Collins and Dalton went to the Hibernian Bank and asked Mr. Pelly for "a brief statement"[10] regarding money which had possibly been deposited under the name of some Republicans.[11] They called to the Bank of Ireland at 11.15,[12] and the Land Bank at 11.45[13]. Then they visited various other banking institutions to try to recover £120,000 which the anti-Treatyites had obtained illegally from the Revenue

Commissioners; it was mainly Excise duties belonging to the Customs and Excise offices in Cork. The anti-Treatyites had obtained this money by capturing the official collector and under threat of death making him sign the cheques which the banks honoured. [14]

A few days before this, Desmond Fitzgerald in the Ministry of Economic Affairs had sent a report to "The Commander-in-Chief" and to "The Acting Chairman" which explained that "Banks in Cork City are keeping currency as low as possible ... Cheques are received at the Bank of Ireland noticeable to Excise and Customs and endorsed by Connell in which originally my 231 Customs & Excise is credited."

Fitzgerald noted: "The Irregulars have opened a No.2 account (Customs & Excise account) in the same bank, authorising a rebel named Peter Ryan-Hervey to sign cheques to that account."[15]

In each bank that Collins and Dalton entered, they demanded that the manager should close the doors. They ordered the disclosure of the names of the big business people who were acting as 'covers' for the Irregulars. "We told them we would not allow the banks to re-open unless they revealed the full information," said Dalton. "In this way, we got ninety per cent of the money back." They also got a tip-off about a certain church. "When we went there, the priest, after some persuasion, opened the tabernacle, where we found £3,000, which was being kept by the priest for the Irregulars." After disclosing this information, Dalton, almost holding his breath, felt somewhat sorry he had.[16]

It was past noon when they returned to the Imperial headquarters where, after a quick lunch, Collins with the convoy set out to review the military situation in Cobh. News of Collins' arrival in Cork had already travelled. Republicans in the Cobh district, anticipating that he might travel along the main road, had mined it at the outskirts of the town and had men waiting to ambush the convoy. However, fortune was on Collins' side on this occasion as the mine failed to explode.

After an inspection of the Cobh military post, the convoy returned to Cork City.

Though Collins loved the prestige of soldiering and the status of reviewing military positions, he expected to return to his duties as Minister of Finance as soon as normality in the military position was restored. He had been interested in figures ever since he passed the British Civil Service examination and worked as a youth in the London Savings Bank.

Now he wanted to inform the Acting Minister of Finance about the banking transactions in Cork, so at 3.30 pm he wrote to Mr. Cosgrave:

(1) The Bank position here is slightly obscure. It will require a full investigation and, combined with that investigation, there must be our examination of the Customs & Excise position – all monies paid in and out must come under this. We shall require three first-class independent men. Unfortunately Brennan [Joseph Brennan, Auditor General] [17] has gone to London.

(2) It would be very desirable to make an examination of the destination of certain drafts on the London County, Westminister & Paris, London. Childers (Mr. and Mrs.) kept and keep an account or several accounts at the Holborn (I think) Branch of this bank. I am sure the bank will give details of any recent transactions.

(3) I wired today re Moor Park & Kilworth – see Hogan and let him send down whatever man was dealing with this matter. It is urgent and we must collect back rent even though it may have already been paid to the Irregulars. The people here want no compromise with the Irregulars.

(4) It is wise to postpone the Dáil meeting as already suggested.

(5) You might get before your mind's eye three persons under par. 1, but don't announce anything until I return.

(6) It would be a good thing to get Civic Guards both here and in Limerick. Civil administration urgent everywhere in the South. The people are splendid.[18]

As telecommunications were extremely bad, Collins recorded in his diary that he asked that Frank Dalton should be assigned to the Cork P.O. "with a group of men while repair work was being carried out, in order to protect the work from sabotage by anti-Treatyites". [19]

Collins had come to realise that the country was for the

most part in the hands of Provisional Government forces. His desire to postpone the first session of the new Dáil indicates that he was hardening in his attitude and wanted to finish the fight. This was the impression that Emmet Dalton gathered from their conversation. "If there was any negotiating to be done, it would be from a position of strength. Collins didn't like to see the split which had arisen in the Volunteer force. And like all of us he had hoped for peace."[20]

It was almost 4 pm when the convoy assembled for the journey to Macroom. Collins constantly tried to squeeze as much as possible into every day. "I felt he wanted to do so much in such a short time," said Dalton, who arranged that the "Dublin Liz" armoured car would replace the *Sliabh na mBan* for this journey. The *Sliabh na mBan* was being serviced at Johnson & Perrott's for its tour through West Cork the following day.

The Macroom army post, commanded by Peadar Conlon, informed Collins of constant attacks from some anti-Treaty forces. In order to withstand the attacks, Conlon requested a machine gun and some ammunition, which Collins promised to have delivered early the following morning. He intended spending the next day on an inspection tour of the full command area in West Cork.

He was disturbed about a prisoner who had been taken in by Lieutenant Coppinger and who had died. He queried the circumstances and asked for a report.

Williams' Hotel, occupied by National Forces, was "fortified with sandbags" according to Stephen Brady (A.J.S. Brady), son of the local rector, who was informed by his "excited" gardener that Collins was at the hotel. As Brady made his way through the hotel bar which "was packed with military men standing at ease in groups taking drinks at the long counter ... General Michael Collins was standing at the head of the counter. His aide-de-camp Emmet Dalton was standing beside him." Collins had "taken his military cap off; it was lying crown down on the counter... From the way he glanced constantly around I gathered that he had not yet rid himself of the alertness inherent in a fugitive. Though he certainly cut a dash as 'a brass hat', the uniform seemed, in some way, to be out of character with his rebel past". He heard Collins ordering a drink. Apparently Collins was in a cheerful mood.[21]

Later Collins met Florence (Florrie) O'Donoghue, former member of the IRA Executive. (He had resigned on 28 June 1922, after negotiations with Richard Mulcahy failed.) O'Donoghue had been arrested and put in a separate quarter. He had been arrested, unjustly, he felt, by a pro-Treaty soldier. He had been making his way from Cork to his Kerry home to visit his sick mother. He told Ernie O'Malley that he had borrowed a car and was travelling through Macroom when he was arrested by a "fool" – a "Free State soldier" – and was "put in the clink". He managed to make contact with Collins and was released. O'Donoghue remained neutral for the rest of the Civil War.[22]

When Collins had completed his business in Macroom, the convoy returned to Cork.

Back in Cork, Collins and Dalton went immediately to a another priest's residence in the hope of collecting further money held in safe keeping for the opposing forces. "Our information was correct," said Dalton. "When we told him [the priest] what we knew, he parted with a small box containing a large sum of money."[23]

Commandant Frank O'Friel, who had come down from Shanakiel hospital, was in the Imperial Hotel when the convoy returned from Macroom. Collins queried him about the wounded National soldiers, and asked for the names of those in hospital.

Word had come in, O'Friel said, that a Patrick Corcoran had died in the South Infirmary at 4 am and that a Michael Collins had been fatally wounded when he rushed a machine-gun post at Rochestown. Collins said that this man was his cousin. Before going to bed that night, he wrote in his notebook: *"Michael Collins shot dead."* Within twenty-four hours those ominous words would fit the man who wrote them.

Chapter 5

While Collins headed southwards on Sunday 20 August 1922, de Valera was also in the south. Some days previously, de Valera was in Kilpeadar, near Ballincollig, and had written in his diary: "Any chance of winning? If there was any chance, duty to hold on to secure it. If none, duty to try to get the men to quit – for the present. The people must be won to the cause before any successful fighting can be done. The men dead and gloomy – just holding on. How long will it last?"[1]

He was in the Gougane Barra area on Saturday. The American writer, Peter Golden, found him in the neat whitewashed kitchen of James O'Leary. The house was tucked between the hills in the townland of Gurtafludaig, near Ballingeary.[2] The family were saying the Rosary in Irish when Golden entered the kitchen. De Valera was kneeling against the back of a sugán chair with his face buried in his hands. When the prayers ended de Valera rose and greeted the visitor, who got the impression that he was "heartsick and distraught at the terrible things which had come to the nation and its people".[3] Yet Golden discovered that de Valera hadn't a word of bitterness against those who opposed him. "Not even against those who certainly have not spared him." And though he spoke of the pioneering work for Ireland done by the late Arthur Griffith, he was "fearful that the next step will be a military dictatorship set up by Mick Collins, taking his orders from England".[4]

At this point in the war anti-Treaty military operations were outside de Valera's influence; those rested in the hands of the Army Executive, with Liam Lynch as Chief of Staff.

Lynch had no intention of compromise. "We have declared for an Irish Republic and will not live under any other law" was his comment to his brother.[5] De Valera had met Lynch in Whitechurch. Lynch deluded de Valera by telling him to "see Liam Deasy" even though he felt at this stage that Deasy would be as adamant as himself. Meanwhile, Lynch sent a dispatch to Deasy, GOC of the First Southern Division, in which he said, "Dev passing through your area talking of peace. Give him no encouragement."[6]

De Valera was hoping to locate Deasy, but because of the National Army's seaborne landings off the Cork and Kerry coasts, the principal strongholds of the anti-Treaty forces had been eroded. On 12 August, anti-Treaty forces abandoned Cork when pro-Treaty forces were making inroads through the city, thus avoiding civilian tragedies. They withdrew to secluded regions to the west of the city. Broken into units without any definite policy, they were operating largely on the initiative of individual commanders during the week which followed. Republican leaders felt that the time had come for some cohesive plan.

Fighting in the field as a regular army had failed; guerilla tactics of the previous years were not operative because personnel, hide-outs, and movement-style were often known by local pro-Treaty troops. In addition, there were no established lines of communication between units and between those and the Executive headquarters. Consequently, when officers of Cork No.1 Brigade met in the Arthur O'Leary's Hibernian Hotel, Ballymakeera, on Sunday morning 20 August, Liam Deasy GOC was unaware of such a meeting until the following evening when he was informed by de Valera, who had been present.

Before the officers' meeting word had reached them from the Limerick area that Michael Collins was travelling south on a tour of inspection of Provisional Government forces. The men who assembled felt that because of his interrupted tour of Kerry (interrupted to attend Arthur Griffith's funeral), Collins' convoy might this time travel along the Millstreet/ Macroom route. And because so many important officers from the First Brigade were concentrated in the one area, it would be necessary to set up roadblocks to avoid a surprise attack. The fact that it was an enemy contingent would of itself mean that it should be ambushed. Therefore, roads into and around the area were blocked with fallen trees and other obstacles on that Sunday. Bill Powell waited in ambush position all day in charge of some men on the Carriganima/ Millstreet road, while another section scouted on the Clondroichead direction. Other roads were also being observed and mines were laid on them. The main aim of the senior officers' meeting (chaired by Dan "Sando" O' Donovan O/C Cork No 1 Brigade) was to decide future policy. It emerged that though de Valera (who was present) talked of peace, the others wondered if there was any way of fighting it out. "The men who were present were not for peace for the sake of it. It was hard, rough going, we debated everything thoroughly," said Sando. Finally, it was conceded that if Liam Deasy agreed, he should put out some peace feelers. Then any new situation could be debated. De Valera informed the men that he was trying to locate Deasy.

During the meeting,[7] Michael Murphy, Divisional Officer, and Sando O'Donovan spoke about Collins. Both men were described by Pake Sheehan as extreme Republicans. Paddy O'Sullivan and Dónal O'Callaghan were security guards protecting the members present.[8] The information received was that Collins was on his way southwards, with Cork on the itinerary. De Valera was told that if the convoy entered any hostile area where Republicans were based, the convoy would be ambushed. When the idea was expressed that Collins "may not leave Cork alive", de Valera expressed regret, as he felt it would be easier to negotiate with Collins than with other members of the Provisional Government or the Army, according to Dan Sando O'Donovan.[9]

Very early on Monday morning, 21 August, de Valera, fresh after his night's sleep in O'Leary's Hibernian Hotel, Ballymakeera (Cork No. 1 Brigade Headquarters, under the Command of Dan Sando O'Donovan) set out, with a change of ponies for their trap, hoping to locate Deasy.

Erskine Childers and Riobárd Langford were known to be producing *An Phoblacht*, the anti-Treaty paper, on a handpress in the home of Richard Woods at Moneygave, near Enniskeane. Liana Corcoran was the typist.[10] It was decided to escort de Valera to this house where at least he would get an indication as to Deasy's whereabouts.

Here Seán Hyde, publicity officer for the Republicans, had joined Childers and the brothers Riobárd and Dick Langford. Later that evening Liam Deasy arrived. "They all gathered in the parlour and remained talking for the rest of the evening," said Maggie Sheehan, who was employed by the Woods family. "We brought in a few large pots of tea, eatables and the ware on trays. The men asked not to be disturbed, they said they would manage for themselves. When they wanted more tea, they came out to have the teapots refilled."[11]

Riobárd Langford said they discussed many issues including "the railroading of the Staters into our territory. Dev was a good listener. We knew, of course, we were being beaten at the time, but we somehow hoped our luck would turn. Though we talked and talked, Deasy said that at the Divisional meeting the next day in Béal na mBláth, when we would have officers from several regions, we could come to some positive decision".[12]

Earlier that morning, Liam Deasy had gone to his parents' home at Kilmacsimon and then to Sullivans' of Gurranreagh, the house that had been used as headquarters during the War of Independence. Deasy intended setting up temporary headquarters for the Division at Sullivans' and had notified Liam Lynch. Consequently, among the many dispatches waiting for Deasy at Sullivans' was one from Liam Lynch informing him that de Valera had been with him, and was even then on his way to see him, and in Deasy's own words: "I was on no account to give him any encouragement as his suggestions and arguments were unacceptable to Lynch."[13]

Deasy soon discovered that Joe Sullivan Senior was pro-Treaty and spoke with hostility about de Valera whom he called "The Long Fellow". It was made quite clear to Deasy that though he was personally welcome, he could forget about his intention of reinstating headquarters in the house for the anti-Treaty side. According to Diarmuid Brennan's correspondence (Friday, 13th November, 1970) to Dr. Gerald Ahern, "Joe O'Sullivan was over seventy and a vociferous supporter of Collins and the Treaty".

Former billets had to be examined, intelligence work needed reorganisation, people's reaction in areas frequented by Republicans had to be studied, so that the anti-Treatyites could have shelter in safety and be sure of food; these were all matters which Deasy noted for the following day's meeting.

Because of the warning dispatch received from Lynch, Deasy wasn't completely taken by surprise when he saw de Valera in Moneygave, nor was he surprised at his suggestion of peace offers. "De Valera's principal argument was that we had made our protest in arms and appeared to be incapable of military success; the most honourable course for us would be to withdraw. I told him that we had at least a thousand armed men in the First Southern Division and, from my knowledge, most were prepared to fight on, and would not, therefore, agree to an unconditional surrender." (They hoped their anticipated armaments from American sources would arrive. Liam Lynch had been involved in organizing this.)[14]

The war situation was discussed by the men far into the night so that it was long past midnight when de Valera lay down to sleep "on the settle in the parlour behind the door". Maggie Sheehan took a quilt from "the master's bed for the settle".[15] Outside, Ned Galvin remained on scout duty throughout the night, in front of the house. (The Woods family were friends of Erskine Childers and their house was "a safe house", according to Ned Galvin and was "Headquarters of the 3rd Cork Brigade" during much of the Civil War. From research it has emerged that de Valera did not stay in Sullivans' at Gurranreigh on this occasion, nor was their house headquarters for the Republicans during the Civil War, as has been stated in other writings.) Ned Galvin confirmed in a letter to the author (28/1/1965) that "De Valera stayed that night before the ambush in Woods' house", where he [Ned Galvin] was "on guard duty".

The following day, policy would be discussed further at an important Brigade Council meeting, which was convened to take place at Bill Murray's house at Béal na mBláth. Deasy was glad that de Valera would be present to give his viewpoint. [16]

Chapter 6

Joe Dolan was startled by an early morning shout from Michael Collins on 22 August 1922. He jumped out of bed immediately. Collins was looking out the window. Cork City was silent in the sultry August morning. This was the beginning of the last day of Michael Collins' life.

The bell on Holy Trinity Church nearby was sounding the hour. At 6 am Collins crossed himself and paused for a moment in prayer. Not a man to waste time dressing himself, he was, within seconds, down the stairs and in to breakfast which he ate hastily. He put on his officer's cap before leaving and going down the few steps to the footpath where the trim figure of Emmet Dalton, his travelling companion and bodyguard for the day, was pacing to and fro. The convoy of vehicles was waiting.

John O'Connell, who two days previously had acted as a guide on the route between Mallow and Cork, was no longer needed but had requested to remain with the group. He was already in the Crossley Tender when Dalton emerged from the Imperial Hotel "as the hall clock read ten minutes past six". The convoy vehicles had left Johnson & Perrott's where they had been garaged, and had arrived outside the hotel at six o'clock. Lieutenant Smith, the motorcycle scout, was in front, followed by the open Crossley Tender with a complement of two officers, two machine-gunners with a Lewis gun and eight riflemen. After this was the Leyland Eight touring car in which Collins and Dalton would sit behind the two drivers, Corry and Quinn. Bringing up the rear was the *Sliabh na mBan* armoured car driven by Jim Woulfe, with the crewmen and machine-gunner Jock McPeak.

Dalton saluted Collins, with the automatic gesture of a soldier – a formal display between two friends. They spoke briefly while Collins fingered the notebook in his top pocket. Before mounting the Leyland, with poised pencil he glanced at the time, then jotted down: "Left at 6.15 am – Macroom, Bandon, Clonakilty, Rosscarbery, Skibbereen."[1]

While most of Cork City slept, the convoy broke the silence as it drove through the city streets. It headed out along the Western Road and towards Ballincollig. Here they encountered what Dalton described as "an extraordinary amount of bridge destruction and road obstruction". Though they had travelled this route the previous day without much difficulty "it seemed as if the Irregulars had come and set up roadblocks overnight".[2]

Retreating from the city during the previous days, the Republicans had succeeded in making the main road to Bandon impassable by blowing up the bridges outside Ballinhassig and Innishannon. Dalton believed that the obstruction of the Ballincollig Road was an afterthought; what he did not know was that Republicans travelling to the meeting at Béal na mBláth from the Ballincollig district were aware that a sudden swoop could leave many of their units leaderless – it was for this reason that Seán Hyde and a number of Republicans took the precaution of destroying the bridges and creating other blockages. These blockages forced Collins' convoy to make a detour through by-roads in the Ballincollig area. They arrived in Macroom sometime between seven thirty and a quarter to eight. The Lewis gun promised to Captain Peadar Conlon the previous evening was handed over. It was then housed in an archway under the Town Hall. Collins, who had carried out an inspection in Macroom the previous day and had also met Florrie O'Donoghue, was anxious to proceed in the West Cork direction as quickly as possible.

Because Captain Conlon knew the road from Macroom to Bandon was blocked, he suggested that Timmy Kelleher, who hadn't taken part in either the War of Independence or the Civil War, and who was employed as a driver for the Williams' Hotel, would be most suitable as a guide. Kelleher constantly took cattle buyers to all the fairs in the district, and was familiar with the area. A soldier was sent to get Kelleher. Having been out late the previous night, Kelleher was still in bed, but immediately awoke at the loud knock on the door. Once dressed, he was informed by the soldier that he was to go to Williams' Hotel, barrack headquarters, and he was to accompany a convoy as far as Bandon.

When Kelleher arrived at Williams' Hotel he was informed that Collins was the principal passenger. This made him apprehensive. Shortly they were on the road. On 19/4/1974, Kelleher travelled with the author on the journey taken that morning. The interview was done with the recorder running. Places and directions were shown as they travelled on this circuitous route. At the time of interview, as Kelleher mentioned, some of the area had been flooded due to the installation of the ESB hydro-electric scheme (1953–1956).

With Kelleher seated in the front of the Crossley Tender, between Dalton and Captain Conroy, the driver that day, the convoy headed in the Crookstown direction. "I knew all the roads and was aware that two of the bridges on this line were broken, so we took the Dooniskey-Cross route," Kelleher told me. They took the indirect route then a right turn at Dooniskey Stores and drove through the townland of Ballymichael.

At the foot of the hill opposite O'Mahonys' the Leyland stalled, forcing its occupants to alight. According to Jim Woulfe, this was due to dirty petrol. The petrol containers had been refilled without being emptied and had thus accumulated sediment since the beginning of their long journey from Dublin.

Kate O'Mahony was getting up, and had her son in her arms. "It was around 8 am when I saw the convoy through the upstairs window." She also "saw the activity".[3]

Collins was amongst those who jumped out to assist and, when one soldier suggested to his Commander-in-Chief that he would take his place, Collins would have none of it, but pushed the car with the others to the top of the hill and down the small incline, where it restarted.

Seated once more, Collins joked about pushing "the old donkey" as the procession of vehicles proceeded towards Kilmurry. The convoy was again brought to a halt by a herd of cows driven by a farmer called Jeremiah Murphy. Collins was in the heart of Republican territory but wasn't aware of it. Nor were any of the convoy members very alert to the danger. But Kelleher, the guide, suddenly became very aware of their vulnerability. He remarked on this to Conroy, the driver of the tender, as they headed into Kilmurry Cross where some men were assembled, many of whom he recognised: "They're all Republicans over there. It looks as if there's an early morning gathering."

From Kilmurry, it was on to Béal na mBláth. (The spelling and meaning of this name is disputed. *Béal na mBláth* translates as "mouth of the flowers". One reconstruction is *Béal Átha na Bláiche*, meaning "mouth of the ford of the buttermilk". However, Bruno O'Donoghue in his *Place Names of West Cork* says the correct name is *Béal na Blaithe* meaning a "hollow between hills", and this is an apt description of the place.) At Béal na mBláth cross, the driver of the tender halted to check that the remainder of the convoy was following. The dispatch motorcycle rider had also pulled up; he kept in touch with Kelleher who signalled directions to him. According to Kelleher, "When we stopped at the cross we were directly opposite Long's pub. In the upper right-hand window facing us there was a man looking straight at us – it could have been anybody. It was at that moment I became really aware that we were in Republican territory, and that no doubt our passing would be discussed. This thought flashed briefly through my mind, as the motorcyclist waited across the road for my signal."[4]

Realising that the remainder of the convoy was proceeding

slowly but in sight behind, Kelleher signalled a right turn to Smith and so they headed in a direct line towards Bandon.

However, when the touring car reached the crossroads (it had been some distance behind), Quinn the driver discovered that there were four roads radiating from this point. He had lost sight of the vehicles in front so he drove to where a man stood and asked him the best road to Bandon.

Denny "The Dane" Long[5] was standing at the crossroads near Long's public house (now the Diamond Bar). He was a Republican scout armed with a rifle. He had been posted as a sentry at the crossroads because of the large number of Republican leaders who were gathered in the area for that day's meeting in Béal na mBláth. When he saw the motor cycle and tender passing he went into the pub which was at the corner and put his rifle behind the door. He saw the touring car approach and when it halted he felt safe enough because he didn't have the rifle. Instantly, he recognised Collins. Realising the dynamite situation which confronted him – at any minute armed Republicans could step out from the nearby pub or emerge from any of the roads – he quickly sent the "intruders" on their way. "The other lorry is gone straight ahead, and take the second cross to the right in the Newcestown direction," he said.

But what Long didn't know was that further on Kelleher had directed Smith to take the straight road to Bandon, and not a right at the cross.

When Kelleher discovered that the convoy wasn't following, he sensed what had happened, so the motorcyclist and tender made an about-turn at a gap in a field and headed towards Newcestown where they found the other vehicles parked outside the church. Collins was reading the inscription over the door when they arrived. Collins raised his hand and returned to the touring car.[6]

The convoy wound its way beside Curraclough and eventually reached Bandon where it drove down Convent Hill into the town. The August sun, hidden by the clouds since early morning, began to emerge. Their first stop was the Devonshire Arms Hotel, barrack-quarters of the pro-Treaty forces. This hotel had been partially destroyed by retreating Republicans before vacating it. A substantial part of the building was saved and there they had set up headquarters.

Bandon had been captured by pro-Treaty forces some days after Cork was taken. Collins regarded the town as the gateway to West Cork and only heard of the victory on the Saturday as he planned the Cork trip. A newspaper reported: "With the capture of Bandon the last of the Irregular strongholds has fallen but that does not mean that the last has been heard of the Irregulars." When the troops marched into the town on "Saturday evening the resistance offered was very weak."[7] Collins had received the news with satisfaction.

Bandon had been a stronghold of British imperialism since its foundation.[8] It was a garrison town and as such played a strong part in the upholding of British rule during the War of Independence. One of the most dreaded forces of British crown, the Essex Regiment, which was stationed in Bandon, was involved in many bloody conflicts with Tom Barry's 3rd

West Cork Flying Column. Following the evacuation of the Bandon barracks after the signing of the Treaty, the Republican forces had been in command of the town. The Provisional Government was now in possession of the partially destroyed large military barracks in the square as well as both the Devonshire Arms quarters and Lee's Hotel.

This stop-over in Bandon was brief as Collins was anxious to continue his journey westwards. He spoke with Lieutenant Liam Daly, headquarters' officer, and said that on his return call in the evening he would have a more detailed discussion with officers in the regional headquarters at Lee's Hotel. (Now the Munster Arms Hotel).

Breaking from protocol in typical fashion Collins cheerfully spoke to a former neighbour, Jack Sheehy. (Sheehy and Collins were born and reared in houses sharing the same farmyard at Sam's Cross.) Collins put his revolver on the table, greeted Sheehy and took Sheehy's eight-year-old daughter, Mary, on his lap. Their brief conversation ended with a warm handshake – the last Sheehy would get from the man who used to answer Mass and play hurley with him as a boy.

Tim Kelleher, who had been booked to take someone to Cobh in the afternoon, reminded Collins that he needed to get back to Macroom. Collins thanked Kelleher and scribbled a note to hand to a taxi driver with a request to take him back to Macroom and to collect the fee for the trip from barrack headquarters in Bandon. As Collins held out the note, Kelleher asked, "How will you find your way back, Mr. Collins?" Instantly, Smith, the motorcyclist, interrupted, "I know the way back now." To which Collins responded, "Good man!", shook hands with Kelleher and thanked him once more, before stepping onto the Leyland.[9]

As the convoy crunched the stony road from Bandon towards Clonakilty, Collins discussed with Dalton the many ambushes that had been fought in the area. Since 1916, the people in the West Cork region had lived with uncertainty. There was hardly a home that hadn't been affected by the harsh and constant reality that the Irish people were fighting for freedom from British rule. Families who mourned the death of a friend or a loved one, killed either in an ambush or murdered in a Black and Tan reprisal, were united in their fight for independence. But since the signing of the 1921 Treaty and the outbreak of the Civil War, disharmony reigned in many homes. Local people were torn in their loyalties. If Michael Collins had not been involved in the negotiations and subsequent Treaty his friends and neighbours in West Cork have maintained that most, if not all, of the region would have decided to take the Republican side. As it was, only a minority had followed him, men who were in school with him, or men like Seán Hales and Ned Barrett who were in Frongoch prison with him.

But now, on this August morning, Collins and his men were travelling through this area recently recaptured by the troops of the Provisional Government, while some key Republicans were heading across fields to a meeting at Béal na mBláth.

Page from Collins' notebook, written the day before he was shot

Collins in 1917

Kitty Kiernan, Collins' fiancée

John (Jock) McPeak, gunner of the *Sliabh na mBan*

Sean Hales, National Army – one of the last people to speak with Michael Collins at Lee's Hotel

Collins greeted by friends

Tom Hales, participant in Béal na mBláth ambush

Tom Kelleher, participant in Béal na mBláth ambush

Bill Powell (standing), participant in Béal na mBláth ambush

Jim Kearney, participant in Béal na mBláth ambush

Last photograph of Collins, taken outside Lee's Hotel in Bandon on 22 August 1922, before heading to Béal na mBláth. He and Dalton are in the back of the touring car, Collins on the left

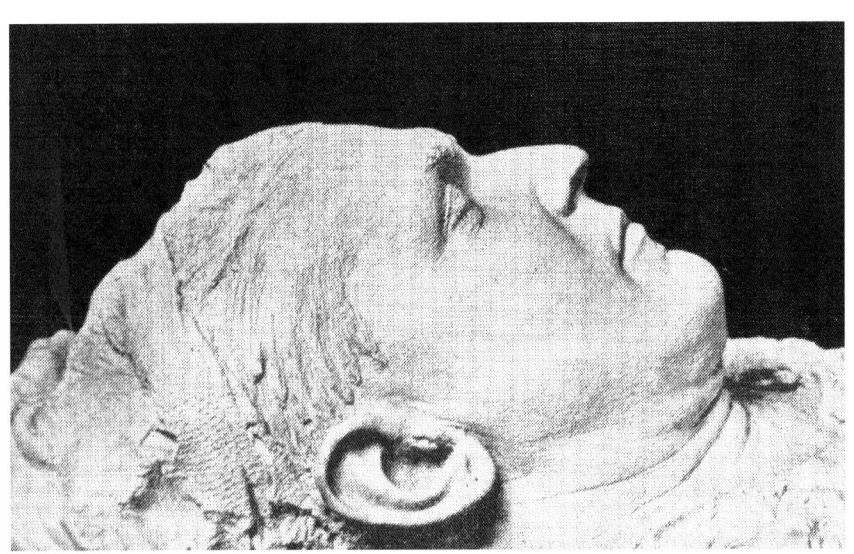

Albert Power's death mask of Collins

Chapter 7

Tuesday 22 August 1922 was an important day for the Republicans. Since the previous evening, men had been billeted in houses around Béal na mBláth in preparation for the meeting to be held in Bill Murray's farmhouse, which was situated on an incline behind Long's public house, near where Collins' convoy had passed earlier.

After breakfast, de Valera, Liam Deasy, Seán Hyde and Jim Flynn travelled in a pony and trap from Moneygave to Béal na mBláth (approximately 3 miles), and arrived around 9.30. (Deasy had arranged that after the meeting Denny Crowley would accompany de Valera in the Glanworth direction to meet Liam Lynch.) When they got out of the trap at Béal na mBláth cross, they were immediately approached by Denny "The Dane", who had been on scout duty since daybreak, having taken over from the night-watch. He told them that a "Free State armed convoy consisting of a motorcyclist, a lorry of troops, a touring car and an armoured car had passed earlier in the morning, and had stopped to enquire the way to Bandon". Denny said that he was "most helpful and sent them via Newcestown, knowing that road wasn't blocked" – that he was only too anxious to get them on their way because of the number of Republican officers who were billeted nearby.¹ Long told them that he recognised Michael Collins seated in the back of the touring car.

"So he's on his way to West Cork!" was Deasy's initial reaction. "Then he'll be coming back this way." Deasy knew that this was the only unblocked road to Cork because both the direct Bandon/Cork road and the "upper" Bandon road via Crossbarry had been rendered impassable, such strategy being necessary because of the many important officers and general staff of the Republicans who had been assembling in the area since the previous night. In response to this information, de Valera asked Deasy what he thought was likely to happen. Deasy said that there were a number of men billeted in the area who had been forced to retreat from Limerick, Kilmallock and Buttevant. "Some were involved in the Cork withdrawal, and because of this they are in a hostile frame of mind." Deasy further explained to de Valera that the area was predominantly Republican and that they would consider the entering of enemy forces as an intrusion. "In five company areas along this Bandon route, not one active volunteer joined the Free State Army. It seems like a challenge that they can't refuse to meet. It's most likely we'll prepare for an ambush."²

De Valera expressed sorrow on hearing this. His aspiration for peace was shattered. He had also hoped that after the Ballymakeera headquarters' meeting and subsequent discussion with Deasy, and the culminating meeting at Béal na mBláth, he would have an overall view of the Republican mentality for the first Dáil meeting which he expected to attend.³

Disillusionment was evident on de Valera's face as he walked up the incline from the cross towards Murrays' house with a few men. Deasy had stepped into Long's public house at the crossroads to meet some of the officers who had spent the night there.

Bill Powell was at the top of the incline near the entrance to Murrays' when he saw de Valera approaching, so he waited. Powell mentioned that Michael Collins had gone past. "I can still picture him [Dev] looking out across the valley, no smile, stem as always, and all he said was, 'A pity! Pity I didn't meet him!' He turned, and we both walked silently along the rough stone of the yard and into Bill Murray's kitchen." Bill Powell was sorry the two men did not meet. "If Collins had been later, or Dev had been earlier, history could be so different. I'm pretty sure, that even though they were on opposite sides in a Civil War, they would have a few civil words in West Cork."[4]

The men who had already gathered in Bill Murray's kitchen were talking about Collins when de Valera walked in. Some who hadn't known de Valera was in the area were surprised to see him. Liam Deasy and other officers entered. There was no great debate – the question was, should an ambush be prepared or not? There was disagreement about this. Tom Hales was "cool and thoughtful," said Bill Powell. He suggested that, on balance, perhaps they shouldn't ambush the returning convoy. (He had been very close to Collins.) However, when all views were expressed, it was finally decided that the convoy was part of an enemy force encroaching on territory which the Republicans still held and that therefore it should be ambushed.[5]

The agenda for the planned meeting was postponed. And de Valera, obviously sensing the mood of the men, left before full orders had been given to take up ambush positions. With his aide, Jimmy Flynn, he took the Cloughduv and minor roads (by-passing Cork City) and on to Mourne Abbey near Mallow.

The men who had assembled at Béal na mBláth were not a column, but officers who were trained in guerilla warfare and who had gathered to hold an important staff meeting. Seeing the opportunity of overpowering an enemy convoy on its return journey, they decided to take up the challenge and ambush it.[6]

Sonny O'Neill, member of the 1st Southern Division, said that they went down to look at the position in Béal na mBláth.[7] "We took up a position there, and held it till late in the evening."

The area chosen was south of Béal na mBláth crossroads, an ideal ambush position as a boreen (laneway) meandered along overlooking the narrow main road. In between there was a marshy field, with high grass and ferns and a little winding river (the Noneen) running parallel to the main road. Off this boreen were smaller boreens running to other roads and houses further north. There were also two gaps in the ditch of the boreen. This all meant ready-made places of retreat, should the necessity arise. On the other hand, the enemy (should they arrive) would be walled in by a thick growth of trees, bushes and a steep, furzy hill field to their backs. Their only protection against the ambushers was a two-foot-high mud wall lightly beaded with ferns, between the road and the little river.

Deasy had to hide some documents and dispatches which he had in his possession. East of the Murrays' house, Jackie and Tom Murray, the sons of the family, were cutting a fallen tree for firewood when Deasy called them.

"There was a safe dump under clumps of briars in the field, and Liam Deasy asked Tom to help bury documents and stuff," says Jackie Murray. Deasy sent Jackie into the house "where there was a lot of commotion". He was handed a dispatch to take immediately to the sentry across the way in Foleys' house where other men were billeted.[8] Sonny O'Neill said that they had heard about the Collins party going through in the morning.

Jim Kearney and Timmy Sullivan (O'Sullivan) were in Foley's kitchen. Under Comdt Tom Hales' instructions, they had come from having blown up Innishannon Bridge, on the main Cork/Bandon Road, two days previously on the 19 August. (Tom Ennis, with pro-Treaty forces, had crossed the bridge before it was blown up and continued on towards Bandon.) The two, with Jack Kelly, had slept for three nights under a chestnut tree close to the bridge as they awaited Tom Hales' order to blow it up. "Tom Hales came himself, accompanied by Jackie O'Neill, and gave us the order. He told us we should head in the Béal na mBláth direction afterward."

Seán Buckley was in Foleys' kitchen when Kearney and Sullivan came there. Then a sentry came to Foleys' with a message from Murrays'. He told the two men to go down to the cross immediately: "You're engineers, both of you are wanted; they're setting up an ambush."[9]

Already Dinny Covney, appointed driver of a 'Model T' motor car, accompanied by Tadhg O'Sullivan and young Tom Foley had brought two mines in wooden crates (a small one and a larger one) from John Lordan's near Newcestown. On returning, they found Liam Deasy O/C and Comdt. Tom Hales laying out the ambush positions. Soldiers were digging a little channel in the road surface for the larger mine.

A barricade was constructed at the northern end (closest to Long's pub) of the stretch of road designated for the ambush. It was made by stopping a Clonakilty man, Jeremiah "The Leaguer" [Léger] O'Brien, who was taking empty mineral bottles from Long's pub in a long horse-drawn scotch-cart (two-wheeled tip cart) to the West Cork Bottling Company in Bandon. The cart was commandeered and one of the iron-rimmed wheels removed and thrown up on the crates of bottles. With the shafts facing east and resting on the ground, the long scotch-car was strategically placed across the road directly beyond a bend. From speaking to ambush participants, it appears that at that time the bend was sharp. Therefore, the barricade was positioned so that the anticipated on-coming convoy travelling from Bandon would be brought abruptly to a halt. Jeremiah "The Leaguer" was directed towards Foleys' farmhouse west of the boreen. He was ordered to take his horse there and to remain there throughout the day.

When Jim Kearney and Timmy Sullivan came to the

ambush site, they found that John Callaghan (O'Callaghan) with the help of Jack Kelly had already laid the larger mine that traversed the main road. It was laid about 50 yards south of the barricade. It was buried at a depth of about a foot and half and covered with the loose chippings and stones of which the road was composed. Now the men, all four trained engineers, laid the cable that connected to the mine which ran from the exploder in the boreen above down through the marshy field, and crossed the river. It was planned that the anticipated armoured car in the convoy travelling north from Bandon would be brought to a halt. The men responsible for activating the cable/mine had a 'marker' in their sights when the car would reach that point. This would mean that it would be blown up, therefore the convoy would be trapped between that and the barricade. Another mine was left inside the little ditch beside the road. It has been stated in other writings that this second mine was placed in front of the bridge, and in some beyond the bridge; this needs clarification. This mine was not used, as it wasn't needed, according to Liam Deasy: "If we laid another mine in front of the barricade, we would only be blowing up our own barricade." Jim Kearney, a trained engineer, agreed with this comment, in a letter to the author, 12/11/1990, and continued: "Also it would be foolish, quite foolish from a military point of view to put the barricade just beyond Glannarouge bridge as the armoured car could drive up the lane and blow us to bits. That was the area where we lay in wait all day."

Deasy GOC Ist Southern Division, Tom Crofts Divisional

Adjutant, and Tom Hales O/C 3rd Brigade, gave approximately forty men (different numbers are given by various sources),[10] the ambush positions. Some of the men were members of local Republican companies who "were rounded-up" for the occasion. (The author spoke to some of these but they did not wish to be named.) It has to be noted that it was Tom Hales who sent sentries to different companies for men, as he was Brigade O/C and was familiar with all the companies in his No. 3 Brigade. (Cork County was divided into three brigades.)

This Béal na mBláth was a small area, merely a place people passed through on the way to somewhere else. The occupied boreen was elevated at the north-western side and this would give the men a vantage field of fire above the spot where the anticipated convoy would be brought to a halt. Behind their backs there were two narrow boreens known as Walsh's Lane and Long's Lane. The men were armed with Lee Enfield rifles (.303), some also had pistols or revolvers, and a few, one being Liam Deasy, had Thompson guns. The men who prepared the ambush "were officers and expert at their job". It was prepared "in a minimum area for a maximum result". They placed the Command Post on 'The Rock', the highest point known locally as 'Poul Séc'. All the men settled down to wait – perhaps for a few hours, perhaps for the day. They didn't know. Visibility was good. At that time there were no Sally trees or bushes. It has to be noted that this area has all changed over the years with bulldozing of fields, the widening of roads and also the building of a Collins Monument. (In a letter to the author from Jim Kearney,

13/11/1990, he wrote: "I was in Béal na mBláth last Friday with my niece and saw that the place has changed quite a bit, with all the growth, not the same view that we had in 1922. The road has also been widened, and that sharp bend is gone.")

Already, May Twomey of Cumann na mBan and a friend had been sent by bicycle to Bandon to find out if Collins' convoy was travelling further or if it appeared that they were returning directly. By midday the two girls had returned and told Deasy that the convoy had gone on to West Cork.

Some of the men who had travelled from the Clonakilty area the previous evening told Deasy that Republicans had blocked the main Clonakilty road with fallen trees. Therefore, it was felt that the convoy might have to turn back sooner than anticipated.

During the day the men maintained their ambush positions, beneath a sultry, at times sunny sky. They did not allow anybody to bring tea, as "nobody was allowed on to the site" once positions were given.

The minutes ticked into hours, and so the day wore on. It was past 7.30 when a light mist began to fall upon the valley, though this didn't last long.

By this time, the men were a little weary of waiting and they wondered if indeed there would be any ambush. Deasy had returned some time previously. He had spent much time during the day securing documents. Hales and Deasy consulted. Hales, aware that Collins, his friend, would be one of the targets of the ambush was initially a slightly reluctant participant, but agreed it was right and offered a great opportunity for the Republicans. Now he was glad when Deasy suggested calling off the ambush temporarily. Deasy thought that the convoy had possibly got held up somewhere and must have decided to rest at some barracks depot for the night. He walked around to the men. "From what I know of Collins he is not going to come back tonight," he said, and told his men to go to billets close by. The engineers, Jim Kearney, Timmy Sullivan and John Callaghan, were instructed to roll up the cable. "We'll have another try in the morning," said Deasy.[11]

De Valera had reached Clashbee near Mallow by this time. Siobhán Creedon[12] was in bed, having returned from work with a heavy cold, when a dispatch rider arrived with a letter from Liam Deasy asking her to go immediately to Batt Walsh's home in Clashabee, "I was to bring some form of transport. De Valera would be there so I was to arrange his accommodation for the night. The next day a blue car would come to take him over the Tipperary border because he was returning to Dublin." According to Deasy's order, she was not to give the job to anybody else but to do it herself. With her brother Michael, Siobhán set out in the pony and trap for the eight-mile journey to Clashabee. The Walsh home was heavily guarded and de Valera was having a meal with Liam Lynch when they arrived. Some of the discussion centered around Michael Collins as it was known that he had passed in a convoy in the Whitechurch area the previous day on his way to Cork.

"When the convoy had stopped at Monee to put petrol and water in the touring car," said Siobhán Creedon, "a local man who casually asked one of the soldiers whose convoy it was, was informed it was Michael Collins on an inspection tour of Cork County." Soon the Republicans were the recipients of this information obtained from an "indiscreet soldier."[13] A dispatch was sent immediately to their comrades in the Middleton/Cobh area where some men had been billeted after the fall of Cork. The Republicans, thus alerted, mined the road the following morning before Collins, they believed, was due to pass through. The discussion in Walshs' kitchen centered around the ambushes that had been set up in the areas of Ballyvourney and Ballingeary two days previously. The news from those areas was brought by de Valera. He also told them about the decision taken that morning by the men in West Cork to lay an ambush at Béal na mBláth.

The possible reasons for Collins' visit to Cork were debated. De Valera told them that Deasy and the West Cork men were extremely surprised that Collins should travel through such Republican country and that therefore they looked on this as a challenge.[14]

Chapter 8

Dalton felt that "normality and law and order should not be too far off. We were in possession of the principal towns in Cork County. Michael Collins and I discussed this on the journey through West Cork." Much of the conversation along the route "dealt with events that had happened, there were suggestions as to the future, and there was some small talk about the countryside; whenever he was familiar with a district, he mentioned this. I remember the early part of the journey as being very pleasant. He was certainly happy as we drove towards West Cork. It was a beautiful August day. Because there were still daily ambushes, I was in trepidation of what could happen, but Collins saw no danger."[1]

On the road to Clonakilty, Collins spoke about some of his former friends and colleagues who were now "on the other side". He mentioned Tom Hales whom he had visited in jail during the Treaty negotiations. Collins knew that Hales regretted that the signatories did not hold out because he regarded Lloyd George "as a bluffer". Collins told Dalton that each time he met Hales, and especially during the discussions on army reunification, Hales maintained that a "federal Ireland" would perhaps solve the problem. "He spoke of Tom Hales with affection tinged with sadness. Their broken friendship appeared to have affected him."[2]

On the outskirts of Clonakilty the convoy was brought abruptly to a halt because the road was blocked by newly felled trees. All the men in the convoy "did splendid team work in pushing aside the barricades, but," according to Emmet Dalton, "Collins was more concerned that local people would be unable to get into town the following day, which was Fair Day, than he was that we would get on our way." It was typical of the man who constantly had time to think of others. Hatchets and saws were taken from the Crossley Tender and Collins lent a hand in the clearing operation. Collins "always ready for emergencies, great or small, directed the work, and took a hand in carrying it out." Active and powerful in body as in mind, "he handled axe and saw with the same vigour as he could exhibit in the direction of affairs of the State, military or civil".[3]

One of the party, John O'Connell, was trying to break through a heavy limb with an axe when Michael Collins came over to him, "Show me that axe, boy. It's not the first time I have used one." O'Connell handed over the axe to the senior man, "whereupon the Commander-in-Chief made short work of the tree".

Having spent about an hour sawing trees and pulling them into the dyke with the aid of a wire rope and the armoured car, Collins stopped, looked around and realised that it would take too long to remove the obstruction even enough to allow them to make a pathway through. "There are plenty of idle soldiers in the area, we'll rout them out to clear this," he said, then suggested that they retrace their movements and travel along a narrow boreen, familiar to him, to the town.

The convoy pulled up outside O'Donovan's Hotel, which was a meeting place for some Provisional Government officers and men. While Collins spoke to Maurice Collins and others, word spread that he was in the area, and shortly a crowd gathered. Former friends came to welcome him home. Though he was invited into some houses he declined and said, "Next time!"

John O'Connell had never been in West Cork before and now saw the hooded cloak for the first time. These pinch-pleated hoods and gathered black cloaks were the prized possession of many women in the area, worn by women after marriage and often the product of hours of tedious work in the months preceding marriage; they were an unusual spectacle to the visiting soldier. Believing that the outfit belonged to some religious community, O'Connell asked a local soldier, "What sort of order of nuns are these? Or what do they represent at all, they seem to be so plentiful?" The soldier laughed and warned him to be careful, according to James Cahalane of Clonakilty, who told them "That's the way the women dress, and they can be mighty handy and have been used to hide many a revolver".

Collins and Dalton, according to James Cahalane, lunched in the home of Collins' cousin, Maurice Collins, then went to O'Donovan's Hotel and met some of Collins' companions of former school years. They recounted many highlights of their youth and spoke with affection of their now ageing and retired schoolmaster, Denis Lyons. Lyons, an old Fenian like Michael Collins' father, drummed into his pupils a desire for an independent nationalist policy; stories of the 1798 Rebellion got new impetus with each telling. Over lunch Collins spoke of the Fenian movement which saw Jeremiah O'Donovan Rossa, a neighbour of his from Rosscarbery, who is considered to epitomise Fenianism, rise to prominence mainly in America. Ever since Pádraig Pearse delivered the oration at O'Donovan Rossa's graveside in Glasnevin in 1915, his words, which inspired not only the 1916 leaders but many IRB members, were spoken of on numerous occasions. Now they were mentioned by Collins, who quoted Pearse: *"They have left us our Fenian dead. And while Ireland holds these graves, Ireland unfree shall never be at peace."*[4]

James Cahalane remembers Collins making the link between "the Fenian idea which had lit the flame, and the War of Independence. He regarded the Treaty as the first step towards freedom. He regretted the split, but that day he said, 'It's almost over'."[5]

Without undue delay the convoy, hailed by a cheering crowd, headed for Rosscarbery. Collins had an important call to make in this region. Two men lived around here who had been involved in supplying information to the British occupying forces during the War of Independence. The men had succeeded in supplying the information without their action gaining the attention of any of the 3rd Brigade men. Collins called to these two men; local people regarded it as a gesture of friendship, believing that Collins possibly knew them in London where they had spent some of their earlier years. Nobody yet knew the nature of their business. It is understood that Collins too was unaware of their involvement with the RIC, but they had offered their services to Collins to supply information on anti-Treaty activities. "Collins spent some time in private discussion with them."[6]

The convoy rumbled over the bridge and into the town of Rosscarbery. The loud hum of the armoured car stirred the inhabitants and brought forth people from their shops and houses. Though this was Republican territory, most people either knew or had heard of Michael Collins and certainly showed no animosity towards him. The barracks that had once dominated the town was now a burnt-out ruin. The destruction of this building on 30 March, 1921, by Tom Barry's Flying Column, meant that the IRA during that period had control over an area of roughly two hundred and seventy square miles free of the enemy. It was one of the major guerilla activities that brought praise in the form of a letter from Collins at Dublin headquarters.[7]

Collins had a personal reason to remember the Rosscarbery ambush, because on that same night British reprisal took the form of burning Michael Collins' place of birth, then owned by his brother Johnny. The incident showed the extremes to which Major A.E. Percival and the British Essex Regiment were prepared to go.[8]

Michael O'Brien and Jerry Collins, two of Michael Collins' first cousins, were among the men rounded up to carry out the burning. "There were seven, eight or nine of us taken at gunpoint by the military," said Collins' cousin, Michael O'Brien. "When we pleaded with them to save some of their belongings, they wouldn't give in, except they left us throw out some of the bedclothes, that was all. We had to take in straw and shake it out around the house, then sprinkle petrol on it. Percival left out the horses before ordering the dwelling and outhouses to be set alight. I cry when I think of it. Percival held us there until the house was engulfed in flames."

Michael O'Brien believed "It was possibly the best thing that was done for the cause. Because in this locality and throughout West Cork it bonded people into a united determination. They thought the episode would turn Mick Collins against Tom Barry, since after all it was a reprisal for the Rosscarbery ambush, but it only strengthened their relationship throughout the remainder of the Tan war."[9]

Collins was to remember the incident with nostalgia when he spoke to Kathy Hayes in Rosscarbery on that day. Even though Kathy was a staunch Republican and friend of Tom Barry, she approached him as he dismounted at the square. There she unhesitatingly told him that he should not have signed anything which still asked for allegiance to a British king. Collins smiled. "That won't be for long, Kathy."[10]

He went into O'Donovan's shop and met Anne Lehane O'Donovan, who had been in Cumann na mBan and had been a good friend of Collins' since their schooldays. Following shaking hands with many locals and a few words with his contacts, Collins once more mounted the Leyland and the convoy headed for Skibbereen.

It was a surprise for Jeremiah McCarthy, the officer in charge of the Skibbereen garrison "when I saw my old friend Mick Collins walking in the yard towards me". Captain Tadgh Sullivan, the other officer in charge, was equally astonished at Collins' unexpected visit. Collins met other friends[11] and had a joke and a pleasant word for all his comrades. The soldiers assembled for the normal military inspection, after which Collins conferred with the garrison officers. According to Emmet Dalton, "He listened to their complaints, gave them advice, and assured them of effective co-operation from the Army authorities on matters which needed attention."[12]

Having eaten a meal with the men Collins was on his way out of the Eldon Hotel shortly after 4.30 when local writer Edith Somerville approached him. She introduced herself and the pair shook hands as Dalton, Jim Woulfe and the other escort men stood by. "Keep your armoured cars away from my haven," she said jokingly. "I can't bear to see my little island being destroyed with those monstrosities."[13]

Marguerite Buckley, who was with her sister Susan O'Driscoll, had got a bunch of flowers and handed them to Collins. "With a smile, he gladly accepted."

Chapter 9

The convoy left Skibbereen and set out for its homeward journey, back via Rosscarbery and on towards Sam's Cross. Collins pointed in the direction of the ruin at Woodfield, with its gaping windows and rugged stone walls silhouetted in the distant field against the evening sky. "There," he said to Dalton, "was where I was born. That was my home."

The convoy wound its way "back home" near his brother's place, to the Four Alls public house at Sam's Cross. On his way into the public house situated at the crossroads, Collins met his cousins Michael O'Brien and Jeremiah Collins.

When he came in, he stood just inside the door, took a look around, smiled and said, "How's everybody?" He then approached the counter and enquired for his brother Johnny. Michael O'Brien told him that he was "down in the field". Immediately he asked O'Brien to tell Johnny to come up right away: "I can't go down with all this army around me," he said with a laugh.

As O'Brien turned to go, Collins shouted, *"How's my aunt?"* Almost in the same breath he said he would go across the road to see her. Collins had great affection for his aunt (Michael O'Brien's mother) with whom he had spent much of his younger days.

She was sitting on a low stool in front of the open fire when Collins approached her. She rose and with "her two hands, she grabbed his". It was she who had encouraged him to be "a good scholar". However, the two were not left to talk about old times for long. It seemed as if everyone wanted to grab "Mick's hand". [1] They wanted him to come across to the pub to chat with them, not about the affairs of state or army, but about the past, their past, his past.

"He was a bit of a schemer in his youth," Michael O'Brien maintained, "always up to tricks. We all went to The Pike school and later we were on the altar. We'd cycle to Mass and when we'd come out our bikes would be gone. Mick would have rushed out and hid them for devilment. Then we'd have a tussle on the grass, in the church yard. He always loved to tussle – all his life, it was part of the boy in the man – even that day he seemed to want a roll on the ground. It was a measure of the fun which was within him."[2]

He had a fondness for children also and they came to him on that day. Here was the man whom they had heard their parents speak of, the man who their school teacher had told them was making history.

A little boy pushed past the protective cluster of soldiers, determined to see this Commander-in-Chief so that he could tell his school pals.

Collins paused in his conversation and swung round, "Well, what does the *garsún* want?"

"To see you, sir."

"How do you do!" A warm handshake and he pushed a

sixpence into the cupped youthful hand.

When Johnny came in the door, the brothers looked at one another. The elder brother who had taken his father's place as head of the family welcomed "Mick" home. The two moved aside from the crowd and talked for a little while.

They discussed the work at Woodfield. Johnny was in the process of "fixing up someplace" but was staying with the O'Briens meanwhile. The members of the family who returned home on holidays really had no definite home, but work progressed in Woodfield farm. There were reminders of the days when young Mick would trot along the furrows while his father guided the horses as they pulled the plough and exposed the sods of dark earth under which the potatoes or the grain would be planted. When Johnny told him he was milking seven cows, Michael spoke of the many times he'd also sat under a cow and brought into the kitchen the frothed milk for the evening tea. "His mother was always singing songs in Irish as she milked the cows."[3]

The kitchen at Woodfield had always been a venue where patriotic exchanges took place. His father would speak of past leaders, men like Wolfe Tone, Daniel O'Connell and Michael Davitt. With the neighbours the chat would eat into the night as the children sat and listened around the open hearth. Landlords' agents still collected rent and showed no mercy to those unable to pay or buy out their holding. The threat of eviction hung over many families, not least the Collinses of Woodfield. Michael was to recall this on the last day of his life – a personal reason why in his youth he disliked landlord's agents. Men who had heard the story before listened as if for the first time to the hero amongst them tell of a day when his father was sick and young Michael was sent to pay £4/6/8 rent. In a shop window in Clonakilty on his way to the agent's house, he saw a football that was marked one shilling. Secretly he hoped that the agent would give him the shilling discount – something that was occasionally done for prompt payment. But no such luck. The agent's response was an abrupt, "Tell your father he is a fool to trust such a small lad with so much money." Little wonder that "the young Michael, whose father died when he was only six, became determined when he grew up to make sure there would be no agent".[4]

During this great homecoming day, one of his former schoolmasters was among the welcoming crowd. Collins' respect for age and learning was always high. In the intervening years the schoolboy had gained wide experience and was now Commander-in-Chief of the Army. He spoke with ease to the older man of learning.

Collins was very kind to old people. They smoked clay pipes and on one occasion he sent a dozen clay pipes to the old people in the neighbourhood. During this, his last day in Sam's Cross, he received words of gratitude from some of those people who were present to welcome him. Here, he was at home amongst his own people. Every one of them had a memory of him. He knew them, he called them by name. He had come to the Four Alls with his companions on many another summer's evening in the past following a cross-country race or a game of bowling. As young lads they'd discuss the reason they lost or the reason they won. Competition was important, but winning wasn't everything. Today, with his friends and his escort, he would sample a pint of the Clonkilty Wrastler. Near the counter beside the small window he stood, the boyish glint in his eye, and he told how different were "the good old days of growing up" from having to live "on your wits in Dublin".

They looked up to him. He had made it to the top in Dublin and in London. Michael O'Brien said he saw in the paper where Collins told Churchill "to do his own dirty work". "I said, 'Mick you were right'!" These words encouraged Collins to close his fist in front of Michael O'Brien's eyes with all the boyish roguery that he could muster. "It was clear to all that here were his roots, and it was here he was happiest."[5]

But all too soon the time arrived to say goodbye to his friends and relatives. *"Don't let it be too long until we see you again, Mick!"* came a shout from the back. He assured them it wouldn't be.

His brother Johnny, Michael O'Brien, Jeremiah Collins and a few more relatives walked with him towards the waiting vehicles. "I hope you're travelling in the armoured car, Mick, because there's still danger around," said Johnny.

"Not at all, this is my bus," said Collins, pointing to the open touring car.

"Be careful of yourself," said the older brother.

"You need have no worries about me – didn't I elude the Auxies all these years?"

He told his brother: "I'm going back to settle this thing. I'm going to concentrate on a Republic."[6]

Chapter 10

As the convoy set out from Sam's Cross at 6.15 on that dull August evening of 1922, the farewell to Michael Collins held an element of rejoicing and also of hope for peace among the Irish people. Collins had told his brother Johnny and his cousin Michael O'Brien "that he wouldn't rest with the settlement of the Treaty, that he would go further with the British Government once there was peace here". His principal aim now was "to concentrate on ending the Civil War". He said: "The British have given up their claim on us. When we begin to work together we can help those in the north-east."[1]

For his aunt, his brother, his cousins and friends who stood outside the pub and across the road near the briar-covered ditches, it was a special evening, and a special evening also for this man who was affectionately known as "The Big Fellow". To them, he was not alone Commander-in-Chief of the Army but also head of the Provisional Government. However, the farewell would be just another happening were it not for subsequent events. These would cause each individual to recall in detail the picture of the stately soldier's smile, his gestures, his words. Irish historical events of the period would be dated from this day. This day would be remembered as *the day Michael Collins was shot.*

From Sam's Cross it was back through The Pike and towards Clonakilty. This time the convoy wasn't taking any chances. Again they went through the fields, through the broken gaps which they had widened in the morning and then back on the main Clonakilty/Bandon road. Collins was as happy as Dalton had ever seen him: "He was able to let himself go, and also I think he felt things were now moving his way. He didn't say much as we travelled along the flat road towards Bandon." He appeared lost in "the myriad thoughts of a crowded and successful day".[2]

Luck was on his side when he arrived at Lee's Hotel in Bandon. Among those he met were his friend and colleague, Major General Seán Hales, Column Commander of Government Forces in West Cork, and also John L. O'Sullivan. John L., speaking for both of them, said, "When we entered Skibbereen, we met strong resistance, some intense fighting, and it was evening before we captured it. We captured most of the towns in West Cork – as we moved on from Skibbereen then Rosscarbery, Clonakilty, Courtmacsherry and we went on to Kinsale." He continued: "With our army we had just taken Kinsale. We had crossed the river under fierce fire on the Sunday and when we tried to get out of the town again we found the bridges had all been blown up, including the metal bridge, so with the use of some boats we ferried our soldiers out of the town, making several trips. It was difficult. We travelled on to Bandon as we were aiming for the Dunmanway direction."[3]

When Seán Hales and his men arrived in Bandon on 22

August they went first to barrack quarters in the Devonshire Arms Hotel. Hales had some military instructions and information as to his next manoeuvres. He sent John L., Maurice Collins (Michael Collins' cousin) and a few men to Lee's Hotel where Michael Collins was to arrive on his return journey. Hales would follow shortly.

When John L. and Maurice Collins got to the hotel, the Collins convoy had already arrived. The two men announced their presence and waited outside. After a short while an officer came out and said: "Michael Collins would like to see you." Collins was seated at a table. He was warm in his praise of their achievements. The men responded to his questions on the military position and, after some further conversation, he said, "I'm trying to put a finish to this business."

When Seán Hales arrived, he was warmly greeted and congratulated by his superior officer and friend.[4]

The conditions of the roads were a constant threat to the progress towards capturing areas. "It makes our task extremely tedious," said Hales. "We are almost boxed in on the eastern side as several roads are impassable."

However, according to John L, "Our conversation was extremely optimistic. We all felt the war was drawing to a close."

Collins was going back to Cork on the Crookstown road, the direction he had travelled in the morning which was the only road open to them as Innishannon Bridge was down.[5] (Planks had been put there for the temporary crossing of local traffic, but this was unsuitable for heavy vehicles.)

The men told Collins that he would be heading through

dangerous country. "It's Republican territory," said his cousin Maurice Collins, "and your convoy doesn't look big enough to take them on."

Collins just shrugged and, with his customary smile, said, "We'll deal with them – we came that way in the morning."

In a further discussion, he told them that the enemy appeared anxious for peace "judging by feelers he had been getting during the full trip from Dublin. He was in high spirits and would be glad, he said, to see an end to this dreadful business."[6]

He rose and drew Seán Hales aside for a short private conversation. Collins proposed to introduce columns into certain definite areas. These columns would work inside a ring of posts, so that there would be no portion of the Command in any region "left without the constant presence of an operating column within a reasonable distance", thus granting all districts of the Command the security of a column that would come to their assistance in the event of an ambush or other difficulty. (Hales had, a few days previously, requested a Lancia.[7])

Then, accompanied by Dalton, the men went towards the door.

"Keep up the good work! 'Twill soon be over," was Collins' parting salute.[8]

Outside, a local photographer clicked his camera as the Commander-in-Chief, seated beside Emmet Dalton, was about to embark on his final journey.

Collins had left for quite some time before Seán Hales, John L. O'Sullivan, Maurice Collins and a substantial number of soldiers marched out of Bandon towards Ballineen and Enniskeane. "We captured eighteen men on the way and took them to Dunmanway Barracks. In fact, we were back at Dunmanway, which was two days later, when we heard of Michael Collins' death. It would be impossible for me to express the sadness, dismay and grief which fell upon us. Our leader was dead."

John L. remembers Hales being most upset. "Together they had been interned in Frongoch for a number of months after the 1916 Rising and were always extremely close. Another question which was left unanswered for Seán was, where was his brother Tom that evening?"[9] A few weeks previously, Collins had said in a newspaper interview, "I'd rather have Tom Hales with us than twenty others." He had also paid "a high tribute to the character of Liam Deasy".[10] Both men had waited in ambush positions at Béal na mBláth throughout the day for Collins' convoy to return.

At approximately 7.30 pm the convoy drove up Convent Hill and out of Bandon, taking a circuitous route, but the only one open towards Cork City.

It has been alleged that Collins was anxious to get back to Cork on the night of 22 August to attend a meeting to make peace with the anti-Treaty forces. However, research shows that this is mere speculation. Father T. F. Duggan[11], a teacher of Greek in Farranferris at the time, "was trying to arrange a meeting in the Imperial Hotel when he heard Michael Collins was in the area," according to his sister, Professor Lucy Duggan. "Tom O'Mahony and Florence O'Donoghue were among those who were neutral. They wanted to get something started. They certainly were involved in peace initiatives, and asked Emmet Dalton to convey their intention. But, apparently, Collins was slow to make any move. It should be remembered that this was at the height of the Civil War. As far as I am aware, there was no formal arrangement for any meeting on the night of the twenty-second of August."[12]

In none of Florence O'Donoghue's writings is there mention of any scheduled meeting for 22 August. However, he was anxious for peace, and hoped to reconcile the two sides, as he, like O'Mahony and Duggan, was totally opposed to the Civil War.

Collins, in a letter to Cosgrave asking for postponement of the Dáil, had stated his belief that by 24 August, when the Dáil would reconvene, the military "would have occupied sufficient additional posts in the South to dominate entirely the positions" in each area – this would indicate their ability "to deal with the military problem" by being free from the restraints of "parliamentary criticism".[13]

Dalton said there was no mention of a peace meeting organised for that night: "As far as I am aware, Collins had no intention of compromising. He wanted me to find out further what was behind the proposals of peace. I don't think

Lynch, or any of the die-hards had any intention of agreeing to the suggestion of unconditional surrender."[14]

No original documentation to the author's knowledge exists, nor is there any indication that Collins was about to make peace at the expense of abandoning the Treaty, of abandoning the Provisional government, or of abandoning the "splendid progress achieved" by his forces. He was returning to Cork for the night and would travel to Dublin the next morning.[15]

Already a light mist (which did not remain) had begun to fold in on the evening as the vehicles wound their way along the ribbon of road that led from Bandon towards Crookstown.

Despite the fact that they were travelling through Republican territory, the convoy had no contingency plan should they encounter hostilities along the way. It appears, however, that Collins had some intuition while driving along this sparsely populated area – also, Hales' parting words may have flashed into his mind. For whatever reason, he said to Dalton, "If we run into an ambush along the way, we'll stand and fight them."

Dalton did not respond. Being more familiar with ambushes and guerilla fighting than Collins was, he decided he would "cross that bridge, if and when, we came to it".[16]

The armoured car was travelling approximately "four poles behind the Leyland which was the required distance."[17] In front the scout rider, Lieutenant Smith, led the convoy towards Béal na mBláth valley.

Having expressed to Dalton his satisfaction at the success

of the trip and unaware of any hidden dangers, Collins sat back and rested his hands on the rifle which lay across his knees.

Note: *The account of the events of the ambush which follows was compiled from a vast number of author interviews of the participants on both the pro-Treaty and anti-Treaty side. The recorded interviews done singly are dated. However, there were several undated interviews done singly or collectively in homes, or other locations or at the ambush site over a period of time, some when the author brought comrades together, just one or two or perhaps three at a time, and went over and over locations; also, notes taken during interviews plus responses to author's questionnaires; in addition, material obtained from other written sources.* [18]

SEE MAP 2 & note orientation: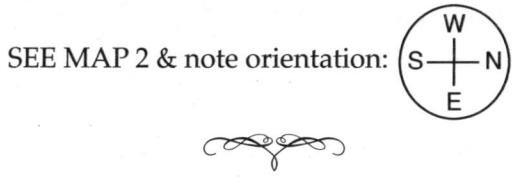

Meantime, further north on the road at Béal na mBláth, the Republicans had dispersed. Some went towards houses where they hoped to get a meal and perhaps billet for the night while others went in the direction of Long's public house at the crossroads. Most of the men either sauntered along the road or up one of the boreens.

Tom Foley and Charlie Foley (not ambush participants)

had gone to collect the horse for Jeremiah "The Leaguer". Tom Hales, Tom Kelleher and Jim Hurley went towards the barricade and began to move the cart containing the crates of bottles to one side, so that local passing traffic would not be disrupted. When they had moved the cart nearer the dyke, Jim Hurley said he was going "for a bit of grub". Hales then asked Kelleher if he would join him for a drink, but Kelleher said he would prefer "a bite to eat" and would follow Hurley back to Longs' house. (This is the Long family who lived on the boreen to the north-west – not to be confused with Long's public house at Béal na mBláth crossroads.)

Kelleher shouted to Jim Hurley to wait for him. Hurley stopped, and just as Kelleher reached him the sound of motor vehicles rattled the air.

"*They're coming!*" Hurley shouted.

South along the road, the convoy headed into the Béal na mBláth valley. Suddenly Smith spotted the rolled-up cable, "*Mine! Mine! Mine!*" he shouted, jolted his bike around and darted back to alert the convoy. Almost immediately the sound of gunfire hit their ears.

Kelleher (north along the road) looked around and, believing that Hales was trapped, yelled to Hurley, "*Better fire a few shots! Hales is at the barricade, he'll be destroyed!*" With speed the two men ran over the northern Glannarouge (Carroll's) bridge, wheeled around and fired a few shots into the air.

Hales leaped when he heard the vehicles in the distance

and ran to catch up with Bill Powell and John Lordan. Powell and Lordan had been chatting further north in the middle of the road when the sound of vehicles and their companions' warning shots hit their ears. Any second they could be mowed down. The two men ran, leaped over the little ditch at the eastern side and began to grope their way up the steep incline of furze and bushes. Hales followed almost immediately. (This little ditch was to the right – coming from the Bandon direction – a continuation of the ditch which would be to the back of the convoy army men, and beyond the northern Glannarouge/Carroll's bridge).

Further north on the road, Pat Buttimer and Dan Holland had been strolling when they heard the sound of gunfire. They jumped over the continuation of that little ditch, also to the eastern side, hid behind a cluster of bushes and remained there.

Nearer to Long's public house, Liam Deasy and Pete Kearney were sauntering along. The sound of gunfire made them leap to safety. They were further north but on the same side as Powell, Lordan and Hales. The growth was not too dense, but it took them some time to make their way towards the hilltop.

Many more Republicans were strolling on the road nearer to the Béal na mBláth pub. Now they rushed in, joined their comrades inside and sped out the back.

Meanwhile, further south along the road, Jim Kearney, Timmy Sullivan and John Callaghan had been walking abreast, away from where the mine had been laid. They had disconnected the cable. Sullivan had picked up the mine and put it on his back. The other two men had rolled up the cable and had thrown it on the low ditch, deciding that they would come back after they had eaten. The three men had begun to walk south towards the Ahalarick bridge (the side nearest Bandon) when suddenly they heard the loud sound of vehicles.

"*Whist! They're coming!*" Callaghan shouted.

The three men made for Ahalarick bridge and rounded the corner just as they heard the motorbike buzz past on the main road, only a few yards away. Within seconds, they heard the scout-rider shout, "*Mine! Mine! Mine!*" when he spotted the cable. At that instant their companions' shots (Kelleher & Hurley's) rent the air.

Smith, having dashed back to the tender, warned the driver, then he about-turned and sped ahead, followed closely by the tender. Both drivers slowed. Were they surrounded? In the stillness, and with the loud hum of their vehicles, they were unsure of the direction of the threatening gunfire.

John Callaghan, Jim Kearney and Timmy Sullivan ran for cover round the bend of the boreen just beyond Ahalarick bridge only seconds before the convoy headed into the valley.

"*Drive like hell!*" shouted Dalton to the driver of the touring car.

"*Stop! We'll fight them!*" retorted Collins.

Immediately, the order was obeyed. The driver of the tender, which was just crawling by this time, halted. Behind him he saw Collins and Dalton jump from the Leyland. Men were seen running up the laneway, according to Dalton. Instantly, the soldiers vaulted from the vehicle and tried to get into position. Already there were resounding gunshots from a selection of armaments. Confusion struck as machine-gunner McPeak pointed the Vickers gun to his left and opened fire.

Callaghan, around the Aharlick bridge bend in the boreen, dropped to the ground and began to crawl. At first Kearney, who had dived close to the ditch, thought that Callaghan in front of himself and Sullivan had been hit because at that moment machine-gun fire "began to mow the little bushes and ferns".

Tom and Charlie Foley had been coming down the laneway with the horse "when the sudden sound of gunfire erupted. Then the horse went mad," and they had "to double back on the trot".

The main road where the convoy halted was rough-stoned, running south to Bandon, north to Crookstown. On the western side of this road (facing the convoy) the Republicans had waited in ambush positions on the north-western section of the narrow secluded curved boreen all day, but during the past half hour or so they had been dispersing. Tom Kelleher and Jim Hurley, having fired the first warning shots, ran and headed further along the northern side of the boreen. They took up positions on the height.

On the road, Hales, running to catch up with Powell and Lordan, jumped in beside the ditch at the eastern side, vaulting over a low section. Eventually he caught up with Bill Powell and John Lordan further up the furzy incline.

Kelleher wondered if the enemy would move further north

along the main road in the direction of the barricade and get closer to them. Slowly both Kelleher and Hurley tried to edge towards the south along the boreen with the intention of helping their comrades in the Ahalarick bridge area from where they heard firing emanating. They fired further shots to distract the enemy because by this time there was continuous shooting in the distance. Jim Hurley missed the motorcyclist with a shot, Tom Kelleher believed he got the touring car. Joe Murphy, Bill Desmond, Dan Corcoran, Paddy Walsh, Sonny Donovan and more soldiers, who had been strolling further up Walsh's Lane to get a meal and perhaps a billet for the night, had now halted and fired shots into the air. They continued to do this periodically to distract the enemy during the engagement.

At the southern end of the boreen, Jim Kearney, Timmy Sullivan and John Callaghan had taken up positions some distance beyond Ahalarick bridge and the ford. They were closest to the line of fire from the convoy.

Under the command of Seán O'Connell, the men in the Crossley Tender opened fire with the Lewis gun. The Thompson guns and rifles which the convoy soldiers carried were all quickly brought into action. They were firing at the southern end of the curved boreen, beyond Ahalarick bridge – here Kearney, Sullivan and Callaghan were positioned. Others had been retreating further up Foley's Lane.

O'Connell it seems saw some men running in that direction, so he instructed some convoy soldiers to target that area, while others moved in the direction of the partially removed barricade.

The armoured car had first moved north and halted. At some point it appeared to have halted somewhere in the general area where the mine had been in position all day – though quite a distance from it. Much to the consternation of the three engineers, Kearney, Sullivan and Callaghan, the cable was now disconnected. If the cable had remained in place, Callaghan in his crawling position could have easily moved to the location of the exploder, where he and his comrades had been all day, and so activated the mine. Had this been possible, not alone would the armoured car and its occupants have been blown up but, because of the ammunition contained in the armoured vehicle, the explosion would most likely have claimed other soldiers. Certainly, it would have caused some destruction for the convoy. (When Jim Woulfe, the armoured car driver, returned with the author to the scene of the ambush over 50 years later, he was horrified at how near he and his comrades had been to death. With such a vantage point, overlooking the road on the north-west, he described it as "a perfect ambush position".)

In a war situation, soldiers fight to win. And just as the Republicans regretted their failure to blow up the armoured car, the gunner Jock McPeak in that car bitterly regretted the problem he was encountering with the Vickers gun. (A few months after this ambush, McPeak deserted to the Republicans, taking with him the *Sliabh na mBan* armoured car which he manned on that eventful day. See Chapter 16) This operation was his first service since he joined the army of the Irish Provisional Government. McPeak was an ex-British-army gunner, recruited in Scotland. On 18 August, he got an order to go from the Curragh to Portobello Barracks where he was told to be ready for a long journey on the following Sunday morning.

Speculation has surrounded his handling of the gun, which after a short time fired only sporadically despite his having in the armoured car two belts of .303 ammunition, each containing 250 rounds and one box of 1,000 loose rounds which were to be used for replenishing the two belts when they became empty. However, there should have been a relief gunner (a No 2 gunner) in the armoured car, who would refill the belt should the need arise, but no such person accompanied McPeak. McPeak believes it was because there was no other machine-gunner available the day of the convoy's departure. Trained machine-gunners were scarce in the National Army.

Driving into Béal na mBláth, Jim Woulfe, driver of the armoured car, saw Lieutenant Smith returning. Once McPeak came into the ambuscade, and into a position he opened fire. Looking through his gun-sights he sprayed the area from the revolving turret. The armoured car moved north, then reversed south a little; it remained stationary, moved, settled somewhere in the general area (though a distance further south) of the disconnected mine for a short period.

McPeak aimed the gun snout with the revolving turret so that it mowed down the ferns, grass and little bushes from the shelter bank where the few men from the opposing forces were taking cover. (This has been confirmed by these men, who were on the hill – around the boreen beyond Ahalarick bridge.)

Woulfe, the driver, then reversed the armoured car south along the road. On McPeak's instructions, Woulfe backed the car to the entrance to Ahalarick bridge "because most of the gunfire appeared to be coming from this corner". He was not, nor were any of Collins' convoy aware of the strength of the enemy, which was a disadvantage for them. McPeak, now in his position as a gunner, was unable to see out the front slit-window. Woulfe tried to drive up the narrow entrance but soon he discovered that it would be impossible to negotiate this rugged track with the heavy vehicle. The armoured car weighed four and half tons and had only a ground clearance of ten inches.[19]

"We could get bogged down, and then we'd have a problem," said Woulfe, who realised that "if we could get in, even part of the way, we would move them quickly. Somebody shouted from the back of the armoured car, *'That could be mined!'* The risk was too great." So Woulfe reversed the car, and moved it in the northerly direction.

Kearney and Sullivan had suddenly realised that they might be trapped. "Have you a handkerchief?" Sullivan had pleaded with his companion.

"What for?" asked Kearney.

"We'll have to hold up something [surrender flag]. If they drive up here we're finished."

Kearney and Sullivan were relieved when the armoured car reversed, and felt further relieved when it moved north along the road. The two men breathed more easily and reloaded their guns. Instantly a hail of bullets came in their direction.

Soon the shots coming from the armoured car were uneven.

Dalton called out from the distance to McPeak, *"Why are you not firing?"*

"The gun is jammed, sir!"

While it may not have been technically correct to say that the Vickers gun was "jammed", there were stoppages in the firing. As there was no No. 2 gunner to assist McPeak, two staff captains had remained in the armoured car to assist him, and when McPeak had finished one belt and was using the second, he asked one of the captains to refill the first empty belt with cartridges from the 1,000-round box. McPeak warned that each round should be absolutely even at the caps. They should have a perfect edge and not be an eighth of an inch out. Being unfamiliar with this work, the soldier did not achieve such perfection. Consequently, there were continuous stoppages, because a round had often to be removed to clear the gun.

McPeak found himself in an impossible position. Having used his second belt, he was now using the one the officer had filled and which resulted in desultory fire. But he was aware there was no real target, and he doubted if smooth firing would have made any significant difference. "I probably wasted the first belt by letting it go. I wanted to let the ambushers know that there was a machine-gun." He wanted to make them keep their heads down. He kept firing very short bursts, two or three rounds between each stoppage until there came a lull in the fighting. "I opened the hatch to get some cool air inside the turret, which was stifling. I had no sooner opened it when a bullet struck the lug which fastens the cover from the inside and sheered it off."

Bullets from the hill hit the armoured car and bounced off its plating; others bounced off the road, some in the direction of the men hiding beside the mud bank. The men on the boreen were not at this stage out for victory, but were anxious that the convoy should be intimidated into deciding to move on. They kept firing.

Michael Collins was mostly remaining in a prone position. Using whatever cover was available, he was taking part in his first guerilla ambush. Apart from being in the GPO in 1916 after some 'underground' training in soldering, Collins had never put these skills to use. Though he was a wanted man during the War of Independence, because he was involved in intelligence against the British forces, his main task was avoiding capture.

General Tom Barry once compared his own life as a guerilla fighter with that of Collins. On the Dublin streets in May 1921, four of Ireland's most wanted men, Collins, Tom Barry, Gearóid O'Sullivan, and Seán Ó Muirthile were returning home in a jaunting car when they were halted by a large party of Auxiliaries. "Act drunk," Collins whispered as the Auxies ordered them out. He proceeded to give a masterly performance, joking and blasting while being searched. Barry, while also trying to put on an act, couldn't help but wonder how callously the Essex Regiment would treat such a performance in the fields of West Cork! Avoiding capture on the streets of Dublin bore little relation to guerilla warfare. Collins "had this boyish mentality of soldering and possibly felt that because he had army men plus machine-guns that they would 'show' them," said Jim Woulfe. Had they come on this spot an hour earlier when the cable and the men were all positioned, the outcome would have been a slaughter. Ambush positions in guerilla warfare are not chosen to favour the attacked. Dalton and some others in the convoy were aware of this, hence Dalton's command of *"Drive like hell!"*

Collins was in unfamiliar territory, taking unfamiliar action.

The windscreen of the touring car had been shattered according the Dalton, prior to his order to "Drive like hell!" and Collins placing his hand on the driver's shoulder, and saying, "Stop! We'll fight them!"

"We leaped from the car, and took what cover we could behind the little mud bank on the left-hand side of the road (the western side)." Dalton believed that the greatest "volume of fire" was coming from the area "on the left-hand side" of the boreen (his left-hand side).This was where Kearney, Sullivan and Callaghan were crouched and firing.

In his interview with the author, Dalton says that Collins was moving around 'a bit'. He was with the soldiers who were taking cover in a prone position, in front of the little mud-bank ditch. From this position Collins fired at the seldom visible enemy. He remained there firing for some time. "As firing continued, after a period he moved south the road, taking cover beside the Crossley Tender." Later he moved behind the armoured car, which was at the time stationary south of the Crossley Tender, according to Eoin Neeson. Around this time, McPeak encountered difficulty with the ammunition belt on the Vickers gun.

Liam Deasy and Pete Kearney were now some distance up a rise and obliquely behind (north-east of) Collins and his men. Because of bushy growth and the humpy hill, and their distance from the men on the road, sight of any definite target, or even of any great movement was impossible for them at this time. They took up positions approximately 400 yards north-east of Collins' convoy. Both men carried Thompson guns. While struggling up the incline they had heard the continuous sound of gunfire. "The lads will be destroyed," Deasy said when they reached the top. He turned, opened fire into the bushes and shouted to Pete, *"Come on, fire! Let's draw their fire in this direction!"*

Shots from the boreen direction bounded around Collins, and other soldiers. At one stage when the armoured car moved south, he also pushed a little south. He and other soldiers returned the fire in the direction of the attackers obliquely opposite on his left (Kearney, Sullivan and Callaghan) but without any definite target. Dalton, with other soldiers, was also taking what cover he could behind the little mud bank. They were facing the enemy on the boreen, Dalton says this was the area from where most of the enemy shots appeared to have been coming.

On the north-western side Tom Kelleher and Jim Hurley were firing periodically in the direction of the men in the convoy. Also, men who had been travelling for a meal or a billet had halted and were periodically firing shots into the air.

Dalton says: "Collins and I were lying within arm's length of each other. Captain Dolan, who had been in the armoured car, together with our two drivers (Corry and Quinn), was further down the road to my right (towards the barricade). General Collins and I, with Captain Dolan who was near us, opened rapid fire at our seldom visible enemies. About fifty or sixty yards further down the road [north] and round the bend, we could hear that our machine-gunners and rifle-men were also heavily engaged." These were firing towards the area from where Kelleher and Hurley were firing, and also the soldiers were firing some shots into the air further west up Walsh's Lane.

Joe Dolan, who had moved into the armoured car at Bandon because "it was warmer than the open Crossley Tender", had been sitting in the back as they headed towards Béal na mBláth. (It was over-crowded at this stage, according to Jim Woulfe.) After an action-filled day Dolan was tired; he relaxed and dozed, his rifle planted between his knees. At the first shots, he was jerked awake. When the armoured car halted in response to the stopping of the Leyland he jumped out and immediately put his rifle into action.

Other soldiers from the Crossley Tender were scattered at intervals along the roadside, taking cover as they crawled on in an effort to find a definite target. Some had British army experience, while others had fought in the War of Independence, and more had been recruited recently and trained. But most were chosen, not specifically, but to make up the number in Collins' convoy. These soldiers brought their weaponry into full play, mowing down the ferns, little bushes, and grass along the bank where the few men on the hill were taking cover.

Both Deasy and Pete Kearney continued to shoot into the bushes.

After some time, there was a lull "down below".

"Is it over?" Deasy asked his companion.

In a distance beyond and further south from Deasy's and Pete Kearney's position, and a long distance east of (behind) Collins' convoy, Republicans from Kerry were hiding in a field. In the aftermath of the taking of Cork by Provisional Government forces, Republicans scattered and moved towards West Cork, or went in that direction on their way heading for their own district. Mike Donoghue was leading a group. They had come from the Sliabh Luachra district in Kerry to defend Cork. After the evacuation of the city they walked, mainly across fields, and reached Upton after some days. Here they were kindly given food.

Travelling again cross-country, they had reached an area east of Béal na mBláth and were travelling along the upper road, further north-east of Bill Murray's house (where the morning meeting was to have been held) when they heard the sound of gunfire down in the valley, west of their position. They dived for cover. One of the men was about to fire a shot in the air when a soldier beside him grabbed his rifle, "Do you want to draw them on us!" he snapped. They did not get involved in the distant sounds of gunfire. This was normal. Republican solders were always warned of the dangers of crossfire when getting involved in any ambush. Furthermore, in this case they did not know what group (army) was firing at another, so they did what they were trained to do. They got into a field and hid.

On the road below, the Vickers on the armoured car was badly jammed and McPeak got frustrated trying to free it.

Meanwhile back in the direct line of fire. to the west of the convoy, Jim Kearney and Timmy Sullivan were crouched fairly near each other, a distance beyond the curve of the boreen while John Callaghan was to their left, a little further north. Leading off this little boreen to their right, and behind their backs, was a laneway going to Foleys' house which ran practically at right angles to the main road. Denis O'Neill, known as Sonny Neill, and Dinny Brien had been walking up this laneway. They had gone a considerable distance when they heard the gunshots in the distance below. Believing that some of their companions were in trouble, they turned back. Sonny Neill jumped inside the ditch and ran down the field towards a gateway obliquely across from and not far behind the position where Kearney and Sullivan were crouched. This gateway and little pillar were practically at right angles to the road, and were located near the corner where the laneway branched off from the boreen. He reached this position just as the firing eased, but he could hear the sound of gunfire from the opposite hillock (Deasy and Pete Kearney firing into the bushes).

Meanwhile Dinny Brien took cover behind some growth slightly further back in the laneway and fired a few shots into the air. Sonny Neill, who had British Army experience, and became known to his colleagues as "a crack shot", stood behind the little pillar, loaded his Lee Enfield rifle and aimed at an enemy target.

The convoy men continued to shoot, mainly at no definite target, while bullets were now emanating only spasmodically from the armoured car.

At the closing stages of the ambush (which is estimated to have lasted approximately 40 to 50 minutes in total), Collins, who had been in a prone position, reloaded his gun and jumped up abruptly when the sound of gunfire coming from an area a distance behind his back could be heard clearly during a lull. This was Deasy's and Pete Kearney's gunfire into bushes up north-east, their motivation being to draw the fire of the convoy in the opposite direction, and so distract them from concentrating on actual targets.

Dalton stated that when a lull in the enemy's attack became noticeable, General Collins jumped up to his feet and walked over behind the armoured car, obviously to obtain a better view of the enemy's position.

"He remained there firing occasional shots and using the car as cover. Then he moved away from the armoured car. Suddenly I heard him shout: *'Come on, boys! There they are, running up the road!'* He had walked a few steps out on the road a distance (north) from the armoured car when he shouted the command. His voice was heard, not alone by his own men, but also by his enemy located around the ford (Ahalarick bridge) in the boreen. He was wheeling around from his right to his left, and hadn't quite completed the semicircle when a shot got him on the poll of the head behind the right ear. He fell awkwardly and slumped to the ground.

Dalton: who was not far away, thought he heard "a faint cry", "Emmet!"

Seán O'Connell, who during the lull had pushed a little further south along the road (just as Collins had done), was instantly with Dalton.

They "rushed to the spot", he said. "With a dreadful fear clutching our hearts. We found our beloved Chief and friend lying motionless firmly gripping his rifle."[20]

Chapter 11

It was still daylight at approximately 8.10 pm on this August evening of 1922, still relatively easy to distinguish people and movements in the distance. Voices carried in this valley of Béal na mBláth. Blood stained Emmet Dalton's hands as he gently tried to lift the head of the Commander-in-Chief. A "fearful gaping wound at the base of the skull behind the right ear" made Dalton recognise immediately "that General Collins was almost beyond human aid". He could not speak to them.

As Dalton bent down he noticed the sound of further gunfire. "The enemy must have seen that something had occurred to cause a sudden cessation of our fire, because they intensified their own."[1]

Kelleher and Hurley who were at the north-western end of the boreen (Glannarouge/Carroll's Bridge) began to shoot as soon as they became aware of a lull, but because of their distance from the convoy their vision of events and people was unclear.[2]

Liam Deasy and Pete Kearney, who were high up (northeast) obliquely behind the convoy, continued to fire "at intervals. Each of us emptied a pan of ammunition into the bushes".[3]

The men on the south-western side of the boreen (Jim Kearney, Timmy Sullivan, John Callaghan, and Sonny Neill), who could see what was happening, as they were looking down on them, held their fire at this time "because" Jim Kearney said, "we knew we were outnumbered, so we wanted them to shift off." (Dinny Brien was further west in Foley's lane.[4]) Because of the suddenness of the ambush, these men had been forced into this situation in a section of the boreen which had not been designated as an ambush position such as they held earlier in the day.

Down on the road Seán O'Connell, realising that "the end was near" for Michael Collins, knelt beside "the dying but still conscious Chief, whose eyes were wide open and normal and whispered into the ear of the fast-sinking man the words of the Act of Contrition". Collins rewarded him by a slight pressure of the hand.[5]

Meanwhile, Dalton knelt beside both of them and kept up bursts of rapid fire.

Joe Dolan, who had heard Collins' command some minutes previously, had fired a few shots ahead, at no particular target, then paused momentarily. He heard Emmet Dalton's cry, *"The C-in-C is hit. Keep up a heavy fire!"* Instantly, he responded to the order and remained crouched.

Smith, realising that somebody had been hit, rushed back to the place of commotion. *"Get him into the armoured car!"* he shouted; then he crouched down on one knee and fired a few shots while Dalton, still stooped, beckoned to Woulfe to bring forward the armoured car. Dalton continued with "rapid bursts of fire whilst O'Connell dragged the Chief across the road". While the armoured car jolted forward, its back doors were pushed open by Wally Coote. When it stopped O'Connell caught Collins' legs and, with Dalton and Smith, shifted him the few feet towards it. The blood-covered cap, through which the fatal bullet had penetrated, had by now fallen off; it remained unnoticed by any of Dalton's men. With the tilting upwards of the legs, Michael Collins' revolver slipped from its holster and landed where it was to remain overnight – on the grass margin with his cap.

Aware of the dangerous position they were in while moving Collins, Commandant O'Connell endeavoured to keep Dalton covered by sporadic bursts of rapid fire. The men in the convoy were at a disadvantage as they did not know the strength of the enemy, nor did they have any idea of the boreens which remained hidden from view in this unfamiliar territory.

Dalton believed that there was fire coming "from that hill up behind" (Deasy and Pete Kearney firing into the bushes). He therefore gave the order: *"Keep firing!"*

The men had by this time got the unconscious Collins slightly shielded by the hinged door of the armoured car, but he was still lying on the road beside it. Dalton had called for bandages, which were quickly handed to him by Smith. Having put down his rifle onto his knee, Dalton gently lifted the head of his dying friend and Commander, then tried to bandage it. "It was an impossible task as the wound was so large and gaping. With O'Connell's help I did the best I could and had not completed my grievous task when the big eyes quickly closed and the cold pallor of death overspread the General's face."

Still on one knee and supporting the bleeding bandaged head with the other, Dalton remained for some moments statue-like, numbed in disbelief as "bullets whistled and ripped" the ground of areas around him, according to his description. "How can I describe the feelings that were mine in that bleak hour, kneeling in the mud of a country road not twelve miles from Sam's Cross, Collins' homeland. Here I was, with the still bleeding head of the idol of Ireland resting on my arm."[6] Shocked, Dalton kept looking at the lifeless body he now held. "The weight of the blow must have caused me to almost lose my reason," he said. And as he wondered what to do next, he abruptly looked up and saw tears streaming down O'Connell's face. "His anguish called for my sympathy and support." Dalton took a deep breath, then said, "We'll say another prayer." Because the emotion of the moment would cause their voices to quiver, both said their few words of prayer silently. (Response to author's questionnaire).[7]

Collins was now dead.

The fire of the ambushers had greatly abated, and Dalton assumed that they had retreated. He asked O'Connell to give him a hand to get the body of Collins into the armoured car. Lieutenant Smith, the motorcycle scout who had been close by covering for them, moved forward to help to lift the weighty body. Just as they had got the body up on the platform a bullet whizzed by them, grazing Smith's neck. "It was a nasty graze," said Dalton. Smith had already got a slight graze in his hand.

However, he remained on his feet and pushed the body

further in towards Dalton and O'Connell, both of whom were already inside the armoured car. Then he too got quickly in. The back of the armoured car was now very crowded: as Collins' legs were not fully in, they were unable to close the hinged-door properly and had to hold it temporarily.

Dalton had given the order to mount and this order was transmitted forward. Immediately the soldiers got back into the vehicles. With Quinn at the wheel of the Leyland, it was discovered once again that it wouldn't start. Woulfe, driving the armoured car, passed back the word to his passengers to "Watch out!" He had to reverse a little in order to get in position. The Leyland was then jerked forward by the armoured car and this got it started.

The convoy set out again, leaving Smith's motorbike by the ditch where he had first dumped it. The Crossley Tender jolted the cart with crates of empty bottles (some of which were covered by an oilskin coat), breaking many and, scattering them along the roadside.

When they got around the next bend and they presumed out of the view of the Republicans, they stopped. Under the cover of the armoured car, Dalton said, they proceeded to transfer the body of Michael Collins into the touring car.

What they did not know was that high up on the hill east of them near Coleman's Rock, Deasy and Pete Kearney (who had been firing into the bushes) had a view of the entire procedure. So also had Powell, Lordan and Hales, hidden midway up the wooded hill. "We knew somebody was either dead or badly injured," said Bill Powell.[8]

Dalton had taken off his cap in the armoured car and used it to cradle his dead comrade's head on his lap. In the back seat of the touring car, he again used the cap to support the head, which for the early part of the journey rested against his left shoulder. This stricken group thus left Béal na mBáth valley to return to the city from where they had set out over fifteen and a half hours previously. When they left in the morning, they were "confident and happy, intent on improving the machinery of the only possible government that could bring peace to a sorely afflicted long-suffering people," according to Dalton. The burden of making other decisions now weighed heavy on his mind. He observed that "the darkness of the night began to close. We were silent, brooding with heavy hearts upon us like a shroud, the ghastly blow known to us alone, that had fallen upon the Irish people throughout the world."

Smith was now inside the Crossley Tender, having had his wound dressed by one of the officers, so he was unable to guide – and, in fact, because of his wound, did not think about the road and the indirect route which, with the aid of Timmy Kelleher, they had taken in the morning. Therefore, the convoy followed on the straight road rather than taking the Kilmurry route at Béal na mBláth cross. Shortly they encountered their first difficulty when they came to a crossroad which was blocked in one direction. They intended travelling to Crookstown where Dalton said they would try to get a priest. Taking a right turn they wound their way until they arrived at the outskirts of a village which they thought was Crookstown but which in fact was Cloughduv.[9]

Local man Tim Murphy was returning from a neighbour's house when the tender pulled up. Captain Conroy, the driver, asked, "Where's the priest's house, we have a soldier who needs attention."

Murphy directed them towards the house beside the church, with railings and gravel in front[10]. They stopped; one of the men got out and knocked on the door. Father Timothy Murphy, the curate, came as far as the railings and "took a look at the dead Michael Collins" lying against Dalton's shoulder. "It was fairly dark at this time. I was crying, and so was O'Connell," said Dalton. Both men were emotionally shaken. Dalton began to speak as soon as he saw the priest. "Because I was very upset I spouted out, 'Michael Collins has been shot, I want you to help us'."

The priest turned his back to walk away. As he did so, O'Connell pointed his gun at his back, released the clip and was about to fire. Dalton slapped at it, tilting it skywards. "The shot actually discharged. Had I not jerked it, the priest would have been shot."

Dalton and O'Connell, believing the priest had refused to attend to Collins (thinking it was because the priest's sympathies rested with the anti-Treatyites) were fearful that more moves might be made to ambush them again. They got into the vehicles quickly and drove off. Filled with anguish and a sense of helplessness, Dalton wished to get back to Cork.

Because the men were crying, Father Murphy had sensed the sensitiveness of the situation, so without speaking he had gone back to get the oils of the dying to anoint and perform the Last Rites. (When I told Dalton why the priest had quickly turned around, he said, "I wish I had known all these years!" He paused. "I was so shaken at the time he turned his back, it hurt, it hurt me deeply." Over 60 years later, tears welled in Dalton's eyes, his voice trembled as he spoke between pauses. "I've often thought about it." Emmet Dalton said that years later he went back to Crookstown with his brother Charlie to try to find the church, but the only church he could find was overgrown "with briars and bushes". But I told him that it was in Cloughduv not Crookstown that the incident with the priest had occurred.)[11]

The day's adventures were not yet over for Dalton and the convoy. As they drove along the winding road out of Cloughduv heading in the direction of Kilumney, they encountered a few felled trees, but were able to weave their way around them.

Soon those in the front of the tender noticed a man advancing towards them. Their first reaction was one of suspicion – a feeling that another ambush had been laid. They halted; every man was alerted. The stranger, when he reached them, was confronted by a number of pointed guns held by the nerve-strained men. The man told them simply that they were on the wrong road and that if they continued they would all be killed. At first they disbelieved him. "Honestly!" he pleaded with them. "Come and look!" To safeguard themselves, they took him captive. Then he guided a few of the soldiers some yards to where the road plunged. The

Cork/Macroom railroad was several feet below and the bridge which normally spanned the gulf had been blown up.[12]

The man suggested that they had no alternative but to reverse a short distance. Then they could cross over some fields and get onto the Cork road. At gunpoint they compelled the stranger to show them the direction. It was a distance of three fields and a haggard.

When the Crossley Tender first hit the soft earth of the fields made slippery by the evening mist, its wheels could not get a grip. The men got out, and in the darkness and dampness began to push and heave the vehicle, but the wheels just spun. The engine roared. Another heave was called, but again it would not move. Somebody suggested that they take their greatcoats and blankets from the truck. This they did to make a carpet. Jim Carmody pulled out some petrol containers when he went into the tender to collect the blankets and these were also used as a type of platform. Some of the full petrol containers burst and saturated still further the men's clothing.[13]

It was a laborious struggle to get this first vehicle onto the main road. The soldiers who recalled this particular episode expressed the anxiety and fear which had gripped them. They feared that at any moment there might be Republicans in the area who would seize the opportunity to ambush them – it was for this reason that they held the stranger captive until they were on their way. "We were fearful that the heavy armoured car would not make the journey" but once it got moving with the "carpet of coats" the wide wheels found it easier to negotiate the fields.

There was one more vehicle yet to traverse the fields. The touring car which contained the body of Michael Collins again refused to start. It had to be abandoned. The body of their dead leader had to be shouldered across the fields by the men. They stumbled on the muddy fields many times in the darkness.[14]

On the main road, they released their guide and drove on. In the cold and drizzle Dalton sat with the body of Michael Collins, now in the Crossley Tender; once more he fixed his own cap beneath the bandaged head of the dead Commander and allowed the body to rest upon him.

Collins' body now leaned against Dalton's "in the darkness rigid and dead, with the piteous stain on him – Ireland's stain – darkening my tunic as we jolted over the road. So long as I live the memory of that nightmare ride will haunt me."[15]

While they journeyed on, Dalton remembered that in the morning they had encountered some road barricades near Ballincollig. "I remember hoping there would be no further problem, praying and chastising myself. I regretted I hadn't countermanded Collins' order, and driven like hell out of Béal na mBláth. I felt so empty during that journey back to Cork. I felt as if I too had been hit by a bullet." (During subsequent years Dalton puzzled as to whether or not he could have or should have countermanded an order given by his Commander-in-Chief.)[16]

Luckily, when they reached Ballincollig, the trees which they had moved aside in the morning were still in the same position. The men breathed more easily as Cork would shortly be in view.

Approaching the city, Dalton thought of the priests in the Sacred Heart Mission Church at Victoria Cross, Western Road, which was on their route. The convoy pulled up on the roadside and Dalton remained seated with Collins' body while two soldiers were instructed to ask a priest to come with them because an officer had been shot dead.

A priest having promptly responded to the soldiers' call, asked them to wait a moment, then brought the oils and administered the Last Rites to the dead Michael Collins. [17]

It was a despondent convoy that arrived back at the Imperial Hotel headquarters. Their burden was great and the trials of the day had been many. Commandant Seán O'Connell, Sergeant Cooney and Lieutenant Gough went into the hotel while the remainder of the convoy stayed outside. Four soldiers were detailed (two at each side) to stand guard beside the tender which held Michael Collins' body on Emmett Dalton's lap; these men had saluted the vigorous Michael Collins in the same location early that morning. [18]

Inside, when told "that Michael Collins was dead" the words were first met with disbelief. Dr. Leo Ahern (Major General) stepped from the Imperial Hotel and went to the tender, and told Dalton he would take care of Collins' body. (After the capture of Cork, Dr. Leo had taken over Shanakiel Hospital for the wounded army men of the Provisional Government, using mainly the annexe for medical services.[19] He had a team of medical men under him, including his brother Dr. Gerald. Some of the medical staff were shared with the Mercy Hospital and the severely wounded were sent to the Mercy as it had better medical facilities.)

"I confirmed that Michael Collins was dead. I told the men to order an ambulance and to take the body to Shanakiel Hospital. We had efficient ambulances, each with a Ford engine – these were at the ready."

Dr. Leo Ahern drove immediately to the hospital. Commandant O'Connell who, Dr. Ahern said, "was very shocked", detailed the soldiers to go to quarters at the Victoria Hotel. Conroy, Woulfe and a few more soldiers took both the Crossley Tender and the *Sliabh na mBan* back to the garage at Johnson & Perrott's, then retired to quarters overhead. Commandant O'Connell and Commandant O'Friel escorted Michael Collins' body to Shanakiel Hospital.[20]

Emmet Dalton now had to attend to many necessary items.

To him fell the task of informing the world that the Commander-in-Chief of the Irish Army had been shot dead during an ambush. "At the time, we were working on short-wave radio which was put together by Dowling, son of the man who was Registrar of the Royal College of Science in Ireland. First, I had to get in touch with Waterville and the message was relayed from there by cable to New York. And from there back to London and Dublin. Because of destruction caused by the Irregulars as they evacuated Cork City, there were no direct telephone links from army headquarters in the city to Portobello Barracks, Dublin, during the hours of darkness."[21]

Dalton had also "to keep in touch with and inform" the many army units in various parts of the city. When he told the soldiers stationed at Victoria military barracks (now Collins Barracks) and word went around, "they got into a very angry mood". The subsequent few hours were very trying as he felt he was going to be faced with a mutiny. He knew a mood for revenge was swiftly brewing. Eventually, with the aid of officers he succeeded "at gunpoint in getting the men to return to their units". He even found that some local officers wanted "to set out on a mission of revenge".[22]

Day was dawning when he got back to his quarters in the Imperial Hotel. It had been practically twenty-four hours packed with activity, turmoil and tragedy. He needed a short lie-down in order to focus mentally on the extra tasks, including funeral arrangements, which had suddenly fallen on his youthful shoulders. Shortly he would have to make his way up to the north side of the city to Shanakiel Hospital. "I couldn't rest. I just kept thinking."[23]

Chapter 12

When Michael Collins' body arrived at Shanakiel Hospital, the Cork "casualty clearing station" sometime after 1am, Matron Eleanor Gordon checked the list and confirmed that all private rooms were full. Dr. Leo Ahern said, "We'd better move some patient." Whereupon Dr. Christy Kelly, who had a room in the annex suggested, "Use my bed."[1]

The body on the trolley was examined by Dr. Leo Ahern, who then asked Dr. Michael O'Riordan and Dr. Christy Kelly to help him in carrying out an autopsy. The bandages with which Emmet Dalton had encased the crown and poll of the head had to be removed to ascertain the extent of the injury and the type of bullet which had caused Collins' death. He saw the large wound in the back of the right poll; both of them were able to examine it. Clean bandages were substituted. Nurse Forbes and Nurse Nora O'Donoghue made ready the bed in Room 201 where the body was then taken.

The dead Commander-in-Chief of the Irish Army was laid out in his uniform and boots. The empty holster was removed. Later it was casually thrown into a locker by one of the nurses who was tidying the room. A sixteen-inch-high silver crucifix (mounted on a stand, seen later by author) was placed on a table to the right of the body.[2] Six large "mourning" candlesticks and candles were strategically positioned, three at each side of the bed. The curtains were drawn, the candle lights flickered and a guard of honour was mounted in the room. Dr. Christy Kelly, who had a camera in his wardrobe (this was his room) decided that he would like to have a picture.

Dr. Leo Ahern, with two officers, had already left by car for Dublin. "Direct communications with Dublin were cut off, so once I had examined the body and organised things at the hospital, I headed for Dublin – a difficult journey, several detours due to road obstructions. Arrangements had to be made for the embalming; also Government officials had to be contacted so that we could await the arrival of the body at the North Wall." He was to be "a pall bearer".[3]

Around 6 am Dr. Christy Kelly went to the Aherns' home at nearby Strawberry Hill. Dr. Gerald Ahern was asleep when Dr. Kelly came into his room, *"Wake up! Michael Collins is dead!"* he shouted. The events of the night were then related as they sat over an unusually early breakfast prepared by Mrs. Ahern. They contacted their brother, Father Joe Ahern, one of the curates attached to Shanakiel Hospital, but he was on holidays in Crosshaven. Dr. Gerald sent word to him, and he returned to the hospital.

Dr. Gerald suggested that his colleague Dr. Christy Kelly should go to bed in his house, but Dr. Kelly wished to return to the hospital. At 8.30 am they arrived back at the hospital and went into Room 201 ("I remember the time because Kelly asked me, 'What time is it?')

Dr. Kelly decided he would like another picture of Collins

from a different angle. When the two men entered the room, there were just four soldiers on guard with rifles. "That's strange," said Dr. Kelly, half to himself.

"What?" asked Dr. Gerald.

"Those things on the chair," said Kelly.

During his absence a greatcoat had been thrown over the back of the chair and a blood-stained cap rested on the seat. They had not been there when he had taken the first picture, nor had he seen them when the body was brought in. One of the soldiers said that these were the Commander's items. Kelly took up the coat and looked at it, then handled the cap. "What puzzled him entirely was that there was no bullet hole in it, though it was smeared in blood. It was still wet." Kelly took yet another picture as confirmation and both doctors left. (Later on in the day he took a further picture of the cortege going down Shanakiel Hill).[4]

Due to the disruption of both the railway line and roads between Cork and Dublin, a boat owned by B&I would take the cortege. The *SS Classic* (later known as the *Kilbarry*)[5] would be used; this had docked at Penrose Quay in the morning, having travelled from Fishguard as part of a regular service, and was scheduled to embark for Dublin in the evening, then travel to Liverpool the following morning.

At 7.30 am Dalton sent a wire to Portobello Barracks which was received at 9.10 am (working P.O. hour). The message read:

"To General Staff, Dublin, Commander-in-Chief shot dead in ambush at Bealnablath near Bandon

6.30 Tuesday evening with me. Also one man wounded. Remains leaving by Classic for Dublin today Wednesday noon. Arrange to meet. Reply. Dalton."[6]

In the afternoon, Cronin & Desmond Funeral Service fulfilled the necessary undertaking duties. Fr. Joseph Scannell, Army chaplain,[7] assisted by Fr. Joe Ahern, recited the funeral prayers. The cortege moved off down Shanakiel Hill shortly after 4 pm, then through the city streets towards the quay.

People from Cork City and surrounds came out in their hundreds to watch the slow march of soldiers as they carried the tricolour-draped coffin of their dead Commander-in-Chief. The long procession of uniformed army men that proceeded down the quay included many of Collins' former friends and colleagues. Along the route and at the pierhead, weeping crowds knelt in prayer. Emmet Dalton observed that, "There were tears in most of the men's eyes as we took the boat slowly down the River Lee."

Soldiers stood to attention, rifles reversed, as the boat moved on its journey. At twilight the boat drew near to Cobh and the high bell on St. Colman's Cathedral resounded over the calm water. Beside the harbour, men from the British destroyer fleet stood to attention on deck. "We were greeted with a salute of trumpets from the sailors; as we went quietly on, they sounded the Last Post." Emmet Dalton would "never forget the sight and the sound. All the windows of the houses in Cobh were lit with either candles or lights of some description – they flickered like fairy lights, and the strains of the music over the water was most impressive – so very touching. It would bring tears to a stone!" Dalton became emotional, there were tears in his eyes as he recalled this scene.

It was a long dreary journey for the men on the *Classic* as the boat wound its way around the south-east coast of Ireland. And for the many who lined the North Wall, Dublin, it was a lingering desolate wait. Members of the Provisional Government and many of Collins' special friends remained locked in their own thoughts. "I began to think, during this seemingly unending wait, what would happen to the country now?" said Ernest Blythe. "We had thought, as Mick did, that the warfare was almost finished; we felt it might be possible to reach some accommodation that would prevent this continued guerilla destruction."[8]

Meanwhile on the quayside "drizzling rain added to our gloom", according to Oliver St. John Gogarty. Hour after hour they stood, "the officers in their uniforms blackened by rain – officers of an Irish National Army."[9]

At last a bright light was seen coming in on the water. (The time of arrival appears to have been somewhere between 2 and 3 am) Grief was noticeable among those who gathered. Many who awaited the arrival wept openly. Oliver St. John Gogarty, who had been friendly with Collins since the War of Independence, when Collins used his house as a place of refuge while "on the run", said he saw women dressed in fur coats who knelt "and chanted prayers into the murky sky".[10]

Troops with reversed rifles formed a bodyguard as the

waiting gun-carriage received the coffin which was draped in the tricolour. Then began the procession through the streets of Dublin, bound for St. Vincent's Hospital. Ernest Blythe was among "the small procession that walked behind the gun-carriage, along the empty dark streets around 3 o'clock. There were a few people at some corners, but in the main it was just members of the government, friends, and some of the army. It was dreary. We were shocked and saddened."[11]

Gogarty, a skillful surgeon who was to embalm the body, wanted to have the task completed before noon. so he decided to have a short nap before he began work. He had just got into bed when he heard a loud knocking on the door. Desmond FitzGerald, Minister of External Affairs, was anxious that the embalming should be undertaken right away. At 4.30 am, Gogarty, not realising that he was still in his bedroom slippers, walked through the empty streets with FitzGerald to awaken the porter of the College of Surgeons. When they got no response at the front entrance they went round to the large gate at the back of the dissecting room. As both hammered loudly with the flat of their hands, a bullet embedded itself above their hands. While they continued to bang, there was "another plunge of lead in pine".

"Leave it to me, the job is not a lengthy one, I will come back at six o'clock," Gogarty assured the minister. Meanwhile, he said he would try the Anatomy School of Trinity College.[12]

When Gogarty reached St. Vincent's Hospital, Seán Kavanagh had just arrived. Gogarty asked him to get Albert Power, the sculptor, to come and make a death mask of

Collins. With snipers active about Dublin streets during an uneasy dawn, the death mask was taken and the embalming begun. Dr. Leo Ahern remembers the skill with which Dr. Gogarty carried out the embalming. Later the body would be changed to a stronger, more decorative oak coffin, so that the Nation could observe the dead hero in full glory.[13]

Lady Hazel Lavery had told her husband, Sir John, on Tuesday evening "All day I have been seeing them carrying Michael covered with blood. Wherever I go I cannot get rid of the sight." Upset at hearing this, he eventually got her to go to bed then "sat with her until well on into the night, and at last she went to sleep. At seven in the morning her very English maid came in with the tea. After she had put it down, she said in a voice showing not the slightest trace of interest, 'They have shot Mr. Collins, my Lady!'"[14]

Later that morning (Wednesday) Countess Elizabeth was sitting with Bernard Shaw's wife beside the fire in the study at Kilteragh House where Michael Collins had dined with them just a few nights previously. Suddenly the door opened and Hazel appeared "in deep mourning".

"I knew it before I saw the papers," she said, "I had seen him in a dream, his face covered with blood."[15]

On Thursday morning, Lady Hazel and Countess Elizabeth went to view the body at the chapel of the Sisters of Charity at St. Vincent's Hospital, where tall candles burned at the head and feet while four soldiers "guarded him in his last sleep. Michael Collins lay in full uniform, and to him death had given her full measure of beauty and dignity, increased by the effect of that white bandage round his head, which hid the wound made by the bullet that had killed him. His face had taken on an almost Napoleonic cast."[16] When she whispered to one of the soldiers, "Where has he been hit?" he responded by touching the back of his own head. The two young women with tear-stained faces stood for some time in silent prayer and then left.

A short while later, Kitty Kiernan, the young woman to whom Collins was engaged and who had expected shortly to be his wife, entered the little chapel accompanied by her sister. Tears trickled down her cheeks as she stood looking on him for a long time.

There were no words now on this Thursday morning of 24 August 1922 – just some silent prayers accompanied by tears.

When Joe O'Reilly, Collins' friend of many years (who had given him the orange drink on the night before he left Dublin, and who shared a room with him in Cork's Imperial Hotel headquarters on the night prior to his trip to West Cork) approached, he stood beside the coffin and burst into uncontrollable crying for some moments. In the stillness, the emotion was picked up by those who stood around. Beside Joe, the newly ordained Army Chaplain Fr. Seán Piggott, turned and whispered to him, whereupon Joe asked Fr. Seán if he wouldn't mind cutting a lock of Michael Collins' hair. O'Reilly had a scissors in his pocket. He took the lock that the priest handed him and put it in a concealed part of his watch, according to Fr. Seán.[17]

It has been said that Kitty Kiernan asked for a lock of his hair – however, this cannot be confirmed. Neither can it be confirmed that earlier she asked a soldier to cut a lock. (In 1925 Kitty married Felix Cronin, a veteran of the War of Independence and Civil War, and an admirer of Michael Collins. She had two sons. There is no record of Kitty ever having a lock of Michael Collins' hair among her possessions, according to her descendants.)

All that day the body remained in St. Vincent's Hospital chapel.

Sir John Lavery regarded it a privilege to be allowed to paint Michael Collins in death as he had already done in life.

He noticed that "the peculiar dent" near the point of his nose seemed to have disappeared.

"He might have been Napoleon in marble as he lay in his uniform, covered by the Free State flag, with a crucifix on his breast. Four soldiers stood around the bier. The stillness was broken at long intervals by someone entering the chapel on tiptoe, kissing the brow, and then slipping to the door where I could hear a burst of suppressed grief."[18]

There were many difficult moments during that painting session, moments when Lavery found the tears welling up in his own eyes. "One woman kissed the dead lips, making it hard for me to continue my work."

In the late evening the body was placed in the oak coffin that was specially made for the dead Commander-in-Chief, by carpenters who had worked through the night. The remains were ceremoniously taken to City Hall for the public lying in state which lasted until Sunday evening. Daily the queues lengthened, often extending to a mile long and moving slowly past the body of a man who had either directly or indirectly affected their lives. "It seemed as if all Dublin wanted to do honours to him in death."[19]

Members of the Squad, Collins' Intelligence Officers, Provisional Government members, Army officers, and other close comrades proudly took their turn to guard their dead Chief.

A black-shawled woman, one of the many from the back streets of Dublin, filed passed the coffin. For a moment she stood, and in the hushed silence of the great hall where hundreds of people awaited their turn, she cried out, *"Michael Collins, Michael Collins, why did you leave us?"*

On Sunday evening the oak coffin was carried to the Pro-Cathedral where it remained under guard overnight. Next morning several priests and bishops officiated.

Dr. Fogarty from County Clare had warned Collins at Griffith's funeral that he (Collins) might be next. Dr Fogarty said to a friend, "Mick didn't see danger anywhere." Michael Collins had dismissed his brother Johnny's concern for him when he told him to be careful as he bid him farewell at Sam's Cross before he left for Bandon and Béal na mBláth. Early next morning 23 August, *The Times* reported that Johnny stated, "The first intimation I had of the death of my brother was from the driver of a Red Cross ambulance which arrived at Clonakilty for a wounded Irregular who had been a prisoner there." Johnny, having heard the sad news, stated that after the wounded prisoner was removed, he "asked the doctor in charge of the car for permission to accompany him to Cork, so that I could proceed to Dublin to my brother's funeral. The doctor kindly gave permission."

On arrival at Bandon "we were told we should take the road to Macroom as the main road as impassable, owing to Irregular operations". About a mile out they were stopped and Johnny was "kidnapped". But shortly afterwards he was released and got to Dublin for his brother's "lying in state" and for his funeral.

Following Requiem High Mass, the coffin was placed on a gun-carriage – the gun-carriage which by a strange irony had been borrowed from the British and used under Provisional Government instructions by Emmet Dalton for the shelling of the Four Courts and which in a sense announced the outbreak of the Civil War.

The Provisional Government purchased four black artillery horses from the British for the occasion. And so the procession set out on the six-mile journey to Glasnevin cemetery. To the slow marching air played by the pipe band, the three-mile-long cortege moved past the thousands of people who lined the route. Many had travelled from counties throughout Ireland, including a large number who had accompanied the body on the boat from Cork.

Some of those who were unable to view proceedings from

the "front line" climbed up on walls, monuments and even rooftops. Women who had picked little bunches of flowers tried to get near the bier so that they could place their tributes on it. "The wail of the pipes and the mournful tapping of the drums added to the impressive sadness of the scene."

Most of the soldiers were unused to the polish of ceremonial drill, yet according to onlookers, "they performed their task of the slow-march pace" by back streets from City Hall to the Pro-Cathedral and from there to Glasnevin "with dignity".

Many of Collins' comrades in arms and in politics now stood at the graveside – men like Dalton, Mulcahy, Dolan, O'Reilly, Cosgrave, O'Higgins, Blythe and many others. His friend and admirer, Dr. Fogarty from County Clare, officiated at the ceremony. Army Chaplain Fr. Seán Piggott and priests from all over the world came to pay their respects.

Richard Mulcahy, who would afterwards take Michael Collins' place as Commander-in-Chief of the Army, was poetic when he delivered the oration over his dead friend.

> " ... those of us you leave behind are all, too, grain from the same handful ... Men and women of Ireland, we are all mariners on the deep, bound from a port still seen only through storm and spray, sailing still on a sea 'full of dangers and hardships, and bitter toil'. But the Great Sleeper lies smiling in the stern of the boat, and we shall be filled with that spirit which will walk bravely upon the waters."[20]

The oration was recorded by Michael Collins' brother-in law, Patrick O'Driscoll (a reporter in Dáil Éireann) on the blank page in the back of his prayer book.

The coffin having been lowered into the grave and covered with soil, the oration having been delivered and the final prayers and rosary recited, it was time for all to move away. Yet, many lingered around the mound of fresh brown soil. Two tearful women met for the first time. Michael Collins' fiancée Kitty Kiernan and his dear friend Lady Hazel Lavery spontaneously embraced. Other friends sobbed softly.

To the remaining members of the Provisional Government and officers in the Army was left the task of picking up the threads of Collins' work and weaving it in their own way.

In a message to Cosgrave, Acting Chairman of the Provisional Government, Sir Nevil Macready, Commander of the British Forces in Ireland, said:

"On the many occasions during the last year when we met on official business, I always found him ready and willing to help in all matters that were brought to his notice in connection with the forces under my command. I deeply regret that he should not have been spared to see in a prosperous and peaceful Ireland the accomplishment of his work."

Winston Churchill, in his tribute to Collins and Griffith, said that they were two men "who feared God, loved their country and who kept their word".[21]

Chapter 13

(*The following is based on eye-witness accounts of the aftermath of the ambush, as given to the author.*)[1]

In the stillness of the evening, the echo of gunfire which ascended from Béal na mBláth valley was heard for miles around. But, when the convoy moved northwards along the road, all was calm once more. For the Republicans that ambush was over. They didn't think any of their men were dead, but they felt there would be a type of roll-call or assessment afterwards, possibly in Bill Murray's, where perhaps the meeting of Southern Command members which had been postponed in the morning would be reconvened. (Republicans who were not Southern Command members, but were members of local companies 'rounded-up' for the day would not be attending.)

Meanwhile the men needed food. After their long dreary wait under the hot August sunshine, a wait that culminated in a swift, sharp, unexpected ambush, they were hungry.

Sonny Neill and Dinny Brien came forward to Jim Kearney and Timmy Sullivan.

"I dropped one man anyway," said Neill.

"You're a crack shot," said Sullivan. "Was it you got the other lad too?"

"Yes," said Neill. "But he jerked from me."

"It must have been our lads who were firing over across," said Sullivan.

"That's what got your man moving," said Neill.

Suddenly Kearney remembered that John Callaghan had crawled further along the boreen sometime after the ambush, and now he wondered if he had been hit later. Kearney and Sullivan said they would look along the boreen, while Neill and Brien said they would go down along the road. Neill also wanted to assess positions which had been held by the enemy, and to review the situation for himself.

As they were about to break up, Liam Deasy arrived. It appears he was disappointed that the mine had been disconnected which he had suggested when they were "tidying up".

There was a misunderstanding between Jim Kearney and Timmy Sullivan about Deasy's initial reaction, as they were some distance apart at this time. Deasy was nearer to Kearney. In a letter to author, Kearney wrote that Deasy asked if "any of us were hurt – I said 'no' that there weren't many of us here to be hurt."

"There is a motorbike back the road," said Liam. "Get it away and be careful, and go and get a cup of tea somewhere."

Sonny Neill came forward. "We got one man," he said.

"Ye were great, to put up such a fight!" said Deasy.

"We were fighting for our lives," said Kearney.

"A pity they didn't come a bit earlier and we would have blasted the lot," said Deasy.

They told him they weren't sure if John Callaghan was hit or if he was "gone for grub". It was decided that they would all make further enquiries.

Deasy said he was going up to Bill Murray's, where the members of the Southern Division would gather after their meal. Kearney and Sullivan and some other soldiers were members of the local companies in the Brigade and not members of the Southern Division, and therefore would not be attending the Divisional meeting.

The men then scattered. They travelled to various houses in the locality where they expected to get food while scouts stood guard outside the houses, as had been the policy since the War of Independence.

Bill Powell had been up to the east during the ambush, in a high bushy field north-west of Bill Murray's. Now, with John Lordan he came out onto the road where some more men were walking. As he walked on, a bullet which accidently discharged from one of his companions' guns scared Powell and brought a reprimand from Deasy. It was obvious that some of the men were slightly tense: the ambush which had been meticulously prepared and well-organised had not materialised as planned; the unprepared manner in which a few men were forced to take on the enemy left an air of temporary dissatisfaction among the men.

As Bill Powell, Sonny Neill, Dinny Brien, Tadhg O'Sullivan, Con Murphy, John Lordan and a few more men sat down to tea in Bill Murray's kitchen, they began to analyse the events of the day. "Fifteen minutes earlier and the lot would have been wiped out," said one. All agreed. It would have been a successful ambush. No wonder Deasy was unhappy – he wanted some success to cling to, they said. And he would have to answer to Liam Lynch. If only he hadn't ordered the engineers – Jim Kearney, John Callaghan and Timmy Sullivan – to disconnect the mine "until after the grub". So the discussion continued.

Sonny Neill, who was seated to Bill Powell's left, said that at least he had "dropped one man". And they all agreed that "getting" one man showed they were still an active armed force. One enemy was as good as another to the man with a gun in his hand.

Liam Deasy, Pete Kearney, Dan Holland, Pat Buttimer and a few more men were eating their meal in the parlour.

The men in the kitchen had finished their meal when Shawno (Seán O') Galvin came in. *"Michael Collins was shot!"* he said.

Bill Powell felt Sonny Neill's grip on his left arm, and knew what that meant.

Immediately, one man in the tension-packed room jumped up. "There's another traitor gone!"

Neill, Powell, Murphy, Lordan, Tadhg O'Sullivan and the other men said nothing.

Shawno Galvin told the men that the convoy had called on Fr. Murphy in Cloughduv. Afterwards the priest's housekeeper, Anne White, sent him the information.

When he finished speaking a silence followed for a few minutes.

"He's dead," said Sonny Neill. "May the Lord have mercy on his soul!" Then he got up and walked into the night.[2]

Word was sent to other houses around.

Jim Kearney was sitting at the table in Jim Murray's house, which was across the valley, west beyond the boreen where the ambush took place. "Sitting inside the table with their backs to the wall were Tom Hales, Jackie O'Neill [Sonny's brother] and another man I didn't know. On the outside was Jack Corkery and myself."

They had almost completed their meal when a girl ran in saying, *"Do you know who's dead? Michael Collins!"* One man grabbed his cap from his knee, and triumphantly threw it up. Again, a first reaction, one of the enemy! Tom Hales joined his hands, lowered his eyes and said nothing. Then he blessed himself and remained with head bowed for some time. The other men around the table sensed the tension in the room.

Back in Corcorans' of Newcestown, Tom Kelleher, Jim Hurley and others heard the news a little later.

Some of the men who had eaten in neighbours' houses returned to Bill Murray's where the postponed meeting was expected to be reconvened. When the group assembled, it was with heavy hearts that the men received confirmation that Michael Collins was dead. "It was only when we thought of the implications, and also when we thought of the man that it began to dawn on us the whole thing was a tragedy," said Liam Deasy. "The original purpose of holding a meeting was suddenly changed. Our meeting that morning was to decide on our future policy. We intended, with de Valera present, to consider his views. Now we felt future policy was being decided for us." Liam Lynch would have to be fully informed about the ambush.[3]

Later that night Tom Hales, Liam Deasy and Tadhg O'Sullivan walked silently down the road from Murrays' house. Over the past number of years all three had been close friends of Michael Collins, "We wondered why of all the men in the convoy did it have to be Collins who received the fatal shot. I remember we said little; we parted without much discussion."[4]

Kearney walked north along the road and into Long's public house where he met "Tom Crofts who was with a few more men in a back room". Kearney had an exploder, also a roll of cable over his shoulder. "The mood was very subdued," according to Kearney. Crofts wanted to know the details of Kearney's account of the ambush. Liam Deasy and a few more of the men had already left. Crofts and the men already knew what Sonny Neill had told Deasy, Jim Kearney, Timmy Sullivan and John Callaghan. (That he "dropped one man".)

Crofts said to Kearney, "It's not safe to stay here tonight. I feel there could be a big round-up."

Kearney asked if anybody had seen John Callaghan. Nobody had. Kearney decided he would go back to the ambush site to look for him. As he walked south along the main road, he saw some activity in the boreen. He spotted flickering matches – men were obviously searching.

"Who's there?" asked Kearney.

"Is that you, Jim?" came Timmy Sullivan's voice.

"Yes, hang on," said Kearney who went around to them and asked if they had seen John Callaghan.

"We found his hat," said Foley.

As Kearney, Foley and Sullivan walked south on the main road, they saw, with the aid of matches, the motorbike and what looked like a cap but they decided they would get a few hours' sleep and return in the morning to investigate.

After a few further enquiries they discovered that Callaghan was alright. He had left the scene of the ambush immediately afterwards. Because of inadequate cover, the hat would have given him away so he abandoned it. He moved away from the ambush scene as soon as it was over. He had got an injury in the buttocks, but did not discover it until sometime later. (John Callaghan died in 1924. During the War of Independence he fought with the Republicans and was very active. He was arrested and sent to Spike Island where he got a woeful doing, as did all the men who were sent to Spike Island. Some never recovered to full health afterwards.)

The following day at the ambush site Sonny Neill and Jim Kearney conversed.

"I used the wrong bullet," said Neill.

"What do you mean?" asked Kearney.

"It was a dumdum!"

Kearney knew what that meant. (These were bullets used by the Auxiliaries which were picked up by the IRA –

ammunition captured after ambushes during the War of Independence and retained by the men.)

Neill, who originally had two clips with five bullets in each, told Kearney he was going to dump the remainder.

Lieut Col. Eamonn Moriarty explained to the author on 23/11/2002: "A dumdum bullet wound was nastier than one created by a conventional bullet."

Chapter 14

On Wednesday, 23 August, the day after the Béal na mBláth ambush, Liam Deasy sent a dispatch to Liam Lynch.

Lynch stated in his acknowledgement:

> "Considering the very small number of men engaged this was a most successful operation, and they are to be complimented on the fight made under such heavy fire, and against such odds.
> Considering you were aware of the fact that the convoy contained an armoured car, it is surprising you had not mines laid to get this."[1]

There was a mine laid, but, as has been established, it had been disconnected before the convoy arrived, as the ambush had been called off. Why then did Deasy not inform Lynch of this?

"This was just a brief dispatch," he said. "Lynch was informed afterwards of the full facts."

Liam Lynch believed that the stand the Republicans had taken was correct but, in his acknowledgement, he expressed regret. "Nothing could bring home more forcibly the awful unfortunate national situation at present than the fact that it has become necessary for Irishmen and former comrades to shoot such men as M. Collins who rendered such splendid service to the Republic in the last war against England."[2]

Lynch had no intention of talking peace. He wrote: "It is to be hoped our present enemies will realise the folly in trying to crush the Republic before it is too late."[3]

A few weeks before his death, Collins had been equally adamant: "When the Irregulars – leaders and men ... give up their arms and cease their depredations on the persons and property of Irish citizens, there will be no longer need for hostility."[4]

Both sides had continued to fight for what they saw as "Ireland's future". A few days after Collins' death, Frank Aiken wrote to Mulcahy expressing his sympathy, despite having been "in arms against him lately. My sorrow for his death is greater because I believe that in a month or so he would have seen that he was on the wrong side, and I don't believe he who most of all was responsible for building up the strength of the nation would – when he saw that he could not win out – have disappointed that strength in a hopeless struggle."[5]

Because of the strong beliefs of people on both sides, there was a determination to win. On the day the ambush was planned at Béal na mBláth, another was being organised on the Cork/Fermoy road near Watergrasshill, because this was the road the Republicans in that area felt that Collins would travel back.

So Collins was at risk from several ambushes during his trip south. There was every possibility that he would get killed during one of these ambushes. Yet the bullet which took his life at Béal na mBláth has aroused controversy, mainly because of the large wound in the back of his head behind the right ear, at a time when it was believed he was facing his ambushers. This has led to several different theories:

– that he was hit from behind by one of the Republicans who were returning to Kerry
– that he was killed by a member of his own convoy, either by a close-range bullet from a Mauser pistol or by a bullet from the armoured car
– that the fatal wound was caused by a ricochet bullet
– that a bullet fired by a Republican killed him

Because the type of wound Collins received has never been confirmed, these theories require analysing. But first it is necessary to establish Collins' position when he was fatally hit.

The road where Collins and his men were engaged in ambush was in a valley. During the final stages of the ambush, after Collins had got up from his prone position, turned to his right, walked a short distance north-east along the road, he wheeled around and gave an order. His back was now to the men around the ford bend of the boreen from where, according to Timmy Sullivan, he and Jim Kearney could see "the soldier out on the road" as they looked out between little bushes. Dalton says that during the ambush, "there was gunfire coming from the direction facing us, coming from our left [boreen]. There were echoes, but I had the awful feeling that there was fire coming from somewhere behind us – back over to the right of my prone position". This was Liam Deasy and Pete Kearney up north/east firing into the bushes. It appears that Collins moved, and turned when this gunfire could be heard more clearly during a lull.

According to accounts given by Corry, O'Connell and several other men at the scene, Collins stood out when he gave the order and began firing. It is not clear what his exact words were. O'Connell thought he shouted, "Come on, boys! There they are, running up the road!"[6] Jim Kearney, up west on the horseshoe boreen, thought he shouted, "Cut them off on the right!"[7] Timmy Sullivan, on the boreen, wasn't quite sure, but thought he shouted, "Get them on the right!" or "Up there to the right!"[8] Dalton heard him shout something like, "There on the right!" In Eoin Neeson's statement, "There they are running up the road!" In Dalton's statement, "Come on, boys! There they are on the right running up the road!" – and he says Collins may have been standing when he gave the order; but when he next saw him a little later he was in a prone position. Dalton says, "he may have been falling at the time, because when I observed him he had been hit – just after this I barely heard my name being called."[9]

According to Rex Taylor he was 'reloading his rifle' when he was shot, showing that he was preparing to fire. He was south along the road in front of the *Sliabh na mBan* armoured car, and approximately 175 yards from the turn in the boreen around which Kearney and Sullivan were positioned a few yards apart and where Callaghan had moved a little further north. Collins was approximately 185 yards from the further pillar of the gate, inside which Sonny Neill was positioned. From this position (Neill's) there was an elevation. Collins was out on the road in the area where the river flows nearest the road, and was approximately five feet out from the dyke (the water-channel where a wooden cross was placed soon afterwards).[10]

Because Collins had turned and was facing the direction in which the Kerrymen were hiding, they could not have hit him in the back of the head with a bullet. These men had no view of a definite target and, in order to preserve their own safety, they did not fire any shots in that direction. Therefore, this theory can be ruled out.

The theory that there was a traitor in Collins' convoy who saw the opportunity and decided "to get him" at an appropriate moment will now be examined.

It was only on Friday morning, 18 August, that Collins asked Joe McGrath, Director of Intelligence, to organise the convoy. No advance warning was sent to Dalton in Cork, as has been shown, though Collins did inform O'Duffy.[11] Fionáin Lynch believed that Collins was unsure whether or not he would get further than Limerick, though his intention was to go to Cork. Also, for security reasons each stage of the journey would be decided at Collins' own discretion. Therefore, it was Joe McGrath who was responsible for the men delegated to escort Collins. So if there was "a plant" among Collins' escort men, he would need the co-operation of Joe McGrath, who would in turn need the co-operation of Captain Coghlan, because Captain Coghlan was "the Army man" in Portobello Barracks with whom Joe McGrath liaised in selecting the men, the transport and the ammunition for the journey.

We know that Collins was annoyed that the transport was not perfect. He was also displeased with the "unprepared escort", as shown in his diary.[12] They were "not as lively as he would have wished and they were unused to conditions along country roads," according to Dalton."[13] But there is absolutely no reason to think that Collins suspected their loyalty. The men who were detailed to escort Collins appear simply to have been men who were available in Portobello Barracks at the time. Ernest Blythe said, "Many of the good fighting men were in action in other parts of the country – the men picked for the journey south were in action in Dublin."[14] There is no evidence to doubt the integrity of Joe McGrath or of Captain Coghlan.

Still, supposing there was a "plant" and by some coincidence he happened to be picked, or got himself selected for the tour – then he would have to wait for the opportune moment to do "the job".

But if the Republicans had not seen a Provisional Government forces convoy passing through "their" area, on the morning of 22 August, then there would have been no ambush set up; they planned the ambush because their forces had blocked all other routes to Cork due to their Southern Divisional meeting (which had to be postponed as already discussed). This meant that this convoy would have to return through Béal na mBláth.

Also, if Collins' convoy had been a half an hour later on its return journey, there would have been no ambush. When, then, would "the plant" have done "the job"?

But to carry the supposition to its ultimate by suggesting that all things were working in favour of the alleged "plant" and that luck was on his side, was he in the right place to do "the job"?

The position Collins was in when he was killed has been established. He had distanced himself from his comrades and had turned his back to the ambushers, shouting a command when he was hit. At this time he was in front of the armoured car, in view of the driver, Jim Woulfe, and his co-driver Wiggy Fortune. If "a job" was to be done with accuracy, it would have to be a clean one, so a Mauser pistol would be used; this would mean an entry and an exit bullet wound which would have been inflicted when the shot was fired at a fairly close range with Collins about to wheel around. The "plant" would have to be close to Collins at the precise moment to inflict the fatal wound. For him, a blunder would be disastrous. This would mean that the killer would have to follow Collins' movements during the ambush. The killer would have to risk being seen by other members of the convoy, including the men in the armoured car.

Jim Woulfe, the driver of the armoured car, concentrated his gaze through the small slit-window, as his task was to move when machine-gunner McPeak wanted him to or when the necessity arose. Looking on the road ahead he could easily see any irregularity. Co-driver Jimmy "Wiggy" Fortune was in a similar position. Jim Woulfe saw "the soldier fall" (Collins) a little distance in front of the armoured car when he was hit. "He was out on the road when he swung round. I saw him fall rather awkwardly."

"Was he with somebody, or on his own?" I asked.

"He was on his own at the time," said Woulfe. [15]

As Collins seems to have been standing alone when he was hit, there is no evidence to show that a close-range Mauser bullet killed him. If he was hit by a Mauser bullet, it would have created a small entry wound in his forehead and a large exit wound in the back of his head. So supposing that during the course of the ambush the alleged killer succeeded unnoticed in getting close to Collins, then the wound/wounds would establish the calibre of the fatal bullet. But before investigating the wound/wounds we will need to analyse the actions of Jock McPeak who manned the Vickers gun in the armoured car that evening, because it has been alleged that Collins was shot by a bullet fired by McPeak.

McPeak had enlisted in the Argyle and Sutherland Highlanders of the British Army in 1915 but was transferred to the Machine

Gun Corps on its formation in 1916. Wounded at the Somme, he was sent on his recovery to Palestine, where he served until July 1919. When he was discharged, he returned to his native Glasgow. Like six million more soldiers, he was unemployed upon being demobbed. This son of a Tyrone man was in sympathy with the Irish cause and deplored the actions of the Black and Tans in Ireland. Consequently, he became involved in securing arms for the Irish cause. At a meeting with some others to make arrangements to get the cargo across the water, he was arrested and sent to Barlinnie prison in Glasgow, where he remained as a political prisoner until the Treaty was signed.

When the Provisional Government was recruiting in Scotland, McPeak enlisted and came to Ireland to join the Army. "To us, it was still the IRA, we didn't know there was any difference at that time between them and the Free Staters. All we had been told was that they wanted soldiers." Shortly after he and his comrades landed in Ireland, the Four Courts was attacked, and the Civil War began.

McPeak was stationed first in the Curragh and afterwards in Portobello Barracks where the armoured cars were housed. On 18 August, he was detailed for his first service operation with the Provisional Government forces, as gunner on the *Sliabh na mBan* armoured car. He was awakened early on Sunday 20 August, and given instructions to "get ready and stand by". His brief was "to escort Michael Collins" (whom he had admired since coming to Ireland) on his southern tour of inspection.

After the funeral of Michael Collins, McPeak returned to Cork and resumed escort duties in the armoured car for General Emmet Dalton and General Tom Ennis. Then, three months after the day Michael Collins was shot, McPeak deserted to the Republicans, taking with him the *Sliabh na mBan* armoured car. Because of this incident, because of his background, and because of the stoppages which occurred in the machine-gun fire during the ambush, there has been speculation that he was a mercenary "planted" in the Collins convoy. This, McPeak flatly denied to Ray Smith and Jim Nicoll of the *Irish Independent* (18–21 May 1971).

However, if we look at McPeak's situation, it is clear that he would have had great difficulty in firing "a single shot" in Collins' direction – apart from the physical awkwardness of deliberately singling a machine-gun shot, it would have been impossible to do it without being noticed. He would have had to revolve the turret quickly to a 90-degree angle at least, thus risking the lives of many more of his own comrades north the road from him, who would then be within his line of fire.

During the action, Dalton questioned the stoppages. Therefore, it is highly unlikely, indeed it can be denied categorically that a trained gunner would take such a calculated risk under such circumstances. Furthermore, when he deserted to the Republicans and took the armoured car with him, McPeak talked to the men on whom he had fired. And, according to both Timmy Sullivan and Jim Kearney, "he fired to kill". Though he himself says he "fired to frighten". Even the mown-down ferns, grass and little bushes, which the men viewed in daylight the morning after the ambush, bore testimony to the fact that he was doing a job to the best of his ability.

Because McPeak had the hatch closed he didn't know that anything had happened until one of the drivers said, "Collins has been hit."

To conclude this analysis, Jock McPeak did not shoot Michael Collins deliberately. If there was the million-to-one chance that he accidentally fired a shot which proved fatal, it would easily have been noticed in the same way as a deliberate shot. Someone would surely have witnessed such a clumsy operation.

Was Collins killed by a ricochet bullet? It has been alleged that bullet marks on the turret of the armoured car (now held in the Curragh) can substantiate a claim that a bullet fired from a particular position ricocheted off the armoured car and hit Collins. This can be discounted because the gun and turret which are now attached to the *Sliabh na mBan* armoured car are not those which were on the armoured car on the day Michael Collins was shot (as has always been believed). Pat Lynch of Curragh Military Barracks told the author that a replacement gun and turret were subsequently mounted.

After the stealing of the armoured car, the Republicans removed the gun and turret to make it ineffective after they failed to obtain tyres for it. These parts were not on it when it was recaptured by the Army.

Furthermore, it is evident that a bullet hitting the armoured car and bouncing off it would be unlikely to hit Collins, in view of the distance between the car and Collins.

However, a bullet could have ricocheted off the road and inflicted the fatal wound. If a bullet came from the boreen direction (Republicans) and bounced as Collins was turning, it could have hit him in the poll of the head behind the right ear (the location of the fatal wound), because he was wheeling from right to left.

Collins wore an officer's cap. This cap was made of superfine wool so a ricochet bullet would penetrate, blow open the skin, and create a large wound. The ricochet theory has found much favour among writers and historians. We will examine this below.

Next we will examine the theory that Collins was shot by a bullet from a Republican's gun.

At Béal na mBláth on that day some Republicans had Thompson guns, but of the five men who actually participated in the ambush directly, John Callaghan had a Peter-the-Painter, Timmy Sullivan had a Colt revolver, Jim Kearney had a Parabellum. These men were engineers in charge of the mines. Sonny Neill and Dinny Brien, the two men who returned, had Lee-Enfield rifles. After the ambush Sonny Neill was certain that a dumdum bullet from his Lee Enfield rifle killed Collins. This was a long-range shot which was said to have hit the soldier on the road (Collins) as he turned round. Sonny Neill was the only man in the Republican party who claimed to have hit any member of Collins' convoy.

So, it must now be established whether the bullet which killed Collins was:

- a bullet from a Mauser pistol
- a ricochet bullet
- a dumdum bullet from a Republican's Lee-Enfield rifle

Before any conclusion can be reached about how Collins was killed, certain very important questions must be asked:

- How large was the wound at the back of the head?
- Was there a forehead wound?
- What was the calibre of the bullet that killed Collins?

Dr. Leo Ahern was the first doctor to examine Michael Collins' body and pronounce him dead. Shortly afterwards he examined the wound in Shanakiel Hospital. "The wound was a large gaping wound to the right of the poll. There was no other wound," he said. "There was no exit wound ... only the large entrance wound. There was definitely no wound in the forehead." He stressed, "It was important for me to check the wound, and to establish the cause of death. Therefore, the wound was thoroughly checked, as was the entire head area."

An autopsy was carried out on the body. Dr Leo went into great detail about it with the author.[16]

Dr. Michael Riordan was detailed by Dr. Leo Ahern to examine and prepare the body. When he examined the body on the trolley in Shanakiel Hospital, he noted a large bullet wound behind the right ear. "There was no exit wound. I'm certain there was only one large, deep wound, it appeared at point of bullet contact ... Part of the head was blown off. Some badly stained bandages were replaced."[17]

Dr. Christy Kelly, who was present during the second thorough examination, confirmed seeing "a huge wound, with part of the poll blown off, at the right-hand side. It was an ugly wound."[18]

Dr. Gerald Ahern, who was not present for the examination, but who was at the hospital later in the morning (8.30 am Room 201) said, "Dr. Kelly told me that the wound was massive – a big hole behind the right ear."[19]

Dr. Patrick Cagney, who was in the Mercy Hospital at the time, and who also attended patients in Shanakiel Hospital, did not examine the body, and he was not there at the time, but was told by colleagues that it was an extremely large wound, "at the right-hand side of the poll".[20]

When the body was being embalmed by Dr. Gogarty, Dr. Leo Ahern was also present.[21] The extent of the wound in the poll was fully examined by Dr. Gogarty, according to Dr. Leo Ahern who remembers "distinctly" Dr. Gogarty asking him "if there was any other head wound, and I told him there wasn't. He checked the forehead for marks while I held the bandages."[22] Consequently, in Gogarty's writings there is no mention of Collins having a forehead wound. Ulick O'Connor in his biography of Gogarty, has written, "With fine skill he was able to hide the gaping wound in the back of the head and preserve in the dead man's face something of the nobility it bore in life".[23]

Therefore, the theory that the bullet was inflicted by a Mauser pistol at close range can be ruled out because there was no forehead entry or exit wound. "The entry wound was in the back of the head and there was no exit wound."

In view of Dr. Leo Ahern's army experience and also his medical experience in an army hospital, I asked him what type of bullet did he believe had caused the wound. "It must have been a flat-nosed – a 'dumdum' fired from a low velocity weapon. The wound was too great, and too much of the head matter had been blown off, there was too much skull fragmentation," to have come as a result of a ricochet. "A 'dumdum' bullet when it hits a victim cascades within the head as it did in this case, and creates a huge wound."

Dr. Christy Kelly who examined the body in Shanakiel Hospital that night, told Dr. Gerald Ahern that "the large wound and shattered bone-structure" was consistent with "the bloody awful" result of a dumdum bullet. Dr. Gerald Ahern said that in later years they (the doctors present at the time) discussed the extent of the wound. "We knew 'dumdum' bullets were used by the Irregulars and, while we didn't say anything publicly, we were, I would say, convinced that it was a 'dumdum' that killed Collins."[24]

Calton Younger, in his *Ireland's Civil War*, writes that Joe Dolan (in the convoy), firing from the mud-bank area, believed "that the bullet was fired, not from directly opposite Collins, but from further along the valley so that it hit the back of his head at an angle". This account coincides with Sonny Neill's position when he fired the fatal shot.

In a television interview with Cathal O'Shannon, Emmet Dalton said, "It could only have been a ricochet or a 'dumdum' which caused the wound. "There was no entrance wound, it was just a great gaping hole at the back of the head"[25] Note the words "entrance wound". By this, Dalton was referring to a forehead wound – a close-shot bullet from a Mauser pistol.

Dalton went into great detail to describe the wound to me.

When asked which was the most likely cause, he said, "On balance a ricochet wound would be more surface." Yet he could not be sure as he did not examine the wound, but said this was done by the doctors.

Why was there no inquest held? "There was no necessity for an inquest at the time," Dalton said. "Michael Collins was shot by an enemy bullet, whether this was a bullet that ricocheted or whether it hit Collins directly. There was no question but that he was killed in an ambush by Irregulars." Dalton said that "despite all the speculation and conjecture, there was no entrance wound, only that gaping hole behind the right ear. I should know, I had bandaged his head, and afterwards had him resting on my lap. It is only as the years have progressed that speculation and a question mark" has hung over Collins' death.

Whatever the causes of such speculation, controversy and insinuation certainly evolved over the years. Jock McPeak has said, "I suppose every man in a way felt more or less responsible that the Commander-in-Chief should have been killed while the rest of us escaped without a scratch – except the motorcycle outrider, Lieutenant Smith."[26]

Dr. Leo Ahern, who spent most of his life in England, having left Ireland shortly after the end of the Civil War, "when jobs were difficult to find in Ireland", said he never had any doubt, and saw no reason to question the source of the bullet. "The effect, as far as I was concerned, told the story." It should be noted that Dr. Ahern called the wound an entrance wound – he did not know what position Collins was in, in relation to the ambushers, when the bullet hit him.

The author interviewed Bill McKenna on 5 June 1983, (3 pm.). *He said he did not see the wound in his head, as has been stated elsewhere, he "only saw Collins when he was lying in state like so many hundreds more". He said he was only "a lad" of about 15 at the time Collins was shot. He did some messages and "ran around" for Collins and others in Portobello Barracks, but "nothing of importance", and he said that he was never "in the Free-State Army".*

This invalidates what John M. Feehan says in the Preface to his book, *The Shooting of Michael Collins*, where he wrote that Bill McKenna gave him much help *"in assembling the facts of the ambush, by placing at my disposal valuable documents, and by giving me a minute by minute account of what happened on the Free State side"*.

Victor Edmonds, whose grandfather, Sam Edmonds, was in the Collins convoy at Béal na mBláth, in a letter to the author 20/3/2013, wrote, "Bill McKenna does not appear to be on the Irish Army Census."

So, is there further evidence to prove categorically that there was no forehead wound, only a large wound behind the right ear covering the poll area?

The final piece of evidence depends on Michael Collins' cap.

Controversy has surrounded the cap, which is in the National Museum, Dublin. The mud-stained coat and the cap in the mahogany case were sent to the Museum on 27 January 1923. Mr. Oliver Snoddy, Assistant Keeper in the Museum, has stated: "The cap here is that which was sent to the Museum from Mr. Cosgrave's Office as being that worn by Collins at the time of his death."[27]

Dalton believed that the blood-stained cap in the Museum was his own cap which supported Collins' wounded head on the return journey to Cork. How it acquired the hole – as Cormac Mac Carthaig, a journalist and friend of John M. Feehan, told him, he could not say. He did not see the cap. He knew Michael Collins' cap and gun were left behind, so also was his own gun.

Most Republicans in West Cork believed the cap in the Museum was Dalton's because they knew that the cap which was found at Béal na mBláth on the morning after the ambush had been buried. However, the cap in the Museum, stated to be that worn by Michael Collins, has a large jagged hole in the back right side. It is minus the badge, the diamond and the chin-strap/upper-cap strap. This cap has all the markings of the one which was buried in Jim Murray's field by Tom Hales, Jim Kearney, and Timmy Sullivan the morning after Michael Collins was shot. "The circumference of the leather band inside the army cap, said to be that of Michael Collins, is twenty and a half inches approximately." [28] (Measurements given to author by Oliver Snoddy.)

Another cap in good condition, belonging to Michael Collins, is in the Brother Allen Collection in the Military Archives at Cathal Brugha Barracks, Dublin. (The vast collection was assembled by Christian Brother, William Allen, born in Newcestown, Co. Cork.) This cap measures twenty-two inches approximately.[29]

Collins himself handed over his own cap and a Sam Browne belt to be put on the coffin for the burial of Dick McKee on 24 November 1920. (Dick McKee, Peadar Clancy and Conor Clune had been arrested on 20 November 1920 and following the events of Bloody Sunday, 21 November 1920, these men were shot in dubious circumstances while in police custody.)

Jim Kearney, who took part in the ambush, was one of the men who found the cap, and was involved in its burial on 23 August 1922. He travelled to the National Museum for the first time on 30 July 1973. Mr. Oliver Snoddy allowed both of us to examine the cap at close quarters. I still recollect Jim Kearney halting before climbing the steps. He said to me, "If the hole is in the right-hand side of the cap, and has the parts I told you about missing, then it is the right cap."

Jim Kearney later took the cap which Mr. Snoddy handed to him. He paused and looked. "This was the cap we buried," he said. This was the cap from which he himself had taken the chin strap. ("The strap was a chin strap, above the leaf of the cap, and could be brought down around the face and neck on a wild day.") Tom Hales had taken the front badge with diamond – both took them as souvenirs. "The hole in the cap reminded me, the first day I saw it, of a burst in a tyre." This cap, with these parts missing, has a large jagged hole in the right back, to the right of the back stitching in the area which would have covered the poll of the head. The inside leather band has remained intact, but is rather hard and shows shrinkage. There is no evidence that a bullet penetrated the front of the cap; there is no front entry mark.

This cap bears all the marks of being the one that Collins wore at the time he was shot. Is it then the same cap?

Dr. Christy Kelly discovered Collins' holster in his locker in Room 201, Shanakiel Hospital, a few days after Collins' body had been taken to Dublin. He gave the holster to Dr. Cagney who passed it on to Edward C. Smith, [30] who in turn took it to Dublin and gave it to Brother Allen. It is now in the Museum Collection that bears Brother Allen's name.

The gun on the *Sliabh na mBan* armoured car, which was removed from it after the Republicans got the vehicle, was held by them. (See Chapter 16.) Collins' revolver was held by the Republicans and is in private hands. A revolver with the initials E.D. (Emmet Dalton) was found later in the dyke of the road at Béal na mBláth and is in private hands.

Collins had a large head, so if the cap in the National Museum and the one in the Brother Allen Museum belonged to Collins, why is there a difference in measurement? Who originally owned the cap in the mahogany case?

The officer's cap which was buried beside the tree in Murray's field in Raheen, "contained almost a basinful of human matter", according to Jim Kearney, who had found it the morning after the ambush and was involved in its burial, as already described. (See Chapter 1)

Some days later Jim Murray dug it up because he had cattle and some pigs in this field. "My father was afraid the pigs would nose it out of the ground," said Pat Murray. "In any case I didn't want it around. I knew it was Collins' cap." Having washed it in a bucket of water, Murray put it to dry on a ditch beside the house. By this time the blood and residue of human matter was washed off. The cap remained there to dry for some days, beneath the August sun. "When it was fully dry my father brought it in, and put it in a closet under the stairs. It was left there for a few weeks. By then it had shrunk. I remember my mother stuffed it with papers and she tried to put it back in shape."

"The Stations" (a local term for the celebration of Mass in the house) were being held in Murrays' household towards the end of September.[31] Because Jim Murray disliked having this cap in the house, he introduced the subject to Fr. Denis Bernard, parish priest, and Fr. Jeremiah Coakley, curate, during breakfast. Fr. Coakley agreed to take the cap home with him and held it for a few weeks. Then his housekeeper Nell O'Sullivan agreed to take it into the Free State headquarters' officer, Liam Daly, in Bandon. General Seán Hales, T.D. happened to be in the office in Lee's Hotel when Nell O'Sullivan entered. "Mick's cap," he said. Then, according to Nell O'Sullivan, "he bowed his head and remained silent".

Both men were informed of the circumstances in which Seán's brother, Tom (Republican side) had buried the cap. Seán Hales kept the cap until he was returning to Dublin. He then "handed it over to the authorities", who had also taken Collins' coat. W.T. Cosgrave was informed of the details. After Seán Hales was shot on 7 December 1922, the cap was sent to the National Museum. W.T. Cosgrave's private secretary Mr. Banim "was the person of contact" with the Museum, and "no files were sent with it" on 27 January 1923.[32]

The leather band in the inside of this cap was made of calf skin and the material of these officers' caps was superfine wool (hand-woven), according to the Military Archivist, Commandant Peter Young. These were supplied by Callaghan's of Dame Street (later Brown Thomas). Both calf-skin (leather) and wool will shrink when dried in the heat of the sun after having been buried in soil and immersed in water. People in both the wool and leather trade have said that "shrinkage is certain under such conditions". This would allow for the difference in size between the cap in the National Museum and the one in the Brother Allen Museum. Fr. Coakley told John Joe O'Sullivan "that the tear in the cap had the jagged marks of a bullet – just the one hole in the back right-hand side". John Joe O'Sullivan confirmed this in interview with author.

It is now certain that the cap in the National Museum is the cap which was worn by Michael Collins on the day he was shot at Béal na mBláth. The cap supports the fact that Michael Collins had "one large wound" behind the right ear. Therefore, it is evident that Collins was killed by a bullet which originated from enemy lines. Sonny Neill, one of the ambushers, had his Lee-Enfield rifle aimed at the head of a soldier on the road. Neill's shot knocked that soldier. He saw him fall, as he told the men in Murray's kitchen that night: "I dropped one man". The bullet in Neill's Lee Enfield rifle was a dumdum – a flat-nosed bullet. This type of bullet, according to the evidence of the doctors who examined Collins, would expand, cascade, when it hit the poll of the head (bone structure). The wound caused by the bullet which hit Collins' poll is consistent with a dumdum bullet impact. The large open wound and the bone fragmentation in Collins' head show that the wound could not have been caused by a ricochet bullet.

Lieut Col. Eamon Moriarty explained, 'These were captured from British sources … it was a low velocity round … and did not have great penetrative power. On impact it would flatten and its cross-section area would increase significantly thus causing a gaping wound with great internal damage." In addition, "these were what the medical report called 'explosive bullets' – these were expanding bullets. Service bullets with the point (scored) and doctored to open on impact, and were used by the Auxiliaries. These bullets would expand on impact thus causing considerable damage, bone-fragmentation and nasty wounds. When this type of bullet is discharged, its destructive effect on bone and tissue is greater than that caused by an internal charge."[33]

The doctors confirm the cause of the wound and the calibre of the bullet which killed Collins. Their evidence corroborates the information which has emerged from my investigation into his death.

Seán Hales, in a statement to Seán McGarry in December 1922, said that afterwards, "They knew they had killed an officer of high rank." The author has this statement, given to Seán McGarry.[33] Liam Deasy confirmed: "We knew it was Sonny Neill's bullet! We knew that night that he 'had dropped one man'."[34]

The Republicans who had assembled in ambush at Béal na mBláth on the day Michael Collins was shot, knew afterwards who shot him. Sonny O'Neill's sister confirmed, "We knew that Sonny had fired the fatal shot that killed Collins. He was fighting in the ambush like all the other Republican soldiers."[35]

Over the years speculation has been mooted that Michael Collins was 'assassinated'. From research and investigation no substantial evidence has emerged. No individual has been named, nor a named individual being at the right place at the time to do "the job".

Manus O'Riordan wrote in *History Ireland*: "Collins was neither 'assassinated' nor 'murdered'. Ignoring the advice to drive on to safety, Collins chose to stop the car, step out and exchange with the Republican ambush party. Collins was no more assassinated than had been his anti-Treaty opponent Cathal Brugha in July 1922, nor, indeed, The O'Rahilly in Easter Week 1916. To employ the term 'assassination' in such circumstances of two-way exchanges in warfare is not only historically inaccurate but also does a disservice to the memory of Collins, who, if incredibly reckless was undoubtedly brave. We can say of all three – The O'Rahilly, Brugha and Collins – that they were killed in action, having chosen to engage in combat, each with a gun in hand.[34]

- Michael Collins was not assassinated.
- Michael Collins was not shot by a bullet from a Mauser pistol.
- Michael Collins was not killed by a ricochet bullet.
- Michael Collins was shot by the Republican who said, "I dropped one man".

George Bernard Shaw wrote in a letter to Hannah Collins, Michael Collins' sister, after his death:

> "How could a born soldier die better than at the victorious end of a good fight, falling to the shot of another Irishman, an Irishman who thought he was fighting for Ireland – a Roman to a Roman?"

Chapter 15

The author believes this chapter is necessary, for many reasons, some of which were letters to newspapers following the launch of the original edition of The Day Michael Collins Was Shot *(1989), when efforts were made to eliminate Jim Kearney's name from the participants of the Béal na mBláth ambush. Also since then, on occasions his name has been eliminated from ambush accounts by authors and writers, some with denial that he was there, when in fact, from the author's research, he was one of the principal trained engineer soldiers who lay in ambush position as the men awaited the anticipated National Army (pro-Treaty) convoy throughout the day, and who then played a vital part in the ambush and the aftermath with colleagues, with Comdt., Tom Hales, and Liam Deasy, Officer Commanding (O/C) Southern Division.*

In a letter to the *Evening Echo* 19/9/1989, the author wrote:

The man who hit an enemy target knew subsequently that the one man he 'dropped' was Collins. He had used his dumdum bullet – bullets captured during the War of Independence. This is the fact of history and we have (I hope) now reached a stage where we are prepared to accept the facts even though they may disturb us.

Our past plays a part in what we are as a people and

when we accept the manner in which this State was born, then we have reached maturity.

These men and women who now form part of our history deserve our understanding that each individual fought for his/her personal beliefs.

... One factor that struck me very forcibly during the course of my interviews with the men who fought on both sides of the Civil War was their absolute conviction that the stand (side) they took was the correct one. None of the men wanted to hide from the truth that they were soldiers fighting for a cause.

Meda Ryan

In a letter to the *Cork Examiner* 28/9/1989, John M. Feehan wrote:

In your issue of September 18, you report a Mr. Jim Kearney claiming to have taken part in the ambush at Béal na mBláth. ... I interviewed Tom Kelleher and Jim Hurley... Mr Kearney states he was one of the engineers laying the mines. Jim Hurley told me that a man named O'Callaghan dismantled the mine which had been laid earlier that day. Hurley helped O'Callaghan. There was no mention of any Kearney.

In the interest of historical accuracy, I would be grateful if Mr. Kearney could furnish details to substantiate his claims.

John M. Feehan

Published the same day, 28/9/1989, Mrs Essie O'Driscoll (née O'Neill) wrote:

> Ms. Meda Ryan has stated that she gives sources for her allegations that Sonny O'Neill shot Michael Collins. I have been unable to find these. Would she define what she means by sources?
>
> ... The bulk of the evidence goes to show that the fatal bullet was accidentally fired by Collins' own escort. This was believed by the majority of the Cabinet at the time as well as by a large number of his escort. But this circumstantial evidence cannot be validated until his body has been exhumed and the distance from which the bullet was fired medically established.
>
> Mrs Essie O' Driscoll née O'Neill

In a further similar letter to the *Southern Star* 30/9/1989, Essie O'Driscoll, née O'Neill, wrote:

> Ms. Meda Ryan ... Would she define what she means by sources? Has she a single signed statement, authenticated by any of those who were proven to be present at the ambush, to back up her allegations?
>
> I have contacted Captain John M. Feehan, author of *The Shooting of Michael Collins*, who interviewed most of the survivors at length and none of them ever mentioned the name of Sonny O'Neill. They discussed the whole ambush in detail. Captain Feehan was a friend of Liam Deasy ... yet never once did he mention the name of Sonny O'Neill. He

did mention a suspect, but that was not Sonny O'Neill.

... The bulk of the evidence goes to show that the fatal bullet was accidently fired by Collins' own escort. This was believed by the majority of the Cabinet at the time as well as by a large number of his own escort, but this is circumstantial evidence and cannot be validated until his body has been exhumed and the distance from which the bullet was fired medically established.

Essie O'Driscoll née O' Neill

In a reply to the above letters the author wrote to the *Southern Star*:

Mrs Essie O'Driscoll asks what I mean by sources. Sources are documents or other means of knowledge from which information, especially historical, is directly derived. Under the heading "Notes" at the back of my book, I have given the origin of my sources with dates, where available.

Many of these are recordings – voices of primary sources whom I interviewed. (I kept a diary and wrote a journal in addition to regular notes, while researching for my book ...)

I quote fifteen people who saw no point in hiding the truth of the dumdum bullet which killed Michael Collins. In fact, the one factor that emerged from all my interviews with these men was their conviction that the truth had to be told – these men trusted me, so they said. I am from the area and my people were involved in the movement.

Regarding the doctors: having spoken extensively to Dr.

Gerald Ahern and examined his papers, I wrote a series of questions for the doctors in England to respond to before I decided to travel to England to interview them – each stage was done to get a fuller understanding of the subject.

Regarding the Cabinet: Members of the Cabinet knew it was an anti-Treaty shot that killed Collins. Ernest Blythe, a member of the Cabinet, confirmed this to me, and incidentally so also did David Neligan, one of Collins' intelligence men. Furthermore, Liam Lynch confirmed the ambush as a "most successful operation" in a well-publicised letter, as did Seán Hales (pro-Treaty) in a statement to his brother, Tom Hales (anti-Treaty) (both sources August 1922 – see book).

The Republicans who lay in ambush positions in the bóithrín that day at Béal na mBláth (August 22) knew they were waiting for Collins' convoy … These men were seasoned guerrilla soldiers, to them all soldiers whom they saw as their enemies could have expected equal treatment – vice versa was also true.

We should not be unfair to the memory of men who fought for their beliefs, to throw doubt now on their word – they declared they were telling the truth, about what happened at Béal na mBláth; they wanted to dispel further speculation.

… Jim Kearney is the sole survivor [1989] and now that the story is public, he has the courage to stand up and be counted. No doubt if his comrades were around now, they would do likewise.

… Sonny O' Neill performed a soldier's act, he was brave

enough to return to help his comrades knowing they were in trouble. (Two machine-guns and other weaponry being used on them). Respect is due to Sonny O'Neill. His sister accepted the role taken by him and that of his brothers – all strong Republicans, she said, when she told me the story which Sonny told her of what happened at Béal na mBláth. I now hope this part of history will be seen within its context.

Meda Ryan

In response to another letter from Essie O'Driscoll, the author sent a similar letter to the *Cork Examiner* 23/10/1989, with some final paragraphs.

To understand that part of our history (1922-1923) is to understand that this country has grown out of a civil war. I do not intend, nor do I wish to hurt anybody, and regret that undue emphasis has been focused on just one specific point in my book.

My objective in writing this book was to record history and I was encouraged to do this by men such as Tom Barry, Liam Deasy, Timmy Sullivan, Jim Kearney in order to set the historical record straight.

The circumstances at Béal na mBláth were part of the scene. It was an ambush in which grown men accepted the responsibilities and fought for their beliefs, and innocence and guilt is not part of this concept. Therefore, men who fought on both sides are worthy of our respect.

In a letter to the *Sunday Independent* 14/1/1990, the author wrote a letter of response to another query, and in a further paragraph, wrote:

My attention has been drawn to another letter which appeared some time ago in your paper asking me to define what I meant by sources in my book, and also any medical information which I had regarding Michael Collins' death.

The author repeated a similar response as in the previous letter to the Southern Star, and further wrote:

Key men whom I interviewed (primary sources) who were directly involved in the ambush – men who were in ambush positions throughout the day ... signed a declaration form of truth. Being from the area I was trusted by these men. The one factor that emerged from my interviews was their conviction that the truth had to be told ... They gave me details of what happened as they saw it, only on condition that I would not manipulate their story to suit any particular slant ...

Meda Ryan

Shortly after the letters were published in the *Cork Examiner* and the *Southern Star*, Liam O'Donoghue, a retired teacher, contacted me. He told me that John M. Feehan called to him and asked him about Jim Kearney and if he knew "whether or not he was a participant in the Béal na mBláth ambush".

O'Donoghue informed him that Jim Kearney, his friend, had told him the story and on several occasions talked about it – that "Jim Kearney was very lucid, and his story never changed. He took me there on a few occasions and showed me the area they were in, and told me all the details." He said he also suggested to Feehan that he "call to Jim Kearney himself".

Jim Kearney wrote to the author on 1/10/1989:

Feehan has given me an order to furnish details to prove I was there. I am going to ignore him for the time being. You are the person who has all these details, so you can deal with that. I'll have a go later at Feehan. Don't you say he visited me for the time being, I will deal with that later.

Essie O'Driscoll also called to Liam O'Donoghue who told her he was confident that Jim Kearney was "one of the trained engineers who participated in the Béal na mBláth ambush". He "advised her to call to Jim Kearney", he said.

Jim Kearney told the author about Essie O'Driscoll's visit and said he explained about his and other volunteers' participation in the ambush. He said they had a cordial chat and she seemed to be satisfied with the details.

In a letter to the *Southern Star*, 7/4/90, the author wrote:

I refer to recent correspondence to your paper regarding Tom Kelleher's knowledge of the Béal na mBláth ambush. I wish to state that from my conversations with him the vital part of his story dealing with Michael Collins' death has been written in my book … Tom Kelleher and his comrades were fully aware of the information held by Republicans regarding the circumstances in which Michael Collins was killed.

I wish to state clearly that the details in my book of the part played by Jim Kearney and the other men were confirmed to me by Republicans who had participated in the ambush ... on 22 August 1922. I have those men's interviews on tape including that of Tom Kelleher who states "I'm telling you the truth" in reference to his information about Sonny O'Neill and the other men who took part in the ambush.

The men whom I interviewed said they were telling the truth because they wanted to set the historic record straight. They had been Volunteers of the Irish Republican Army, having fought for their beliefs and were adamant that the truth be properly conveyed.

For their own personal reasons some may have given different stories to other people. All I can record is the information which these men gave me, because they said they trusted me not to twist the truth.

Meda Ryan

On 21/6/1990 Jim Kearney wrote to the author:

If you put yourself in my shoes you would understand. The more I think of that day [Béal na mBláth ambush] I do believe that Liam Deasy did not want to ambush Collins. They were great friends, you know ... But then the enemy were entering Republican held territory . . . he was just a soldier on the road ...

On 28/6/90 Jim Kearney wrote to the author:

"... Put yourself where I am [then] you would

understand. The more I think of that day I see the fear, and wonder how the few of us just fought for our very lives.

On 24/1/1991 Jim Kearney wrote to the author:

... I will fight to the bitter end to put things right ... there is a lot of fighting to be done yet, and I am fit and healthy.

So God bless and best wishes.

Jim Kearney sent the author a signed PUBLIC STATEMENT dated 27/3/91. The contents of the statement are similar to the following letter by Kearney, published in the *Evening Echo* 25/1/1991, dealing with just a section in one chapter of Tim Pat Coogan's book *Michael Collins*:

As one of the three engineers with the column that day who had the responsibility of laying the mine, as the only survivor, I give the other two names here: John Callaghan and Timmy Sullivan.

The four of the men who participated in the ambush (in the direct line of fire) were John Callaghan, Timmy Sullivan, Sonny O'Neill and myself.

Our ambushes were organised under a strict disciplinary code. For example: We would not have allowed anybody who came on the ambush scene to leave the scene. We would have held 'intruders' in a 'safe' house in case they carried stories to the enemy. *[He then deals with other facts]*

We had experienced soldiers on that day, such as Jim Hurley, Pete Kearney, Sonny O'Neill, Bill Powell, Liam Deasy, G.O.C., First Southern Div., Comdt, Tom Hales, O.C,

3rd Brigd., Comdt. Tom Kelleher, O.C. 5th Batt. and many more …

I have given the facts of the Béal na mBláth ambush to another author (Meda Ryan): my comrades in arms have done likewise …

I am prepared to make a statement on oath, as I feel in duty bound to do so on behalf of my comrades, and to end the continuing speculation, and to establish for posterity the true history.

Jim Kearney [Signature]
Peace Commissioner

On 27/3/1991 Jim Kearney sent the author a signed letter:

<u>To Whom It Concerns</u>

I sent the enclosed statement to the National Newspapers on 22/1/91. As only a few of the newspapers published the full statement, and because I believe it is important that students should have the correct version of history I have decided to send a copy of the statement to [many of] the Universities and Keepers of Manuscripts.

… I am the sole survivor of the Béal na mBláth ambush and am adamant that truth should be foremost when it comes to history.

Sincerely,
Jim Kearney [signature]
Jim Kearney. P.C.

On the 11/4/1991 Jim Kearney in a letter to the author wrote:

Remember there was no ambush [as had been set-up]. **It was only the few of us who had to fight for our lives. This is something that some people seemed not to know.**

On the 3/5/1991 Jim Kearney wrote to the author:

I'm still prepared to make a statement on oath what more can I do. This is not a 'white elephant' statement. I'm going to get that organised.

Jim Kearney P.C.

In a further note he wrote to the author:

I must reply to John M. Feehan. I will send it to Archives.

God bless, if they had me out of the way God only knows what they would write & say.

Next day 3/5/1991, he wrote another note to the author:

Feehan's book did not appear yet as far as I know. I believe (from the papers) that he is only writing an addition to his last book. He is taking Sonny O'Neill out of Bealnablath altogether that is the plan. It's too late now to try that.

The oath would be worth a lot...

On the 27/6/1991 Jim Kearney wrote to the author:

I have done a public statement, a response for Feehan to substantiate my claim that I was at Béalnablath. I have sent it to The National Archives, National Library and Trinity College, Dublin.

Tom Foley was not a member of the IRA, he was not a runner or message boy for the ambush party during the ambush wait. We would not send a young lad for messages or allowed him to be at the ambush site. No person man or boy brought us tea, during our wait. ... He with others were engaged in doing some messages at the preparation stage and afterwards.

It was Liam Deasy who came along the road and gave us the order to roll up the cable leading to the mine ...

On 25/5/1991 Jim Kearney wrote to the author saying that he "had prepared a letter for the *Southern Star*, on Sunday, I didn't know John Feehan was dead."

[This was in response to the author's note to him, re his letter prepared on Sunday, for the Southern Star. *Our letters seem to have crossed in the post.]*

He replied to the author.

Anyway he has done the harm to you and to me as well. I thought someone would have told you immediately. You seem to be afraid of them, if so I'm not. I think you are wondering was I there [ambush] at all. I'll still fight on my own for the sake of history.

Best Wishes,
Jim Kearney

In a letter to the *Southern Star* 29/6/1991, Jim Kearney wrote:

It had been brought to my notice that the late John M. Feehan had added a few extra pages to his 'old' book of Michael Collins before his recent death. In these pages my name has been mentioned several times – I am challenged in the interest of historical accuracy to substantiate my claim that I participated in the Béal na mBláth ambush. I have already done this in a public statement. The statement is available in the National Archives, Four Courts, Dublin, Reference No. 899/592, also the Historical Collection of Trinity College Library and the National Library Manuscripts.

In that public statement I said I was prepared to give a statement on Oath because I was a participant in the Béal na mBláth ambush and an eye-witness to the events.

I stand by that statement.

I want the public to know that I have received threatening letters warning me to keep my mouth shut, but I won't be intimidated. I feel that the public today, and future generations, deserve to hear the truth.

I want to state also that we had no young lad of sixteen years at Béal na mBláth ambush that day, as is stated in John M. Feehan's book. As Tom Foley was not a member of the Irish Republican Army, he could not be privy to "the exact location of all the participants, neither could he know who these men were – this sixteen-year-old boy could not be running around attending to soldiers in ambush positions, as is stated in Mr. Feehan's extra pages.

There were men at Béal na mBláth that day from many areas of the First Southern Division, some I had never met before, so to state this sixteen-year-old boy knew all does not make sense.

It should be noted that on the morning of 22nd August,

1922, Timmy Sullivan was with me in Foleys' house when Liam Deasy sent for us, prior to laying the ambush – this has been recalled by Charlie Foley. Also, late that night his brother Sonny secured a billet for both of us in Dave Long's at Béal na mBláth.

Jim Kearney, P.C.

In a letter in relation to above, Jim Kearney wrote to the author:

I got a surprise when the girl who opened the door said 'Well, look who's here, Jim Kearney'. She was Nellie Long, a cousin of the family, who was on a holiday with her cousins and knew me since school days.

In an interview, Nellie Long confirmed to the author that this is correct, that these men had participated in the ambush.

In a letter to the author 26/9/1991, Jim Kearney wrote in connection to a query re the chapter on the ambush in Liam Deasy's book *Brother Against Brother* which was not published until 1982. Liam Deasy had died in 1974.

There was only one Brigade Officer and that was Comdt., Tom Hales, not four as given in his book. ... The other item is that he knew about Sonny Neill's direct shot that got the soldier on the road, as I was there when Sonny told Liam, so was Timmy Sullivan. In a *[further]* conversation, Liam told us to get a cup of tea and to take away the motorbike that was left on the road, ... as I told

you before Liam Deasy was a very popular man with most people and a great leader. So too was Tom Barry.

Did you ever see that Document – Tom Barry's reply to Deasy – it was very cutting?

[This was in connection with Liam Deasy's book, *Towards Ireland Free* and Tom Barry's Document/Booklet "*The Reality of the Anglo-Irish War, 1920-21 in West Cork: Refutation, Corrections and Comment on Liam Deasy's* Towards Ireland Free".]

Several of the men were unhappy with that letter which Feehan published. It is at the beginning of Deasy's book. [*Brother Against Brother*] **As far as I know it was on the newspapers around the same time, sent I was told by Feehan. I believe it was a priest who was involved in it ... Do you know his name? It caused a split between Barry and Deasy, which was a pity, as they were great, really great friends.**

In a Biographical Note to that book, it states that Barry, "wrote a rather hysterical pamphlet which was immediately rejected by a group of surviving ... members of the Third West Cork Brigade" who wished "to disassociate" themselves "from the contents of [Tom Barry's] booklet." There are 14 signatories.

From interviews with many of the signatories the author is aware that they signed a letter presented to them by Fr. John Chisholm, who had previously written much of Liam Deasy's book *Towards Ireland Free*. The men who signed the letter published in Deasy's, *Brother Against Brothe*, got the impression that they were signing about Liam Deasy's competence. In an interview with Fr. Chisholm 5/9/1983, he admitted that he was involved in drafting its contents. "They signed," he said. See *Tom Barry: (IRA Freedom Fighter*, by Meda Ryan.)

The following are some snippets of various dates, from letters sent by Jim Kearney to the author:

On 21/6/90, he wrote:

I am very upset. I don't know what I can do to stop this rotten lie. *[denying his participation in the ambush.]*

On 9/3/91, he wrote:

I've told you all this many times before. Are you giving me a test? My memory is great ... God Bless and keep going ...

On 13/7/91, he wrote:

My head is still very active and my memory great ...

On 29/8/91, he wrote:

I'm fighting a lone battle all on my own ...

On 26/9/91, he wrote:

I'm flying it T.G. full of fight.

On 1/10/92, he wrote:

How often in letters to the Press have I stated that I was prepared to swear and that my statements were true ...

On 2/10/92, he wrote:

As regards this oath I will have to give it a lot of consideration to do it right *[correctly]* ...

On 23/4/93 he wrote:

I am fit for any fight T.G. ... so keep writing and fighting.

In that letter he wrote: **If the military men come again I will ask them about records of Collins' death. They seem to**

know the man who fired the fatal shot, and of course I also told them who it was. They invited me to visit the Museum in Cork. I don't know if they expect me to call first, I'm not clear on this.

[Members of the Dept. of Defence visited him.]
On 19/7/1993, he wrote:

Thanks for your letters they cheer me up. God bless.
On 28/9/1993, he wrote:

I am getting stronger every day T.G.

It has to be noted that during my research I interviewed many Béal na mBláth participants. I brought many of them back to the ambush site (on different occasions), sometimes with just myself and the person present, and at other times with Jim Kearney, and we went over details of the ambush. There was never a question mark over Jim Kearney's name. I heard him speak vividly about his fear and "dread" when armoured-car bullets were "clipping the grass bank" in front of them. "We were in fear of our lives," he wrote in a letter to author. Tom Kelleher told of his experience and his fear as he believed soldiers were trying to advance up the laneway towards them. Liam Deasy talked about his experience and his fear for the men on the site – he wasn't sure how many. I still recall Liam's recollection of how he spoke to Jim Kearney and how he told him to "roll up the cable", believing they wouldn't return that night; also recollecting their conversation following the ambush and Deasy's vivid recollection of telling Kearney about a motorbike down on the road which should be removed. They discussed what happened to it later. (The Republicans "had it around".) They discussed the cap. Tom Kelleher also heard that story from Jim Kearney, on the site, as did Pat Buttimer – all three together in my presence. (Tom Kelleher and Pat Buttimer were great friends all their lives.)

I wish to record that one day Tom Kelleher rang me and asked if I would join Pat Buttimer and himself for lunch when passing through Cork City. He said they generally had lunch in a restaurant and asked me to give him a ring. I joined them both one day; this led to many lunches over time. We chatted about many things, but especially events of history, and of course that day at Béal na mBláth. All the men had a vivid memory of the events of that evening at Béal na mBláth. It appeared to have left an indelible mark on their brains. Like any traumatic event this is understandable.

Of course, the "fatal" bullet and Sonny O'Neill's participation in the ambush were all part of the discussions.

These are among my many notes and recordings. The reason they kept quiet over the years was, they feared for themselves – sometimes due to Civil War animosities "around". They were always glad when "the blame", as they called it, was placed on "the other side", or the "ricochet" cause for Michael Collins' death was made public.

Jim Kearney was reluctant to mention in public that he was a participant in the actual ambush. He even didn't want to talk about Sonny O'Neill's involvement to me initially. Having spoken to other participants of the ambush following my preliminary contact with Neilus Flynn, he agreed, as did other participants that the time was right to tell the story "to somebody" whom they "trusted", they said.

They spoke with affection for Collins, especially Liam Deasy, who knew him well and worked with him. I saw tears in some of the men's eyes as Collins was discussed. (At times, I had to close my eyes and picture them as young men, and could understand.)

These men had a clear recollection of that day's events.

In my interviews, there are statements such as: "I want to make it quite clear. I was there." – Liam Deasy.

Liam Deasy, G.O.C., 1st Southern Division was adamant that there should be clarity that "the true story should be told". He wanted to dispel the rumours.

"I was there, and I'm telling you the truth," – Tom Kelleher. He spoke to Sonny Neill afterwards, he said. I asked Kelleher why he had made contradictory statements to journalists on a few occasions; he replied he just wanted to "confuse" the issue to take away any "blame" that might be attributed to the men who fought there. They were often in fear of their own lives, hence the word "blame" was used. He knew Jim Kearney well, and mentioned him on many occasions (in recordings and notes). It was he who took me to Tom Kelleher's house initially, as he [Kearney] knew where he lived, and both are on a recorded interview on that first day together.

"I've told you this many times before." – Jim Kearney.

Others are similar on their clear-thinking and telling.

I could see from Jim Kearney's letters that he was

frustrated that he would not be believed. Furthermore, during our many chats, it was clear he was frustrated that his attendance and participation in the ambush was so patently disbelieved. Though he never showed his annoyance in my presence nor, I understand, in his family's, it was clear that internally he was upset and exasperated at times. Certainly, he was incensed that the initial letters of denial to newspapers had begun to become established. This was shown towards his family on few occasions. History and facts were important to him; he read widely on the subject.

On one occasion when architect Curly Cahalane came to the ambush site and we were looking at positions, Jim Kearney, Bill Powell, Tom Kelleher, Pat Buttimer and other participants were there that day.

Jim Kearney told the author he often met Tom Hales "in town" (Bandon); they would go to a local pub for a drink and a chat. (Kearney did not drink alcohol – never in his life broke his "Pioneer Pledge". He told the author that on most occasions he just drank orange or lemonade or water.)

In a letter to the author, 6/2/1989, Jim Kearney wrote: "Tom and myself often spoke of this fight."

Meetings/chats have been confirmed by Eily Hales McCarthy (Tom Hales' daughter, and a close friend of mine since early childhood). In many of our regular phone conversations, mainly about history, she would say things such as "when my father met Jim Kearney in town". They would talk about his souvenir of Collins' cap badge which was in his house, also the burial of the cap as well as other events of the Béal na

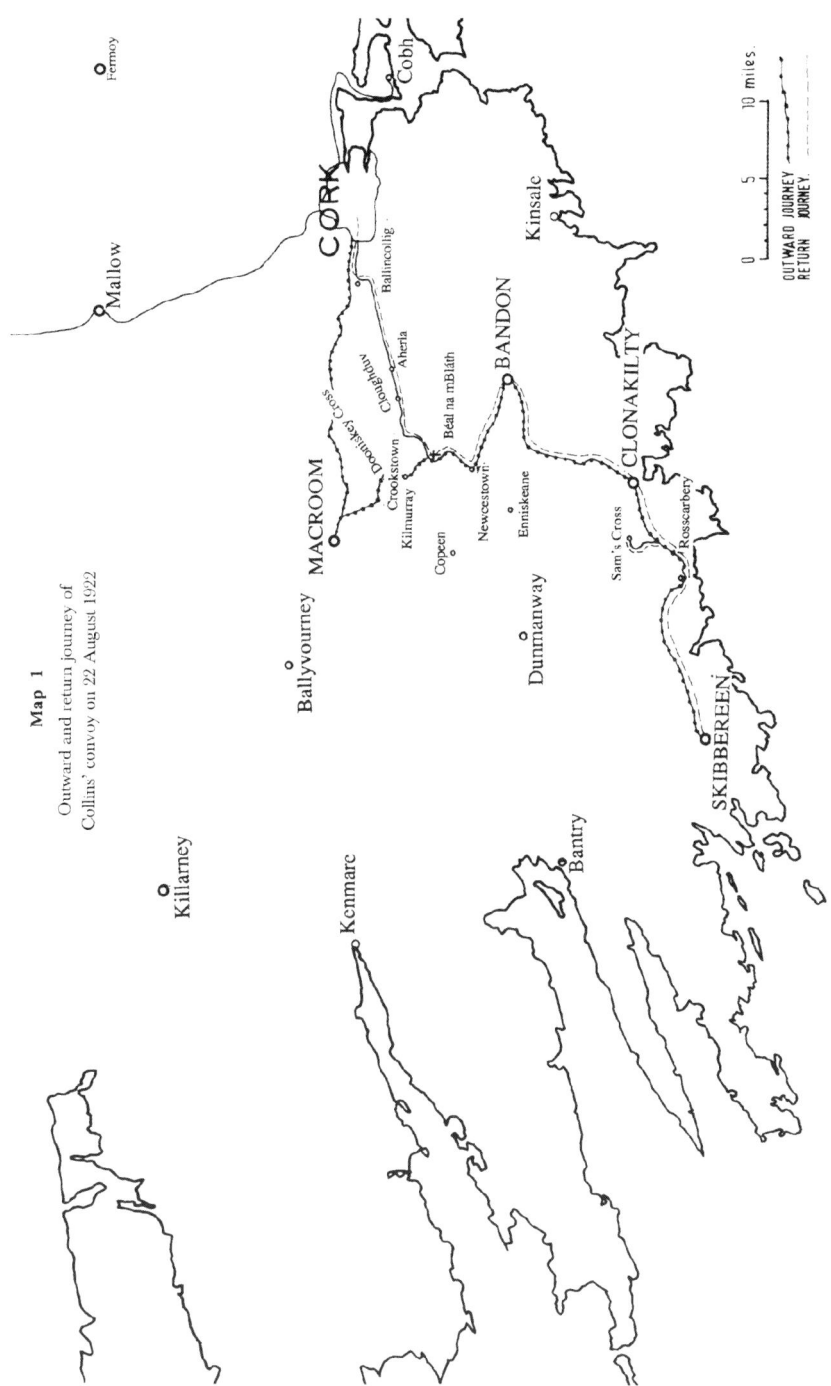

Map 1
Outward and return journey of Collins' convoy on 22 August 1922

Maps © Curly Cahalane

Map 2.
The ambush at Beal na mBlath
Approximate Positions.

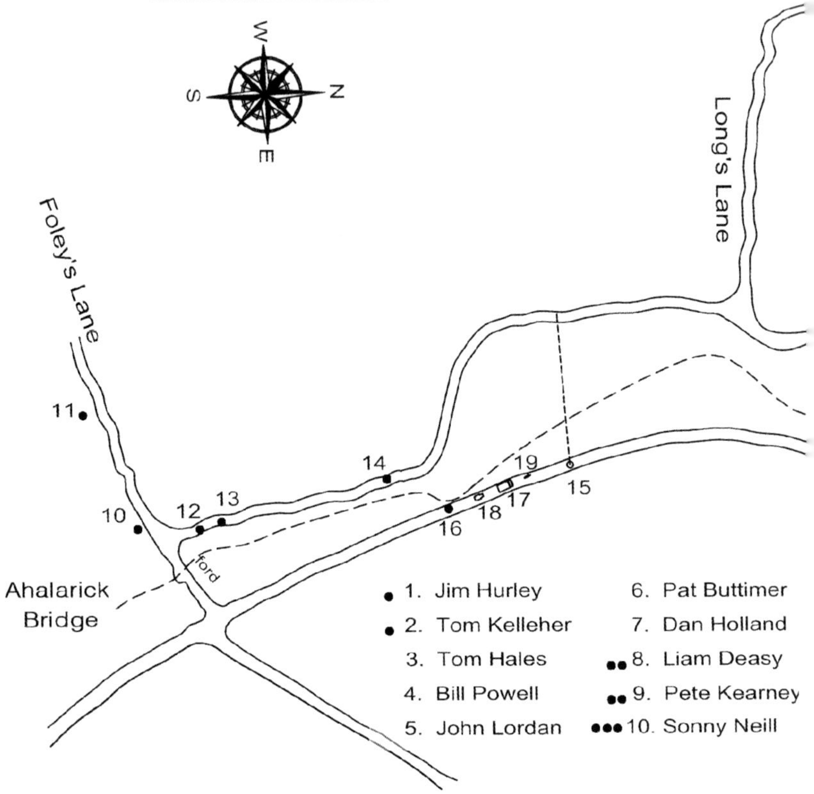

Foley's Lane

Long's Lane

Ahalarick Bridge

ford

- 1. Jim Hurley
- 2. Tom Kelleher
- 3. Tom Hales
- 4. Bill Powell
- 5. John Lordan
- 6. Pat Buttimer
- 7. Dan Holland
- •• 8. Liam Deasy
- •• 9. Pete Kearney
- ••• 10. Sonny Neill

Maps © Curly Cahalane

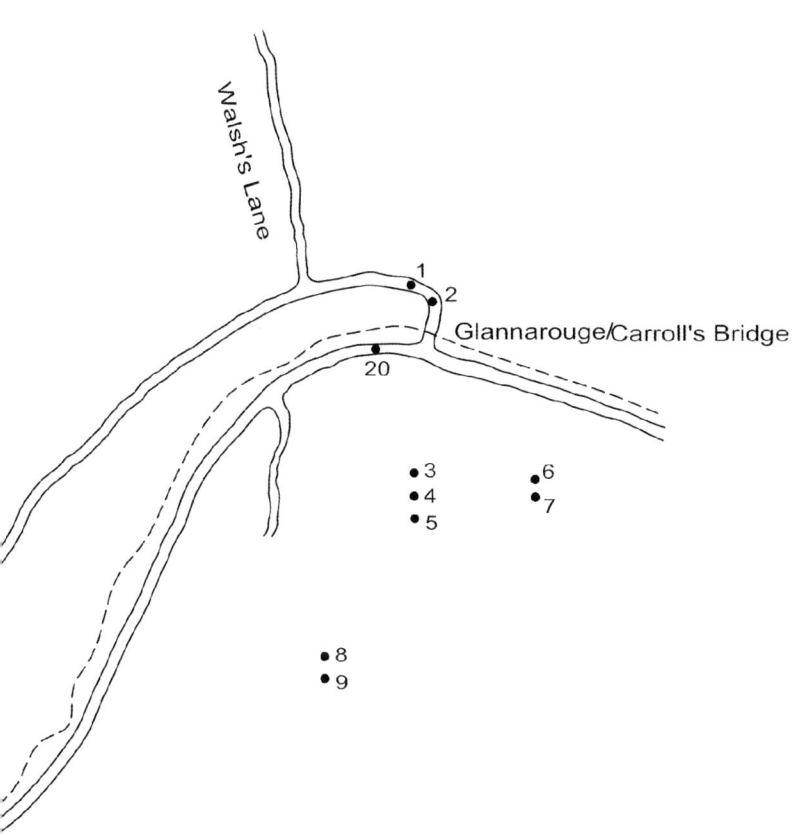

11. Denny Brien
12. Jim Kearney
13. Timmy Sullivan
14. John Callaghan
15. Disconnected Mine
16. Collins's final position
17. Crossley Tender
18. Touring car
19. Motorbike - against low ditch
20. Barricade

• (warning shots)
•• (attempt to draw fire of convoy)
••• (behind post / pillar)

Note: ford is turn (bend) on Ahalarick bridge where 12, 13, were located
Armoured car: south of stationary vehicles, position varied during the ambush
-- Approx. position of little river Noneen

Maps © Curly Cahalane

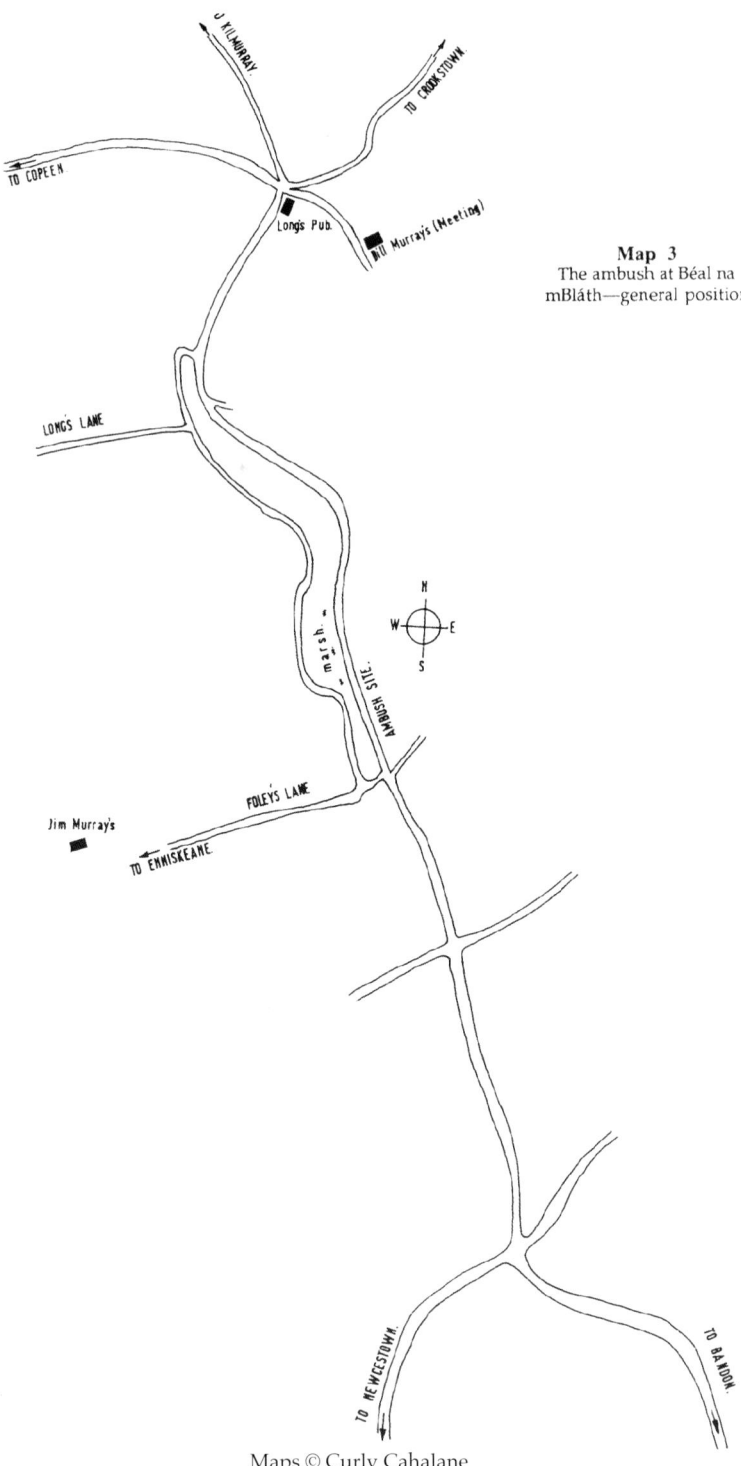

Map 3
The ambush at Béal na mBláth—general position

Maps © Curly Cahalane

mBláth ambush. They discussed many events of the past including Tom's awful experience with Major Percival, following his arrest during the War of Independence, and his suffering when his nails were pulled off. "Jim Kearney and Dad were great friends," Eily wrote in a card she sent. Both men were in Tintown detention camp during the Civil War, after arrest. In his letter to the author, 6/2/1989, Jim Kearney wrote; "Tom Hales and indeed his brothers were great men, and great fighters too." Eily said, "it may sound strange" but her dad attended many of the annual Michael Collins commemorations.

Jim Kearney and Bill Powell were neighbours and certainly, according to Powell's son Dómhall Mac Giolla Phóil, they 'often and often' chatted about the events of Béal na mBláth. He heard them talk about Sonny Neill (O'Neill) and what "an excellent character he was, and his great courage as a soldier, and as a person". Dómhall knew from an early age about the ambush, and his father's participation in that ambush as well as his other struggles in the fight for "Irish freedom". Dómhall travelled with both of us (the author and Bill Powell) on a few occasions to the ambush site. Jim Kearney was with us on a few occasions.

One comical incident occurred when Jim Kearney with the author called on Bill Powell. His family were out and he was on his own. Rather than make a cup of tea he said he was giving us sherry. When he produced two little sherry glasses and the bottle from the cabinet, Jim Kearney said he didn't drink. Powell said, "Ah Jim, a glass won't do you any harm." Though Kearney explained about his Pioneer Pledge, Powell began to pour two gasses. The conversation between the two was amusing. We began to laugh. When Bill left the room Jim looked around and spotted a geranium pot on the windowsill and poured his glass into it. Bill returned and noticed Jim's empty glass, and proceeded to fill it despite Jim's protests. Bill had plugged in a kettle and again left the room. Jim said to me, "Drink up yours and I'll throw some into it." I was only sipping. He, again, watered the geranium plant with half a glass, and nursed the rest while there.

Following some laughter, we eventually got down to the serious business of the ambush.

Though sincere and serious when discussing facts, Jim Kearney also had a great sense of humour. During many of our chats he recalled anecdotes of incidents that occurred while 'out with the boys'.

In a letter to the author, dated 1/10/1992, Jim Kearny wrote:

How often in letters to the Press have I stated that I was prepared to swear that the statements were true and nobody challenged me to do so, because they knew I would, they also knew I was telling the truth.

Next day, 2/10/1992, Jim Kearney sent the author a copy of his Affidavit that he had prepared.

I James Kearney swear by Almighty God that I took part in the Béal na mBláth ambush on 22 August 1922 and I am the man who found the cap Michael Collins wore when he was shot, and I am the person who buried the cap which was later dug up and now rests in the Museum in Dublin.

I also wish to state that the statement I made to Meda Ryan as to who fired the fatal shot is true and correct.

Signed: James Kearney, P.C. [*Signature*]

In a letter to the author 13/7/1993 Jim Kearney wrote:

Keep at it and don't let anything stop you. My head is still very active and my memory great ...

Jim Kearney kept writing to the author about history and people who called to see him and also incidents up to 29/7/1995.

On 3/10/1995, he wrote, "**Call soon, we have so much to talk about.**" He was still as lucid as ever; he had a wonderful memory, and his story about his participation in the Béal na mBláth ambush never changed. He wrote about his arrest and some details of his release.

To set the record straight, I believe that this chapter is necessary for the sake of Jim Kearney's memory and for his relatives, neighbours and friends. Recently the family told me that "he has been written out of history". Jim's daughter-in-law, Angela, and his son J.J. were most helpful, and generous to me on so many occasions whenever I called to their home to speak with Jim. His grandchildren deserve to have his memory respected.

A brief account of Jim Kearney

Jim Kearney was a member of Kilpatrick Company, and was in 1st Batt. of the 3rd West Cork Brigade. Under Comdt. Seán Hales, he fought in the Brinny ambush and other ambushes with the Bandon Battalion. He was a participant in the Upton train ambush and afterwards Kearney, Tom Kelleher and Flor Begley shouldered across fields the injured Charlie Hurley and Dan O'Mahony. Though it was a difficult task they managed to bring them to safety. Kearney became a member of Tom Barry's Flying Column. As a volunteer he attended Barry's lectures on their future – they would often be hungry, they must be prepared to sleep rough and be ready for action at any time. The Ballymurphy training camp was held in a field near Upton in October 1920. Kearney recalled Barry's "sharpness and courage, his hair blowing in the wind". He fought with Barry in ambushes and took a leading part in a successful "shoot-up" in Bandon one evening.

In the interregnum between the War of Independence and the Civil War, he with Timmy Sullivan, John Callaghan, John Kelly and others took an intensive engineering course. At the outbreak of the Civil War he took the Republican side. With his comrade Timmy Sullivan, he participated in many ambushes. "To become an engineer required special training over quite a period. It was a long difficult training," he wrote. They had to be familiar with mines, explosives, cables etc. Curly Cahalane, who has drawn maps for this book, recalled: "Con Callaghan taught my father, Dan Cahalane [Republican supporter,

Dunmanway] how to lay a mine and cables and so on."

During the Civil War, the major engagement that Kearney was involved in (apart from the Béal na mBláth ambush) with his comrade Timmy Sullivan, was the "taking" of the twin villages of Ballineen and Enniskeane under the Command of Tom Barry (who had escaped from prison). It was over a four-hour-long battle when eventually they captured 18 prisoners. These were taken to a local school. "Fr. O'Connell was a major help," according to the report. These villages remained under Republican control for the duration of the war.

Kearney was also involved in helping Jock (John) McPeak who wished to get back to his Scotland home place. Part of his agreement with the Republicans was to steal the *Sliabh na mBan* armoured car. Jim Kearney was friendly with Billy Barry, who eventually helped Jock McPeak escape. On one occasion Kearney with Pat Dempsey stood at Coolmountain Cross while Tom Kelleher was at Tinker's Cross awaiting the car. Jim Grey, driver, was to flash the lights three times to announce their approach; however, that initial plan fell through. (See Chapter 16)

Jim Kearney was arrested on 2, January 1923. He wrote: "Things were quiet, the 1st was a Bank holiday." He was with Timmy Sullivan. They called to a pub, met a few pals and only stayed for a short while. "We decided we would spend the night in my house. Next morning, I got up around 9.30 and was having my breakfast in the kitchen when the door opened and in walked a few Free State soldiers. They looked at me and one ran out, saying to the others outside: 'Our man is here.' A number of them rushed in and I was taken out. They also had another prisoner outside. Next to come out was Timmy Sullivan. They allowed him have a cup of tea, while others were tearing the house apart. They took my bike and my sister's watch, and marched us off to Innishannon. We were taken from there to Kinsale that night and held for a week in the old workhouse or hospital. Our bed was straw, more furze than straw."

They were then taken to Moore's Hotel, Cork, and tried. They were sentenced to death by shooting, then taken to the Female Gaol, No. 6 Wing. He wrote: "Tom Kelleher and lots more were there, to be shot. We ended up in Newbridge Military Barracks, Co. Kildare. We never knew the hour when we would be shot. It depended a lot on what might be happening outside in any part of the country. We were hearing every day of executions in different parts of the country. One day a man named Healy from Cork, I knew him well. He was in Newbridge. He taken out and shot, he was one of the many."

Liam Deasy was captured and tried by military court and sentenced to death. Then General Mulcahy took Seán Buckley and Liam Deasy to Dublin to sign a letter of unconditional surrender. Seán Buckley, who was in Newbridge, didn't sign it as he had no power to do so. These letters were sent to all members of the IRA Executive which were delivered by Fr. Duggan, Cork. They all replied 'NO' including Liam Lynch. I must say Liam Deasy was fully prepared to face the firing squad. But seeing the futility of the Civil War he did sign a surrender form for the IRA, though he was facing death bravely."

For Kearney and Sullivan "came the sad news of Liam Lynch's death, our Chief of Staff. He was shot on the Knockmealdown mountains on 10 April 1923".

When a hunger strike was organised, Jim Kearney and Timmy Sullivan joined and were among the decreasing number still in prison.

"The first few days of hunger were very difficult, but we persisted. A great way of helping us was, during the break we'd talk about a meal, such as bacon, cabbage, and potatoes, or roast beef. We could almost taste it, as all would add their own views."

"We had fasted 40 days when finally the strike was called off in October. Shortly after this Timmy Sullivan was released."

Kearney and few more prisoners were moved to Tintown Prison camp, also in Kildare. "There were only around twenty of us left in the finish. Cosgrave, in a reply to a question, said: 'The prisoners we are holding are the most extreme of the extremest.' I was finally released at the end of February 1924."

Jim Kearney continued to write to the author up almost to the end of his life.

On 29/7/1995 he wrote: **"Write soon. Keep fit."**

On 6/9/1995, he wrote: **"I hope to see you soon we have so much to talk about."** Another similar letter 28/9/1995 asked me to call. A few weeks earlier he had written that he would like to record some details of the Hales, Knocknacurra, family history. (Tom, Sean, Bob, Bill, Dónal, Madge) **"Bring your talking machine with you,"** he wrote.

Jim Kearney was a Peace Commissioner. He was married to Mary Frances Connor (O'Connor). They had six sons and two daughters. His wife died suddenly when the children were quite young. Relatives and neighbours were a great help, he said. His two daughters died quite young, and one son predeceased him.

In his obituary it is stated that he "gave of himself throughout his life to make the dream of Ireland a reality". In the War of Independence, "he fought for the freedom of his country with his comrades in the 1st Batt. 3rd West Cork Brigade".

Jim Kearney was one of the founder members of the Fianna Fáil Party in Bandon, and guided many of the leaders and encouraged others to join. He helped to build up the organisation in the Bandon area. During the Emergency he joined the Irish Defence Forces, reaching the rank of Corporal. He later became a member of the "Old IRA".

A keen athlete and sportsman, he not only participated at track and field events but also helped to establish new athletic clubs. For a period, he was Chairman of the Cork County Board N.A.C.A.I.

He was a prolific poet and writer had pieces published in many newspapers and journals. He was intelligent, and so accurate with details, and dated all his letters when writing to the author. He had a wonderful memory right up until the end of his life, according to his family. Towards the latter part of his life, he lived with his son J.J., daughter-in-law Angela, and grandchildren.

He died on 23rd December, 1995. During his long life he touched many and participated in, and witnessed, so much history. On 24 December, Christmas Eve, he was laid to rest. Full military honours were rendered.

Regarding Sonny (Denis O'Neill) Neill

In a letter to the Irish Times 4/1/1990, in response to a reviewer of my book asking why I did not interview Sonny O' Neill, I wrote:

Sonny (Denis) O'Neill died in Nenagh on 5 June 1950 … I interviewed Sonny O'Neill's comrades in arms who were assembled at Béal na mBláth on August 22, 1922. These men had memory of that important day – the day of the death of their former friend Michael Collins who became their opponent in a Civil War. These men gave me every co-operation because of their desire to set the historical record straight.

Despite what the reviewer says, I found that Liam Deasy's views concurred with those of his comrades. It should also be noted that Jim Kearney, who was one of the four men who were unexpectedly forced to take on Collins' convoy (the ambush having been called off), is the sole survivor. Though he is 87 years, I find him as lucid and accurate on details now as he was when I first interviewed him 1973.

> Most historians agree that eye-witness contributions which are properly assessed are a valuable asset to history.
> Meda Ryan

Sonny O'Neill's sister, Mary O'Neill Walsh, confirmed to the author (16/6/1974) that it was Sonny who fired the fatal shot that killed Collins. She said it was well known and that "he had no problem in telling it, later. He felt it was important for those who fought with him." She also confirmed this to the author in Jim Kearney's presence (25/6/1974). The two talked about the ambush. She listened to Jim Kearney saying, "We were fighting for our lives." Mary's other brothers were IRA volunteers John (Jackie) a Béal na mBláth participant, Daniel, Jeremiah and Michael (Mick) O'Neill who was fatally injured in Hornibrooks' loyalist home in Ballygorman on 26 April 1922, while on IRA duty.

Sonny Denis O'Neill (Sonny Neill), a native of Maraboro, Timoleague, was a resident of Nenagh in the 1920s. He fought in the British Army during the First World War, having previously served in the RIC for a number of years and resigned 1915, then attended the College of Science in Dublin. He fought in the War of Independence from 1919. He was intelligence officer for the IRA. He acquired information on Kilbrittain Castle RIC upon their occupation there, when he "became free with them" thus gaining intelligence on them which helped in an ambush afterwards, leading to the IRA obtaining a considerable number of rifles. He got a job in the British Army stores of Cork Barracks. Photographic material was kept there. At the time the IRA were looking for a Captain Kelly who worked in the Barracks. O'Neill obtained the photo; however, Republicans "did not get him". Previously O'Neill had spent a short period on Bere Island, constantly gaining intelligence for the IRA; meanwhile, he trained local IRA units "in Drill and Musketry", due to his previous experience as "Musketry Instructor" in the British Army.

Eugene Igoe, Head Constable, Commander of County Mayo's RIC, was drafted to Dublin to "organise efficient resistance to Collins". (See Tim Pat Coogan, *The Twelve Apostles*, pg.163-71). O'Neill was sent to Dublin Castle, and visited local RIC and British Forces haunts, gaining "valuable information" relative to "Igoe's Gang" and movement, including Igoe himself. Paddy Kennedy and Joe Dolan kept in constant touch with O'Neill, while he identified members of the "Murder Gang" who were spying on Michael Collins and the IRA.

Initially, Liam Deasy had recommended him to Collins due to his knowledge and experience of the British Army. According to his Military Service Pension application, he secretly met Michael Collins. He admitted he "nearly got plugged" a few times.

During the Civil War he was with the 1st Southern Div. after Cork City was taken by the National Army in early August 1922. He was first based in Mallow, then transferred to Buttivant and North Tipperary, where he engaged in rigging up a field kitchen in an isolated unit. He obtained rifles and grenades and formed a cavalry column in Ballincollig. He was O/C Training Cavalry due to his British

Army experience. On an occasion they "held a line" with cavalry in Bandon. In addition, he was "constantly on intelligence duty" giving valuable information to the IRA. Naturally he had to be extremely careful.

Later he was appointed to Staff 1st Southern Div., 3rd Cork Brigade. Approximately around mid-August he got a despatch to meet some members of headquarters staff in Newcestown, where a Brigade meeting was held on Sunday night 20th August.

For the 22 August he was called to an IRA Brigade headquarters Divisional Staff meeting at Murray's in Béal na mBláth. On arrival with his men, a decision had been taken that an ambush was being organised there, following the knowledge that Michael Collins and a convoy had passed through in the morning and was expected to return by the same route later in the day. Therefore, he became a participant in the ambush.

In March 1923 he was promoted to the rank of "Senior Officer" by Frank Aiken on Tom Barry's recommendation. He has stated that he was "on the run" up to 1926.

During the early 1920s he worked in Nenagh. Initially he resided at Rohan boarding house at 35 Michael Street where he met and later married Mary Anne Rohan. He then lived at the Nursing Home she co-owned with her sister, Mrs Brigid Thompkins. They successfully ran the Nursing Home at 5 Mitchel St. and later the Ormond Hotel.

He acted as director of elections for Fianna Fáil in most elections from 1926 onwards. He also represented North Tipperary in the National Executive of Fianna Fáil, and helped in building up the organisation in North Tipperary. For many years he was a member of Nenagh Urban District Council and the Board of Health.

Sonny O'Neill died 5 June 1950. It was well known in Nenagh as well as within IRA circles and locally that Sonny Neill said afterwards that he "dropped one man". That man (soldier) on the road was Michael Collins, whom he had known well and worked with him during his Intelligence work.

Living in Nenagh he frequented a successfully run pub known as the Widow Ryan's. The owner of that pub was Anastasia Ryan who originated from Ballyvaughan, Co. Clare, and was widowed at the age of 22. (She had four young children.) In an article in a Sunday newspaper it stated that it was "the best pub in Ireland for a pint". She told the author that Sonny "had no problem in talking about the ambush and his participation in it". Anastasia's daughter Loretto Hannon said that her mother "was a great fan of Michael Collins" and praised him for his achievement during the War of Independence.

In February 2007, The Ormond Historical Society asked me to give a talk on my book in Nenagh. That night the large room was packed.

Following my talk, discussion was opened "to the floor". During a lively discussion, many people recalled their personal stories about Sonny Neill, who would willingly talk about his involvement in the Béal na mBláth ambush. I don't recall any negative comment relating to his admission that he shot Michael Collins. Each person who spoke just told of their own experience of knowing this "kind" man who was willing to answer their questions. Apparently, he wished it had been otherwise, but "facts were facts", said one person.

The *Nenagh Guardian*, prior to this event, wrote on the "Nenagh Connection".

Florence O'Donoghue was adjutant of the IRA's Cork No. 1 Brigade during the War of Independence and remained neutral throughout the Civil War. He organised a Statement which he took from six members of the Southern Division who participated in the Béal na Bláth ambush. However, this statement was embargoed until 1990.

He recorded:

"**On the evening of Tuesday 15th February 1964 seven of us sat down at the Metropole Hotel, Cork, to try to record the circumstances in which Michael Collins was killed so far as they are known to the surviving members of the Republican forces who participated in the engagement.**

There was present Liam Deasy, O.C. First Southern Division; Tom Kelleher, O.C. Fifth Battalion Cork No. 3; Jim Hurly, Brigade Commandant Cork No. 3; Dan Holland, O.C. 1st Battalion Cork No. 3; Pete Kearney, O.C. 3rd Battalion; Tom Crofts, Adjutant 1st Southern Division and myself (Florence O'Donoghue). All except myself were at Béal na mBláth at the time and I was asked to be present to record what could be established as the truth and because I had been given an undertaking by Capt. Sean Feehan of the Mercier press that

he would not publish Eoin Neeson's book on the Civil War until we were satisfied that the part of it dealing with the death of Collins was in accordance with the facts."

" ... Statements which have been made to the effect that the Division and Cork No. 3 Brigade were aware of Collins' intention to visit posts in Cork and that a general order was issued to kill him are without foundation and completely untrue. His presence in the South was known to the officers of the Division and of the 1st and 3rd Brigade only on the morning of the 22nd and no general order had been issued by either of the command. The ambush was decided as part of the general policy of attacking Free State convoys."

" ... The action lasted between 20 and 30 minutes and, before it ended, darkness had fallen to the extent that it was possible to see the flashes from the gunfire. Conditions were such that it was not possible to get off an aimed shot.

Firing stopped at almost 8 o'clock. The Cork No. 3 Section remained in position and the Free State convoy withdrew under fire. No one in the Republican Party knew that Collins had been killed or that the convoy had suffered any casualty. It was only when Seán Galvin came to Béal na mBláth about one that they got the first report of his death."

It was signed by: **Liam Deasy, Tom Kelleher, Tom Crofts, Pete Kearney, Jim Hurley, Dan Holland.**

Note: For complete Statement, see Appendix V

Though all of these men knew exactly what happened during and after the ambush, it is unknown why the full facts are not given. However, I am well aware that participants were fearful of recording their details during the 1950s and 60s and were reluctant to speak to me in the early 1970s about their involvement until they had consulted each other.

It is to a great extent because of their reticence that writers, historians and the public continued to speculate about the details of Collins' death. For example, in his 1991 book *The Shooting of Michael Collins* (With new chapter "Did Sonny O'Neill Shoot Michael Collins?") John M. Feehan wrote: "Collins was shot by a bullet from a Mauser type pistol which entered his forehead and tore out the whole of one side of his head. He was not shot by a ricochet or dum-dum bullet. A ricochet would make a small gash about" 1"- 2" long and the bullet would remain inside … In the last analysis there is no real evidence to show who fired the fatal shot – whether Free State or IRA, and such evidence will not become available unless his body is exhumed."

In a letter to the *Southern Star* 1997, the author wrote: "**I leave the final word to Tom Barry who spoke at the unveiling of the monument to Michael Collins at Sam's Cross in April 1966. 'Let us leave it that each of us, like I did myself,**

believed in the correctness of our choice. I concede that those who were on the opposite side believed that theirs was the right decision too.'"

As trained soldiers they all fought for what they believed in at all times, fought to win. This was war – a Civil War – many of those who fought in it were reluctant to talk about it immediately afterwards, and for quite some time. Though later, as already stated, they believed it was important for history and important for future generations.

Chapter 16

John McPeak and the *Sliabh na mBan (Slievenamon)*

(Some material from Ray Smith and Jim Nicoll's articles in Irish Independent, *18-21 May 1971; also documents and information from McPeak's Solicitor and McPeak's Reps.; plus many author interviews, especially with Billy Barry, May Twomey and Anna Mulqueen.*

After Michael Collins' funeral John (Jock) McPeak returned from Dublin to Cork and resumed escort duties as gunner in the armoured car, serving with General Emmet Dalton and General Tom Ennis.

Some days later he accompanied a number of soldiers and an intelligence officer on a farmyard raid in Dublin Hill outside Cork city where he witnessed the arrest of two anti-Treatyites who were pushed into a Crossley Tender. Standing in front of the tender, McPeak heard sudden bursts of gunfire, rushed to the rear to investigate and found both men bleeding. Seán Donoghue died instantly and his badly injured companion died later. McPeak openly expressed his feelings of revulsion at such a barbaric deed but he only got a rebuff. From that moment on, he was determined to get out of the National Army and out of Ireland at the first opportunity.

After a few weeks he was transferred from Victoria Barracks, Cork, to the Devonshire Arms Hotel army headquarters, Bandon, and went out on duty in West Cork as driver of the *Sliabh na mBan*.

During this period, the trim 5 ft. 6 ins young man befriended another Scotsman who worked in the mess room, and who was married to a local girl. One evening the three of them went to Gertie Leary's public house on the South Main Street, Bandon, where McPeak was introduced to Anna Mulqueen and May Twomey, members of Cumann na mBan. In conversation, he told them that initially when he was recruited in Scotland, he believed that both "the Free Staters and the Republicans were the same, and fighting for the same cause". (This was prior to the Civil War.)

Basically, McPeak supported the Republican cause, as both his parents had come from Ireland. During the early part of 1921 he was at a meeting with about twenty men in St. Joseph's Hall in Tollcross, Glasgow. The men had obtained arms and had them packed and ready for shipment to Ireland when the hall was raided. All the men, including McPeak, were arrested and sent to Barlinnie prison where they were roughly treated. They were released following the signing of the Treaty in December 1921.

When McPeak and his comrades were recruited under the authority of the Provisional Government, it was the men's belief that they were being brought to Ireland to join the IRA. McPeak was a welcome recruit, having been a machine-gunner in the British Army (he had served in the machine-gun corps with the Argyll and Sutherland Highlanders from 1916 to 1919, having been enlisted in 1915). "We were just told that they wanted soldiers in Ireland."

Shortly after his arrival in Ireland, the Civil War began. Then McPeak was commissioned as gunner in the *Sliabh na mBan* armoured car that escorted Michael Collins on his final journey.

After the incident in the Dublin Hill farmyard, McPeak, appalled by this and other atrocities that were being committed, was determined to get out if possible. He feared that some reaction of his while working within the force would put his own life in danger, so he decided he would desert and hope for the best.

Anna Mulqueen and May Twomey, the Cumann na mBan girls whom he met in Gertie Leary's public house, Bandon, got in touch with Tadhg Sullivan and Dan Holland. The Republicans subsequently contacted McPeak and agreed to help him desert, but to prove his loyalty he would also have to bring with him the *Sliabh na mBan* armoured car. In return they would enable him to return safely to Scotland. Without the armoured car he was of no benefit to the Republicans. Several meetings took place as the two young women liaised with McPeak.

(The *Sliabh na mBan* or *Slievenamon* in its earlier, anglicised form, was one of thirteen 920 pattern Armoured Rolls Royce cars which were acquired from the British by the Irish National Army after the Anglo-Irish Treaty of December 1921. It was at first stationed in Beggars Bush Barracks in Dublin. It was used in Dublin during the first week of the Civil War and was in action several weeks around O'Connell Street. Then it was posted to the Southern Command.)

Jim Grey (Cork) was selected by the Republicans to drive the armoured car and was sent to meet McPeak. Both men agreed that on the evening of 5 October 1922 Grey would be ready to drive the vehicle. That evening Tom Kelleher waited at Tinkers' Cross outside Bandon while Jim Kearney with Pat Dempsey waited at Coolmountain Cross for Jim Grey to flash the lights of the armoured car three times to announce their approach. However, they waited in vain; this plan fell through.

Billy Barry, a motor mechanic, was then selected for the job. He came from Cork and stayed at O'Mahony's of Laragh outside Bandon. It was decided that McPeak would inform the women when the armoured car was "out on a run" so that with McPeak's co-operation, the Free State party could be overpowered.

Nevertheless, McPeak hesitated because he feared for the lives of some of the companions he had got to know in the pro-Treaty Forces. He suggested an alternative plan.

On the evening of 2 December 1922, May Twomey cycled out from Bandon to Laragh, taking with her a Free State uniform that had been secured by McPeak. She told Billy Barry that the time was right. Barry changed into the uniform, took May Twomey's bicycle and cycled towards Bandon. "I was to meet McPeak and Anna Mulqueen walking out the Dunmanway road. When I saw the couple, I stopped and asked if I was on the right road for Bandon."

Immediately Barry recognised the Scottish accent. "Aren't you the gunner in the armoured car?" said Barry. "Yes," came the response, "McPeak is my name."

Barry then handed over the bicycle to Anna Mulqueen and the two men, both now in National Army uniform, walked into town. They went into the Devonshire Arms Hotel army headquarters, and upstairs to a room where Sergeant Thomas Cooney, the most recent driver of the armoured car, was playing cards with a few more men. (The crew assigned to the armoured car on this occasion was different from the crew that had been on it during the journey with Michael Collins from Dublin to West Cork in August)

Lieutenant Peter Gough had issued an order that while the men were in barracks an air-valve should be removed from the engine to immobilise the car, and that McPeak was to hold the lock of the gun.

McPeak entered the room, removed his greatcoat and proceeded to hang it up with the other coats. He quickly searched the pockets of the other coats for the air-valve while Billy Barry remained at the door. One of the men seated at the table shouted, "Mac, would you ever get me some cigarettes?" McPeak gladly agreed.

So McPeak and Barry left, went down town and had a pint. McPeak decided he would say the shops were closed, but that he had cigarettes in his greatcoat pocket.

Back upstairs, while getting out the cigarettes from his pocket, he transferred the parts for the vehicle to his own greatcoat pocket. He pulled the packet of cigarettes from his coat pocket and deposited them on the table.

"I think it's getting cold," he ventured, putting on his coat. He turned and calmly said to an uneasy Billy Barry: "I feel like a walk. Like to come?"

They went down the stairs and into the yard where there was a number of soldiers. A dance was in progress in the hall upstairs. Thinking quickly, McPeak spoke loudly so that he would be heard, "Let's go to the dance!"

As the two men were going up the stairs to the dance-hall an awkward moment occurred when they met a Free State officer, who knew Billy Barry, coming down.

"Oh, hallo!" he said.

"Hallo, sir!" said Barry, saluting him smartly.

Luck was on Barry's side, because on the previous day there had been a slight mutiny in Drimoleague barracks, which resulted in a number of men having been transferred from there to the Devonshire Arms headquarters, and "they were wandering around without guns". Consequently, Billy Barry did not appear out of place. The officer's suspicions were not aroused.

The two men continued as far as the dance-hall door. "This way," said McPeak. They mingled with the onlookers and wove through the room, down a back stairs and into the courtyard.

Smartly they walked to the armoured car and set to work. Billy Barry began to check the engine while McPeak was up on the body. When questioned by one of the men, McPeak said he was cleaning the gun.

Barry, having inserted the loose piece of equipment, closed

the bonnet and jumped into the driver's seat. "I was about to start the engine when I heard the gate closing. An officer came along and posted a sentry in charge of the car. I thought the game had been given away on me. I was a sitting duck!" said Barry.

Immediately McPeak spoke up. "We're going out on a raid, sir. There's a driver in the car. You'd better get the gate open for us."

As they were pulling out, an officer named John Sullivan realised what their intention was and jumped on the back. McPeak failed to persuade him to get off. So they drove with him up Convent Hill and out the Crookstown road. When Sullivan wouldn't get off for McPeak, he told him he'd shoot him. Then Sullivan jumped.

Once the two men passed certain points along the road, Republicans helped them. They were hidden behind ditches and began to fell trees (previously partially cut) so that any pursuers would be impeded, and would be compelled to turn back. McPeak and Barry drove towards Newcestown, picked up Charles Foley, and continued towards Crookstown to meet Tom Crofts. Later they were joined by Jamie Moynihan and Tim Farrell. A carpet of straw had to be used to urge the *Slieve na mBan* through some stubble fields. (It was only some months previously that the same car had to be helped along with pro-Treaty greatcoats, as Collins' body was being shouldered over rough fields.)

"We travelled through bogs and by-roads on to Kealkil to meet Ted O'Sullivan O/C 5th Brigade," said Barry. "The great weight of the armoured car caused it to sink several times. We had to get planks to dig her out when we travelled along Coolmountain bog-road. For two days we travelled without sleep, and drove at night without the headlights. I was young at the time, but still I felt worn."

The men were billeted in a house near Kealkil. Following a substantial meal, they went to bed. A few hours later they were awakened from a deep sleep and told they were to drive to Ballyvoumey and be prepared to attack it. "We couldn't wake McPeak," said Billy Barry, "so we left him. In any case we knew Mick Sullivan of Kilnamartyra would man the gun."

While McPeak was certainly tired he was only pretending to be in "a dead sleep". He was now a reluctant machine-gunner. He did not want to attack the men he had left behind just a few days previously.

Billy Barry, Jamie Moynihan, Foley and a few more men drove through Ballingeary to attack Ballyvourney. "We arrived at 8 o'clock in the morning and attacked the village, which had been held by Free State soldiers."

Mick Sullivan manned the gun of the *Sliabh na mBan*, while Billy Barry was in the driver's seat. Jerry Kennedy from over the Kerry boarder commanded a section of men from Kerry in support of the Cork men during this attack.

"It wasn't long," said Barry, "until the village was ours. We took 125 Staters as prisoners. Tom Kelleher had been captured by the Free State soldiers. We told them we'd shoot the lot of the prisoners we held if they didn't let Tom Kelleher free. It didn't take them long to change their minds." Because the Republicans had no accommodation for the prisoners, they stripped them of their guns, uniforms and boots "and sent them packing into Killarney, making them take their wounded with them. We got an amount of ammunition plus another armoured car – the Lancia car."

All the tyres of the *Sliabh na mBan* had been punctured, so it was half-driven and half-pushed back to a farmyard near Gougane Barra. They removed the turret and gun section, took it away and buried it elsewhere. They also removed some parts from the engine, pushed the car into a shed and covered it with furze.

Over the next few weeks the Republicans tried unsuccessfully to get tyres for the car. In the end it remained beneath the furze. Only a few weeks after the Ballyvourney attack the National Army soldiers went looking for the *Sliabh na mBan*. In December 1922, they found it while combing the area.

Eventually, the *Sliabh na mBan* was towed away to the Curragh minus gun and turret. Though the car has been preserved and is held in the Curragh Army Training Headquarters, the original gun which was used by Jock McPeak on the day Michael Collins was shot, has never been located. Contrary to the general opinion, it is a replacement gun and turret that is now mounted on the *Sliabh na mBan*. Pat (Paddy) Lynch in the Department of Defence kept it in good condition. In the Curragh, at time of interview, Pat Lynch told me the original gun and turret were missing. He took myself and Jim Kearney and on a trip in the *Sliabh na mBan* around the Curragh Military Barracks. He explained details of the car and also explained and showed various types of arms and ammunition to us. The car was used in the film *Shake Hands with the Devil* and the RTÉ series *Insurrection*.

Meanwhile, back in Kealkil, Jock McPeak rose to eat a hearty breakfast/lunch, and then wandered into the farmyard to discover that the *Sliabh na mBan* was indeed gone. He was informed that his companions of the night before had taken it on a raid.

That December evening McPeak was told he was going on a further journey. Exhausted, he arrived at "a safe house" in Kilgarvan, Co. Kerry. After a meal he went straight to bed. At daybreak he was abruptly awakened and told that Free State soldiers were raiding the area. He pulled on his trousers, grabbed his coat and boots and ran downstairs. Through the window he saw that the street was thronged with soldiers.

Calmly, the householder led McPeak out to a turf loft at the rear of the house, and showed him a concealed attic opening. When McPeak had ascended the ladder, the man removed it. McPeak had a tense moment when the soldiers flashed up the lights; he held his breath and remained until he got the "all clear".

Just as he sat down to breakfast again, he heard a sudden burst of gunfire. He bolted to the back door, ran across the yard and over the wall. He waded through a river and up a few fields at the back. He picked his way carefully towards cover and encountered some more Republicans who were also evading capture.

McPeak had only had two meals since he left the security of Bandon Barracks a few days previously. As the days progressed, he had to move further into the Kerry hills, and as he did so the danger of being captured lessened. Over the cold winter months of December 1922 and January 1923, in rain, hail and snow, he learned what it was like to live "on the run".

However, he had a break on Christmas night when he was taken to Ballingeary where Republicans had organised a party. "It was a lively night with singing, dancing, and plenty to eat and drink."

A few weeks later a comrade introduced him to five men who had also deserted from the National army, and who lived in a derelict cottage in the Kerry mountains. This companionable interlude was short-lived. Soon he had to move on and keep moving as the troops had begun to scour the hills.

As the months progressed and the spring days lengthened, he was taken in by Dan Kelleher; here he lived and worked for some weeks on the Kelleher farm, hidden in the Kerry hills. Now he relished the home-made brown bread, bacon and cabbage and all "the other satisfying country cooking" served to him by Mrs Kelleher after his day's work.

Once more word came that his life was in danger, so again he went on the run. As the pressure increased, he wondered and asked how he could get out of the country. By this time, he desperately wanted to get out.

By early June, arrangements were being made for his trip across the Irish Sea. He was escorted one morning to the home of John Sullivan and family, where he stayed for a few days. Dressed in a Republican-supplied new suit of clothes, he prepared for his journey to Scotland.

When the car came to collect him, there was a priest at the

wheel (or a man dressed as a priest, McPeak couldn't be sure) and two women, one in the back with McPeak and another in the passenger seat. The four set out for Cork city. Free State soldiers saluted the "priest" as they passed through many towns and villages. The large bouquet of flowers, held by McPeak's supposed partner in the back seat, shielded his face from view when they were stopped in Blarney.

On the night of 14 June 1923, McPeak stayed in Cork with IRA sympathisers. The following morning, he was escorted to a cattle boat which was sailing to Glasgow that evening. Some members of the crew collaborated. They gave him food on this rather tense journey, and smuggled him ashore just outside his native city.

Fearing arrest, Jock McPeak did not return to his home in Parkhead; instead, he lodged in cheap boarding houses. However, his freedom was short-lived. On 2 July, he was taken in for questioning by the Glasgow police. Shortly afterwards the Dublin Metropolitan Police arrived from Dublin and escorted him to Cork where he was jailed in the military barracks.

Because there were no extradition laws covering the new Free State, John Robertson, a local MP, asked in the House of Commons by what authority McPeak had been deported. The Solicitor-General for Scotland responded by saying that Irish warrants could be endorsed in Scotland under the procedure regulated by statutory provisions.

Back in Cork, McPeak was charged by the military authorities with having deserted from the army. He was remanded in custody for ten days. But McPeak had deserted from the Provisional Government forces and had taken the armoured car on 2 December, 1922. The Free State did not come into existence officially until 6 December, 1922. So McPeak had deserted from a division of the National Army, but was arrested and handed over to the Free State Army authorities. Furthermore, he was a Scottish national and had been arrested without a warrant. When his case came up for trial, the military authorities refused to let the prosecution witnesses testify. His offence of desertion was committed under the jurisdiction of a body which militarily no longer existed. He was discharged.

But as he walked down the steps of the Courthouse in Cork he was re-arrested by the civil authorities, and returned to Cork Gaol. This time he was charged with the stealing of the Rolls-Royce armoured car, taken from Government forces in Bandon on 2 December 1922. The car and its contents were valued at "£1,000 and upwards".

John McPeak's brother, Frank, came to Dublin to arrange legal aid, and got Mr Comyn, KC, a prominent lawyer in Dublin, to handle the case. Frank, who had served in the Royal Navv during the war, booked into a guesthouse for the night. During the night he was awakened by police, arrested, and conveyed to military barracks. He was charged with aiding in the acquisition and the exportation from Scotland of arms and ammunition "for the Irregulars to be used against the Free State". However, despite an affidavit by General O'Sullivan that Frank McPeak had conspired to acquire the armaments, he was released due to "insufficient evidence", and he returned to Scotland.

John McPeak believed that he faced execution. This belief was shared by the Republicans who had helped to get him to Scotland.

Back in West Cork a rescue attempt was being planned. They looked at several different angles. Five men were ready "to jump him from custody" during his court appearance and a full plan had been structured. However, because of the risk to their men, the Republican officers decided it would be suicidal, so the plan was abandoned.

John McPeak eventually went on trial before District Justice O'Sullivan. Captain T. Healy, State Solicitor for West Cork, prosecuted. The evidence disclosed that the parts removed from the armoured car to immobilise it had been secured by McPeak with an accomplice. These had been reinserted, and the car had been taken from the barracks' yard without permission.

McPeak was the only member missing from the Devonshire Arms headquarters when the loss of the car was reported by John Sullivan (who had returned after being pushed off the car on Convent Hill). A search party had been sent "to pursue the car", but six miles out the road had been blocked "by felled trees".

During McPeak's trial there was no mention of the shooting of Michael Collins. He pleaded guilty to taking the armoured car for his own protection; for this he received a sentence of six years imprisonment, and was sent to serve his time in Maryborough (Portlaoise) prison.

During his stay there, he participated in a hunger strike in sympathy with Republican prisoners. During one Sunday

Mass a pastoral letter was read condemning Republican prisoners for their activities. The men left the prison chapel during the reading of the letter, and as a punishment were confined to a diet of bread and water. A hunger strike followed. However, like many of the men, McPeak abandoned the hunger strike when he became weak. Eventually the protest was called off.

In July 1928, John McPeak was released from Maryborough having served five of his six years. Penniless, he returned home to Glasgow. Free but insecure, he decided to use a pseudonym to aid him while seeking employment. Various temporary jobs came his way; he worked as truck driver, crane driver, furniture remover, until finally, because of his unsettled state, he decided to move south to England.

A job with a construction company south of London brought him security. He worked driving a crane with this company during the building of the present Bank of England. He was accustomed to go out with his pals to a local dance hall. One night he met an English girl of Irish descent. In June 1932 they were married. Two children, a boy and a girl, were born to them.

He changed his name by deed poll and lived the rest of his life under the assumed name. He died in 1974 and his wife died a few years later.

Postscript

Whatever hope there had been of bringing a swift end to the Civil War died with Michael Collins' death. In Kilmainham Gaol, on the night of 23 August 1922, Tom Barry noticed a questioning silence when news spread of Collins' death. Shortly afterwards he looked down from the corridor above "on the extraordinary picture of about a thousand kneeling Republican prisoners spontaneously reciting the Rosary aloud for the repose of the soul of the dead Michael Collins, Commander-in-Chief of the Free State forces." He felt there was little logic in such an action but it was a wonderful tribute to the part played by a man who had worked tirelessly in the struggle to gain independence for Ireland. Even through all the bitterness of Civil War "those Republican prisoners remembered that the dead leader, latterly their enemy, was once the driving force and the inspiration in their struggle against the British forces of occupation."[1]

Richard Mulcahy now took over Collins' position as Commander-in-Chief of the National Army and also held his post as Minister of Defence. As the weeks progressed the Civil War conflict continued to divide the two groups who blamed each other for wrecking Ireland's future, while many people who had remained neutral on the Treaty issue tried to set up a platform for negotiations. In Cork, Emmet Dalton endeavoured, in association with Tom Ennis, to find a peace formula. But Liam Lynch, Executive Forces Chief of Staff, treated these moves with suspicion. Dalton, acting on instructions from Richard Mulcahy, was anxious "to make an effort towards ending the present needless strife on the basis of an unconditional surrender".[2]

Dalton wanted the Civil War to end, especially after Collins' death. "I was really sick of it all," he said, especially when he saw "the turn events were taking" with reprisal killings as the weeks progressed.[3]

The Republican deputies did not attend the new Dáil which met on 5 September with W.T. Cosgrave as President. However, de Valera was extremely anxious to bring both sides together and to pursue his aim through political means. In his efforts to find a basis for peace, he wondered if there was any method by which the Treaty decisions could be revised. But Mulcahy informed him that the Treaty was not negotiable.

Control of the anti-Treatyites was now almost totally outside de Valera's influence and he was compelled to do as Liam Lynch suggested. "The fight must go on until there is no question of forcing Ireland into the British Empire, by the enemy, foreign or domestic," Lynch wrote.[4]

By the end of September, Republican casualties had mounted to more than 300 killed or wounded and there were over 6,000 prisoners either in jails or internment camps. Provisional Government casualties up to the middle of September were 185 killed and 674 wounded. The Provisional

Government issued a proclamation on 7 October giving effect to a decision to set up military courts with powers to inflict the death penalty.[5]

On the 16th of the month the Republican Executive attended a meeting in Nugents' house, Ballybeacon, near Fermoy, Co. Cork. Liam Lynch, who presided, read a memorandum from de Valera which suggested that if a decision was taken at the meeting to continue the fight, then the possibility of setting up a Republican Government which would co-ordinate efforts and prevent a Free State Government from establishing itself, should be considered. It would also mean laying claims to any funds or resources of the Republic. He stated that the only public policy necessary was to maintain the Republic and the sovereign independence of the nation.

After lengthy discussions, the members of the Executive, realising that the problem was not solely a military one, expressed an almost unanimous feeling in favour of the establishment of a Republican Government.

The members of the Executive who were able to do so met secretly in Dublin on 25 October, constituted themselves the Republican Government and appointed de Valera as President with a twelve-member Council of State. A Proclamation was issued by the Army Executive on 28th October and it was arranged that documents from the Executive's Defence Department would be signed both by de Valera as President and Liam Lynch as Chief-of-Staff. While de Valera recognised the views of Lynch and the Executive, he made his position clear in a letter to Joe McGarrity: "If the Army thinks I am too moderate, well, let them try to get a better President and go ahead."[6]

After the Republican Army Executive meeting, Liam Lynch expressed his satisfaction and optimism in a letter to his brother Tom: "It was a splendid review of the actual situation all over Ireland ... We are absolutely confident that the Free State is beaten and that it is only a matter of time when they must give in ..."[7]

However, the Provisional Government were determined "to fight to the bitter end".[8] Since Michael Collins' death W. T. Cosgrave had taken over Chairmanship of the Provisional Government. (He was also President of the Dáil.)

On 24 November Erskine Childers, who had been taken prisoner, was executed by order of the Provisional Government. This led to Liam Lynch issuing an order on 30 November (which later fell into pro-Treaty hands and was used for propaganda purposes) stating that "all members of the Provisional Parliament who were present and voted for the Murder Bill will be shot at sight". In this "General Order" Lynch stated that: "As your Parliament and Army Headquarters well know, we on our side have at all times adhered to the recognised rules of warfare. In the early days of this war we took hundreds of your forces prisoners but accorded them all the rights of prisoners of war and, over and above, treated them as fellow countrymen and former comrades. But the prisoners you have taken have been treated barbarously, and when helpless you have tortured, wounded and murdered them ..."[9]

POSTSCRIPT

The Dáil passed the Irish Free State Constitution Bill, and after a year of turmoil the Provisional Government ceased to be and the Irish Free State was officially born on 6 December 1922.

On 7 December, Dáil Deputy Seán Hales was shot dead. (As he was absent, he had not voted on the special emergency powers. Controversy has surrounded this shooting.) Deputy Pádraig Ó Máille, who was travelling in a sidecar with him, received a slight bullet wound. Early next morning, 8 December, four Republicans who had been prisoners since the fall of the Four Courts at the end of June (Rory O'Connor, Liam Mellows, Joe McKelvey and Dick Barrett., one from each of four provinces) were taken from their cells in Mountjoy and executed.

Their execution order was signed by Richard Mulcahy.[10] "You are hereby notified that being a person taken in arms against the Government, you will be executed at 8 am on Friday, 8 December, as a reprisal for the assassination of Brigadier Seán Hales T.D. in Dublin, on 7 December, on his way to a meeting of Dáil Éireann and as a solemn warning to those associated with you and who are engaged in a conspiracy of assassination against the representatives of the Irish people."

(It has to be noted that Dick Barrett and Seán Hales were close friends during the War of Independence and also reasonably near neighbours.)

By now the Civil War had taken a cruel and bitter twist. During the closing days of 1922 and the early days of 1923 there were executions and deaths. Fifty-five executions had been carried out by order of the Free State authorities, and more were pending. (The total number of executions during hostilities was seventy-seven according to records, though Ernest Blythe, in an interview with author, said that he believed "it was many more".)

The Free State began to introduce a policy of sentencing prisoners to death in places where Republican activities were taking place, so the conflict now lacked any human dignity. By this time the guerilla warfare was almost over and the Republicans were reduced to snipings and skirmishes. It was evident that military victory was no longer a possibility for the Republicans, yet doggedly and stubbornly both sides continued the battle.

Liam Deasy, who was captured on 18 January and faced with death, some days later signed an unconditional surrender order. Though Deasy's comrades regarded this action as traitorous at the time, it was later regarded as courageous and just; it saved the lives of many Republican prisoners, many who were on hunger strike. Copies of this order were sent by the Free State Government and to the members of the Executive for their signatures. Deasy had already begun to see the futility of continuing the fight, but his companions "outside" and especially Liam Lynch became more determined, understandably from his point, due to all the "murders" and "torturing" of their prisoners.

However, by 10 April many Republicans had begun to accept the futility of further resistance. When Liam Lynch and other members of the Executive had assembled in Bill

POSTSCRIPT

Houlihan's house outside Fermoy for a meeting to decide on future policy, they were surrounded by Free State troops as they climbed the shoulder of Crow Hill on the Knockmealdown Mountain. They tried to escape but Liam Lynch, who hadn't been well since the previous night, was fatally wounded on the mountains. He begged his companions to leave him. He was captured and had a horrific death, as he was being brought down the mountain on a stretcher and being carted to Newcastle, Co. Tipperary.

On 26 and 27 April the remaining Republican Army Council members met. With de Valera presiding over the meeting, they decided that armed resistance to the Free State forces should be terminated.

De Valera, by this time, felt that a compromise should be made if the Republicans were to work within the frame of constitutional and political realities. Though the Republicans had decided on an unconditional surrender, many were not prepared to hand in their arms and so they still constituted a threat to the Free State. Meanwhile the Free State continued to arrest Republicans, and many of them remained on the run. Jim Kearney and Timmy Sullivan, both of whom had been in the Béal na mBláth ambush, were among the many who remained in prison. While de Valera was addressing an election meeting in Ennis on 15 August 1923, he himself was arrested, put in prison but headed the poll in Clare.

After the ending of a hunger strike by Republican prisoners in most prisons during October and November, the Government began to release people in a "dribble" system.

POSTSCRIPT

Timmy Sullivan was released in October 1923 and Jim Kearney was held until the following February (1924). By then only about 20 prisoners remained in Free State prisons.

The results of the 1923 election legitimised the Free State because the newly formed Cumann na nGaedheal party had 63 candidates elected. Despite the absence in prison of many Sinn Féin candidates, the 44 elected showed continued support for the Republicans. It also showed that the Sinn Féin abstentionist principle was no longer popular and so de Valera, on his release from jail in July 1924, set his sights on a method of entering the Dáil.

The task of establishing order and the concern of bringing stability to the twenty-six counties of Ireland now rested with the Cumann na nGaedheal government which held office until 1932.

Appendix I

Letter from the Provisional Government
at 8.40 pm on 14-7-1922

General Michael Collins

You have been entrusted with supreme command of the National Army and with General Mulcahy and General O'Duffy you have been constituted a War Council to direct the military operations now in progress. The Government's action is dictated by a determination that the splendid valour and devotion of the Army shall be inspired and directed to yield its full fruit for the Salvation of the Nation.

The Government recognises itself as the servant of the Irish People, and as such its duty is to see that the expressed will of the Irish people shall be carried into effect. An armed minority, possessing no authority, is waging war against the people to force them to submit to a dictatorship; and the army which so recently freed the people from a foreign tyranny must now resist this domestic encroachment upon their liberties.

The Irish Army, therefore, is fighting for the same principle as that for which we fought the British, the right of the Irish people to be masters in their own country, to decide for themselves the way in which they shall live, and the system

APPENDIX 1

by which they shall be governed. For that principle they have made, and are prepared to make further sacrifices. Many have died, many have been wounded. They have died and are suffering that the people of Ireland may be free.

The "irregulars'" method of warfare is utterly destructive of the economic life of the nation. Sheer brigandage is a fair term to apply to it. Wherever they go, they burn and wreck property; destroy roads, railways, and bridges; seize food, clothing and supplies even from the poorest people; conscript men into their ranks; and use forced labour. In short they are doing their best to ruin and demoralise their country.

From these outrages the Government and the Army will protect the people. The fight is for the revival of the Nation; for the free expression and effective execution of the people's will; for internal peace and order – in other words for the establishment of all the signs by which a nation is to be held worthy of consideration among the states of the world.

Arthur Griffith
Michael McDonnchada
Acting Secretary to the Provisional Government

(Signed by):
K. O'Higgins
P.J. Hogan
L.T. MacCosgair
J. McGrath

Appendix II

Military Censorship General Instructions-July 1922

1. The Army must always be referred to as the "Irish Army," "The National Army," "National Forces," "National Troops" or simply "The Troops".

2. The Irregulars must not be referred to as "Executive Forces" nor described as "Forces" or "Troops". They are to be called "Bands" or "Bodies" or "Armed men" or "Irregulars".

3. Irregular leaders are not to be referred to as of any rank such as "Commandant" etc. and are not to be called Officers.

4. No news of movements of the troops may be published.

5. No news may be published with regard to the movements of newly enrolled members of the Army, movements of food ships or trains, or transport of arms or equipment for Army purposes.

6. Descriptions of a military operation must not be published while the operation is still uncompleted, as for instance, an encirclement movement.

7. Articles or letters as to the treatment of Irregular prisoners may not be published.

8. The Censors are not to insert the words of their own in any article submitted to them. Their business is to conceal what is objected to. They may however propose to substitute words or phrases, such as "Irregulars" for "Republicans", "fired at" for "attacked", "seized" for "commandeered," "kidnapped by Irregulars" for "arrested", "enrolled" for "enlisted".

9. Letters, news or articles dealing with proposals for peace or negotiations with the Irregulars should not be passed without first submitting them to the Chief Censor.

Appendix III

Peace Proposals – 19th August 1922

The following terms have been communicated to Major General Dalton by a Committee of prominent citizens of Cork, and after consultation with his staff he has agreed to communicate them to General Michael Collins.

1. A week's truce is to be immediately arranged on the basis of the existing military position.

2. During this interval facilities are to be afforded to the Republican Military and Political leaders to hold a meeting to discuss the making of peace on the following basis:

1. Republican opposition to the Government and Parliament is to be on constitutional lines.

2. Members of the Republican Forces who desire to return to civil life will be allowed to return to their occupations without molestation or penalisation.

3. Members of the Republican Forces who wish to join the National Army will be received therein with due recognition of rank and service.

4. Arms and amunitions in possession of the Republican Forces will be handed over to a Committee to be mutually agreed upon.

5. There will be a general amnesty of all Political prisoners.

Collins' Response

On Saturday night Collins wrote a message which was to be wired to General Dalton the following day:

Wireless dispatch received. Will you say by cipher who the prominent citizens responsible for the offer are?

Have the Irregular leaders, political and military, agreed to the offer and is it made on their behalf?

Government offer published in the Press 5th June, and conveyed to the People's Rights Association, Cork, stands. For our guidance the terms of this are:

First: Transfer into the National Armoury of all war materials.

Second: Restoration, without exception, of all seized property and money.

Third: Particulars be furnished, bridges, roads, railways which are or have been mined or rendered otherwise unsafe.

Appendix IV

W/T Office Portobello – 16 August 1922

The following messages from Cork and Limerick have been intercepted here at 9.15.

Gen. O' Duffy to Gen. Dalton: What is your position?

Gen. Dalton to Gen. O'Duffy: All quiet on all fronts. I occupy Cork City, Queenstown, Fermoy, Rosscarbery; have moved on Macroom, and Mitchelstown; believe O'Connell at Mitchelstown will write. Have you Mallow or will I take it?

Gen. O' Duffy to Gen. Dalton: Advancing south, expect to be at Blackwater from Waterford to Kerry by weekend, attack on Mallow proceeding now. Did Limerick ship arrive with 250 men?

Gen, Dalton to Gen. O' Duffy: Ship has returned to Limerick, ship arrived. I will attack Mallow from Fermoy.

Gen. O'Duffy to Gen. Dalton: I am moving on Macroom from west tomorrow.

Gen. Dalton to Gen. O' Duffy: I bet you £5 I will be there before you.

Gen. O' Duffy to Gen. Dalton: Good man, accepted.
Ends

Mulcahy Papers P7/B/70/80

Appendix V

O'DONOGHUE'S STATEMENT

Copy of Statement recorded by Major Florence O'Donoghue
[*This statement was made in 1964. It was embargoed until 1990.*]

On the evening of Tuesday, February 15, 1964, seven of us sat down at the Metropole Hotel, Cork, to try to record the circumstances in which Collins was killed, in so far as they are known to the surviving members of the Republican Forces who participated in the engagement.

There were present Liam Deasy, Tom Kelleher, Tom Crofts, Pete Kearney, Jim Hurley, Dan Holland and myself. All except myself were at Béal na mBláth at the time and I was asked to record what could be established as the truth and because I had been given an undertaking by Capt. Séan Feehan of the Mercier Press that he would not publish Eoin Neeson's Book on the Civil War until we had been satisfied that the part of it dealing with the death of Collins was in accordance with the facts.

The first intimation the Republican Officers received of the presence of Collins in the area came to them on the morning of August 22. Denis Long was on sentry duty at Jerh. Long's public house on the night of 21st and 22nd. Tom Crofts stayed at Murray's and Con Lucey stayed at Long's that night.

In the morning, Denis Long saw the Free State convoy pass in the direction of Bandon and reported it. Liam Deasy and De Valera, who had stayed at Gurraneriagh on the night of the 21st, arrived at Béal na mBláth next morning. De Valera, in company with Séan Hyde, went on apparently to Ballyvourney, but Liam Deasy remained.

Four officers of Cork No. 3 Brigade assembled at Béal na mBláth in the forenoon to attend a Brigade Council meeting to the possibility of an ambush and, in fact, it was not until 11 p.m. that night.

Before the officers arrived at Béal na mBláth, the decision had been taken, on divisional initiative, to lay an ambush 400 yards south of the cross for the Free State convoy, on the assumption that it would probably return later in the day by the same route. When the four Cork No. 3 officers arrived, the position was in the process of being prepared and occupied.

Statements which have been made to the effect that the division and Cork No. 3 Brigade were aware of Collins' intention to visit posts in Cork and that a general order was issued to kill him are without foundation and completely untrue. His presence in the South was known to the officers of the division and of the 1st and 3rd Brigades only on the morning of the 22nd and no general order had been issued by either of the commands. The ambush was decided as part of the general policy of attacking Free State convoys.

The ambush party numbered between 20 and 25. It included Liam Deasy, Tom Kelleher, Jim Hurley, Pete Kearney,

Dan Holland, Tom Hales, Tom Crofts, Con Lucey, Seán Cullhane, John Lordan, Bill Desmon, Dan Corcoran, C. O'Donoghue, John O'Callahan, Sonny O'Neill, Paddy Walsh, Sonny Donovan, Jim Crowley, Tadhg O'Sullivan, Jerh. Mahony. A mine was laid and a covered lorry with one wheel removed was used as a road block on the boreen running almost parallel to the road on the eastern side

The ambush party remained in position during the day but no action took place. In the afternoon, a message was received from Bandon that Collins was there. It was considered unlikely that the convoy would return through Béal na mBláth and the decision was made, probably by Liam Deasy, to call off the ambush and evacuate the position.

When the main party moved, a Cork No. 3 section remained to cover withdrawal and clear the road. This consisted of Tom Hales, Jim Hurley, Dan Holland, Tom Kelleher, Sonny O'Neill, Paddy Walsh, John O'Callahan, Sonny Donovan, Bill Desmond and Dan Corcoran.

They had left their prepared positions and were helping to clear the road, when the noise of a motorbike and lorries was heard approaching from the south. They realised that the main party, moving back toward Béal na mBláth, was in a ravine and in a very dangerous position. They could not have reached the cross before the convoy overtook them.

Immediately on hearing the noise of the approaching vehicles, seven or eight of the Cork No. 3 section took up positions on a boreen west of the road and opened fire on the oncoming convoy. Jim Hurley fired on the motorcyclist and missed him. Tom Kelleher fired on the following vehicle.

The Republican party was armed with rifles and revolvers only. They had no machine guns, but there were two machine guns in the convoy and fire from them raked the section of the fence, from which the Cork No. 3 section were firing. The action lasted between 20 and 30 minutes and before it ended, darkness had fallen to the extent that it was not possible to get off an aimed shot.

Firing stopped at almost 8 o'clock. The Cork No. 3 Section remained in position and the Free State convoy withdrew under fire. No one in the Republican Party knew that Collins had been killed or that the convoy had suffered any casualty. It was only when Seán Galvin came to Béal na mBláth about one that they got the first report of his death.

Signed:

Liam Deasy, Tom Kelleher, Tom Crofts, Pete Kearney, Jim Hurley, Dan Holland.

Notes

List of Abbreviations

P.G. – Provisional Government

C.in.C – Commander-in-Chief

M.P. – Mulcahy Papers

P.R.O. – Public Record Office

D/I – Director of Intelligence

Q.M.G. – Quarter Master General

op. cit. already cited

The Lead-Up

Part I

1. The Irish Republican Brotherhood (IRB) was founded in Dublin on 17 March, 1858, by James Stephens – with John O'Mahony providing funds from New York. As Head Centre, Stephens designed the organisation along secret lines. It lost force for some time but was reorganised in 1873. The Easter Rising of 1916 was planned by a small group of the Military Council. Following the collapse of the Rising, the IRB was reorganised under Michael Collins and, after

≈ NOTES ≈

Thomas Ashe's death, Collins replaced him as secretary. The Supreme Council favoured the Treaty, so the IRB split during the Civil War. Collins was in the organisation until his death.

2. Sam Maguire, b.1879 Dunmanway, County Cork; worked as a clerk in London General Post Office; became a supporter of the IRB, GAA and Irish Volunteers, and was a close friend of Collins. He was Chief Intelligence Officer for the Volunteers in London and supplied arms to Collins for the Irish cause. Being a keen sportsman, he captained the London teams that played in All-Ireland football finals in 1903, 1905, 1906. As a memorial to his GAA work, the "Sam Maguire Cup" was presented in perpetuity.

3. Properly entitled "The Fighting Race" by Joseph I. C. Clarke (1846-1927), Irish American newspaperman, poet, playwright, writer, and Irish nationalist.

4. Michael O'Brien interview with author 15/6/1974.

5. Elizabeth Countess of Fingall *Seventy Years Young*, p. 409.

6. *Ibid.*

∽ NOTES ∽

7. Public Records Office, Dublin

8. National Library, Dublin MS 13329.

9. Executed leaders: 3 May: Padraic Pearse, Thomas J. Clarke and Thomas MacDonagh. 4 May: Joseph Plunkett, Edward Daly, William Pearse and Michael O'Hanrahan. 5 May: John MacBride. 8 May: Eamonn Ceannt, Michael Mallin, Con Colbert and Seán Heuston. 9 May: Thomas Kent. 12 May: James Connolly and Seán Mac Diarmada.

10. May 1, 1916, entered as "Collins M. 16 Rathdown Road, North Circular Rd, Irish Prisoner 48F".

11. Thomas Ashe, b. Kinard, near Dingle, Co. Kerry; active in Gaelic League and Irish Volunteers; for his part in the 1916 Rising in Ashbourne he was sentenced to life imprisonment; released June 1917, became active in Sinn Féin and Volunteers, arrested in August, sentenced to two years imprisonment. He went on hunger strike for political status but failed to achieve his goal. On 25 September 1917 he died while being forcibly fed. Collins delivered the oration at his graveside.

12. According to the IRB constitution, its President, in fact as well as by right, was regarded as Head of the

NOTES

Government of the Irish Republic. However, the constitution of the IRB had subsequently to be amended to take into account an oath required by Dáil deputies and officials, committing them to support and defend the Irish Republic and its government.

13. Dave Neligan interview with author, 30/1/1974. Neligan, one of the G-men in Dublin Castle, later one of the British Secret Service acting as agent for Collins.

14. This episode happened with the knowledge and approval of the Minister of Defence, Cathal Brugha. (Eleven British Intelligence men were shot dead and four were wounded, two Auxiliaries who intervened were killed and another uninvolved officer was also killed.) Collins said afterwards (in London) to Birkenhead, "Our lads would have been wiped out. We got there first." 26 Oct. 1922.

15. Member of the Hales family, Knocknacurra. Dónal Hales was involved in the organisation of a shipload of arms to Ireland. Collins supplied him with material on the Irish situation for his newspaper reporting.

16. Letter to Liam Lynch, 16 May 1921; See also *Liam Lynch: The Real Chief*, pp. 154 – 158, by Meda Ryan.

17. Another member of the Hales family from Knocknacurra.

NOTES

During the War of Independence and the Civil War, Madge Hales (Murphy) communicated dispatches between the Third West Cork Brigade and GHQ. She was the personal link between Collins and her brother Dónal Hales in Italy in connection with the arms shipment.

18. Ulick O'Connor, *Oliver St. John Gogarty*, p. 193.

19. Madge Hales interview with author, 20/6/1971.

20. Tom Barry interview with author, 17/3/1976.

21. Leon O'Broin, *Michael Collins*, p.85 Frank Thornton memoirs.

22. T. Ryle Dwyer, *Michael Collins and the Treaty*, p. 46.

23. *Ibid.* p 48. Also Piaras Béaslaí, *Michael Collins and the Making of a New Ireland*, p. 275.

24. T. Ryle Dwyer, *Michael Collins and the Treaty*. p 46.

25. Emmet Dalton interview with author 3/10/1973.

26. Frank Pakenham, *Peace By Ordeal*, p. 239.

27. Sir John Lavery, *The Life of a Painter*, p. 214.

NOTES

28. Haden Talbot, *Michael Collins' Own Story*, p.144 to 151.
See also T. Ryle Dwyer, *Michael Collins and the Treaty*, p. 44 to 53.

29. Collins to O'Kane, *Freeman's Journal*, 6 Dec. 1921.

30. Sir John Lavery, *The Life of a Painter*, p. 214.

31. Rex Taylor, *Michael Collins*, p. 124. Letter John O'Kane to Taylor.

32. Fifty-seven opposed the Treaty, sixty-four were for the Treaty.

33. See Meda Ryan, *Liam Lynch: The Real Chief*, pp.154 to 168.

34. Seán MacBride interview with author 23/10/1978.

The Lead-Up

Part II

1. Margery Forester, *Michael Collins: The Lost Leader*, p.317.

2. Calton Younger, *A State of Disunion*, p. 154.

3. Ernest Blythe to author 25/10/1973. Collins was in Cork when word of Wilson's assassination reached him.

4. *Ibid*.

5. Lloyd George to Collins, 22 June 1922. M.P. P7/B/244/1; See also Sheila Lawlor, *Britain and Ireland* 1914-23, p.191.

6. Ernest Blythe, interview with author 8/11/1973.

7. Reginald Dunne and Joseph O'Sullivan were hanged at Wandsworth prison, London, on 10 August 1922.

8. Collins to Cosgrave, 6 August 1922, M.P. P7/B/29/62.

9. Cosgrave to Collins, 7 August 1922, M.P. P7/B/29/50.

10. Ulick O'Connor, *The Sunday Independent*, November 2nd, 1980 reviewing *Michael Collins*, by Leon Ó Broin.

11. Emmet Dalton interview with author 2/3/1974.

12. Lloyd George to Collins, 22 June 1922, M.P. P7/B/244/1 & 2.

13. Sir Nevil Macready, *Annals of an Active Life*, Vol 2 pp.652, 653.

14. Provisional Government minutes, P.G. meeting 27 June 1922, M.P. P7/B/244/7.

15. Ernest Blythe interview with author 20/3/1974.

16. *Ibid*.

17. P.G minutes, meeting 2 July 1922, M.P. P7/B/244/23, P7/B/244/26 & 27.

18. P.G. minutes, meeting 13 July 1922, M.P. P7/B/244/30. By 17 July, the number of men in the Army had reached 15,000 approx. Later, further authority

was given by the Government to increase the army strength to 35,000.

19. Collins to Griffith – memo on establishment of War Council, 12 July, M. P. P7/B/177 – also quoted in Hopkinson, *Green Against Green*, p.136.

20. P. G. minutes, meeting (morning) 12 July 1922. M.P. P7/B/244/58; also P.R.O. P.G. 57. 12 July 1922.

21. P.G. minutes, meeting (evening) 12 July 1922. M.P. P7/ B/244/61. *Ibid* .

22. Collins' notebook. 12 July 1922 – abbreviated version of these appointments.

23. Collins – General Instructions, July 1922. M.P. P7/B/52/5.

24. Report from Capt. Stapleton, Observer and Commandant Russell, Pilot, to Collins, 17 July 1922, M.P. P7/B/107/69.

25. Collins' handwritten notes, 14 July 1922, M.P. P7/B/18/29 & P7/B/18/27 & P7/B/18/28. M.P. (Collins' notes: "Immediate Objective – To prepare for an attack on Waterford at once – to have Carrick-On-Suir in mind for occupying almost immediately

∽ NOTES ∽

after." He commanded Gen. Prout to "Supply a gun team to report of Gen. O'Duffy". Collins wanted men to move on Kilkenny, Thurles, Castlecomer, and distribution of men and arms. 14 July 1922.)

26. Collins' notebook, p. 14 & 15, 14 July 1922, M.P. P7/B/ 43/13.

27. Collins to Chief of General Staff, 14 July 1922, M.P. P7/ B/49/50.

28. Collins to Lieut Gen. O'Connell, 14 July 1922, M.P. P7/ B/17/49 & P7/B/17/50.

29. Collins to Quarter Master General 16 July1922. Q.M.G. to Collins (list) 15 July 1922. M.P. P7/B/3/147; compiled 17 July 1922, M.P. P7/B/3/145.

30. Collins to Quarter Master General 17 July 1922, M.P. P7/ B/3/143.

31. P.G. minutes, meeting 12 July 1922, M.P. P7/B/244/58,

32. P.G. letter to Collins signed by A. Griffith, Michael McDonnchada, K. O'Higgins, P.J. Hogan, L.T. MacCosgair, J. McGrath. (Handwritten on top: *"Original sent to Gen. Collins, 8.40 pm today 14–7–'22."*)

NOTES

M.P. P7/B/29/233 and P7/B/29/234 also 235. See Appendix I.

33. *Irish Times*, 19 July 1922.

34. Collins' notebook, 13 Aug 1922. "First day at P'Bello. Staff meeting at 4 o'c. Spent morning rather wastefully owing to delay B. of Works in fitting up rooms for working in."

35. Collins wrote to Acting Chairman (Cosgrave), signing himself Chairman, 31 July 1922: Re British Gov. Stocks kept in Bank of I. in Belfast. M.P. P7/B/29/143; Collins wrote to Acting Chairman, signing himself Chairman, 31 July 1922: Re prisoners on hunger strike in Derry jail, M.P. P7/B/29/131; also, 31 July 1922: M.P. P7/B/29/ 133: Collins wrote to Churchill under the heading of Chairman's Office – Re Diseases of Animals Act, 27 July 1922, Blythe Papers p. 27/65.

36. There are notes written at 12 midnight, 17 Aug. 1922, M.P. P7/B/2/83.

37. Collins to Churchill. 15 July 1922 P.R.O. CO 38573. (Churchill's letter to Collins P. G. minutes, meeting 8 July 1922. M.P. P7/B/244/48.

NOTES

38. Collins to Churchill 25 July 1922, P.R.O. CO 38573.

39. Cosgrave to Collins 25 July 1922, M.P. P7/B/29/184.

40. Chairman Legion of Irish Ex-Servicemen to Collins, 25 July 1922, M.P. P7/B/9/63. "100 Artillery men, 100 Drivers, 100 Machine gunners, 100 Engineers, 100 Signallers" (20 Instructors were selected for the Curragh.) M.P. P7/B/9/52.

41. Collins' memo – General Situation – 26 July 1922, M.P. P7/B/28/45 & 46.

42. Collins' memo, 26 July 1922, M.P. P7/B/28/60, *Ibid.*

43. Collins to Cosgrave – Re bank raids. 9 Aug 1922. M.P. P7/B/29/44; Cosgrave to Collins – position of southern banks, 18 July 1922; Collins to Cosgrave, 28 July 1922, M.P. P7a/50.

44. Margery Forester, *Michael Collins: The Lost Leader,* p. 329.

45. Collins to Director of Intelligence, 31 July 1922, M.P. P7/B/4/90.

46. Collins to Director of Intelligence 3 August 1922, M.P.P7/B/4/74.

47. Collins to Acting Major General Tobin, 20 July 1922, M.P. P7/B/4/123.

48. Cosgrave to Collins – Re purchase in England of "arms by the Irregulars" 29 July 1922. 30 July correspondence of information received from Cope, M.P. P7/B/29/149, P7/B/29/150 also 151 and 152. D/I to Collins, 5 Aug. 1922: "Mr Childers made an attempt to get away to USA on the *Carmenia* from here yesterday ... " M.P. P7/B/4/56; 7 Aug 1922. Collins to D/I suggested, "The idea that would be most suitable would be that he should be arrested as a stowaway." M.P. P7/B/4/54.

49. Emmet Dalton interview with author, 2/4/1974.

50. Collins to Acting Chairman – Interim Report – 5 Aug. 1922, M.P.P7/B/29/87 to P7/B/29/100.

51. Dr. Gerald Ahern interview with author 10/8/1974. His brother Dr. Leo was medical doctor with Provisional Government forces in Portobello Barracks, Dublin. Later Dr. Leo took over Shanakiel Hospital for the forces.

52. Collins to Cosgrave, 5 August 1922, M.P. P7/B/29/87 to P7/B/29/100.

53. Dalton to Collins, 10 August 1922, M.P. P7a/50-S.M.

54. *Ibid*, 11 August 1922, M.P. P7a/50.

Chapter 1

1. Arthur Griffith (1871–1922) joined the Irish Volunteers in 1913, took part in the Howth gun-running in July 1914. He was arrested and spent a term in jail. Having led the Irish team in the Treaty negotiations, he later signed and defended it. Later he was elected President of the Dáil. During the Civil War he died of cerebral hemorrhage on 12 August 1922.

2. D.V. Horgan interview with author 14/4/1982. (One of the bodyguards to Michael Collins.)

3. *Ibid*.

4. Pat Murray interview with author 23/3/1974.

Chapter 2

1. P.G. meeting 12 July 1922, M.P. P/B/244/58.

2. Collins' personal notebook 13/7/1922, M.P. P/B/52/5.

3. Collins' memo, *Organization at G.H.Q.* 19 July 1922, M.P. P/B/41/88.

4. *Collins – General Routine Orders,* 14 July 1922, M.P. P7a/50.

5. On one occasion Lord Birkenhead and Michael Collins were guests at lunch in the home of Sir John and Lady Hazel Lavery. During the meal, Hazel's small Peke dog was pawing at Lord Birkenhead under the table. Hazel realised this, and called the little dog. "Oh, I'm sorry. I thought you were making advances," said Lord Birkenhead. Fuming, Collins jumped up, "D'ye mean to insult her?" Hazel, wishing to calm the situation, said, "Lord Birkenhead was only joking." "I don't understand such jokes," shouted an irate Collins.

6. Collins, *General Instructions,* July, 1922. M.P. P/7/B/52/5.

NOTES

7. *The Path of Freedom*, by Michael Collins p. 99.

8. Collins' notes, M.P. p. 7/29/3 to 19.

9. Michael Hayes, *The Capuchin Annual*, 1972, p. 279.

10. Affidavit of Thomas A. Kelly, Sligo, 26/9/1967 – Private papers held by Dr. Ned Barrett.

11. Ernest Blythe interview with author 19/1/1974.

12. Collins' notebook, Sat. 12 Aug. 1922, M.P. P7a/50.

13. C. in C. wire To Confidence, 14 Aug 1922, M.P. P7/B/70/98.

14. *Ibid.* Handed in 1.20, 15 Aug. 1922, M.P. P/B/70/82.

15. Chief Of General Staff wire to C. in C. 20 Aug. 1922, M.P. P/B/70/57.

16. Collins to O'Duffy, 15 Aug. 1922, M.P. P/B/21/12 & P/B/21/13 & P7/B/21/14.

17. *Ibid.* 16 Aug. 1922, M.P. P/B/39/42.

18. Collins to Q.M.G. 17 Aug. 1922, (a long angry letter) M.P. P7/B/3/42.

NOTES

19. Piaras Béaslaí, *Michael Collins and the Making of a New Ireland*, Vol.ll p. 424.

20. *The Irish Independent* 16 Aug 1922.

21. Chief Of General Staff wire to Collins 15 Aug. 1922, op. cit. M.P. P/B/70/89 also P/B/70/88, P7/B/70/108.

22. Newspaper cutting, 16 Aug. 1922, M.P. P/B/70/74.

23. Report aerial reconnaissance, 13 Aug. 1922, M.P. P7/B/ 39/21.

24. Personal notes written by Collins, 16 Aug. 1922, M.P. P7a/62.

25. *Ibid.*

26. D.V. Horgan interview with author 23/5/1979.

27. Collins 16 August 1922, M.P. P7/B/28/97.

28. Margery Forester, *Michael Collins: The Lost Leader*, p. 331.

29. Collins to Director of Munitions, 19 Aug. 1922, M.P. P7I B/4/11; Collins to Director of Purchases, 19 Aug. 1922, M.P. P7/B/12/l; Ibid. Director of Publicity, 19

Aug. 1922, M.P. P7/B/14/1; *Ibid.* Prout Southern Division 19 Aug. 1922, M.P. P/B/14/1.

30. Personal notes written by Collins, 16 Aug. 1922, M.P. P7a/62.

31. O'Duffy to Collins, 12 Aug. 1922. M.P. P7/B/39/32 & P7/B/39/33.

32. Collins' notes undated, M.P. P/B/28/1 & P7/B/28/2.

33. Commander-in-Chief to Officer Commanding S.W. Command, 17 Aug. 1922, M.P. P7/B/21/8.

34. Dalton wire to Collins, 19 Aug. 1922, M.P. P7/B/70/62.

35. *Ibid.* P7/B/70/63 & P/B/70/65.

36. Commander-In-Chief to Dalton, 19 Aug. 1922, M.P. P7/B/2002. (This was received in Cork by Major General Dalton on 19, August, 1922 at 10.50 am) See Appendix III.

37. Collins' notes, undated, M.P. P7/B/28/1.

38. Elizabeth, Countess of Fingall, *Seventy Years Young*, p.403.

NOTES

39. Piaras Béaslaí, *Michael Collins*, p. 427.

40. Margery Forester, *Michael Collins: The Lost Leader*, p.333.

41. Collins' notes, 19 Aug. 1922, M.P. P7a/62.

42. Collins to Director of Munitions, 19 Aug. 1922, M.P. P7/ B/4/11.

43. Collins to Director of Purchases, 19 Aug. 1922, M.P. P7/ B/12/1.

44. Collins to Director of Publicity, 19 Aug. 1922, M.P. P7/ B/14/1.

45. Collins to Director of Recruiting, 19 Aug. 1922, M.P. P7/B/8/15.

46. Collins to Dalton, 19 Aug. 1922, M.P. P7/B/20/1; Collins to Gen. Price, 19 Aug. 1922 P7/B/3/20/10.

47. Collins to Director of Munitions, 19 Aug. 1922, M.P. P7/ B/4/11.

48. Sir John Lavery, *The Life of a Painter*, p. 216.

49. Elizabeth, Countess of Fingall, *Seventy Years Young*, p.409.

50. Sir John Lavery, *The Life of a Painter*, p 218.

51. *Ibid*, p. 216.

52. *Ibid.*, p 216.

53. Frank O'Connor, *The Big Fellow*, p. 211.

Chapter 3

1. Fionán Lynch to Bill Stapelton, 1950. Stapelton interview with author 8/5/1977; also, Fionán Lynch in RTÉ interview.

2. *Ibid.*

3. Collins' notes, Sun. 20 Aug. 1922, M.P. P7a/62.

4. *Ibid.*

5. Frank O'Connor, *The Big Fellow*, p. 211.

6. Collins' notes – diary, 20 Aug. 1922, M.P. P7/a/62.

7. Hales was in the south at that time with John L. O'Sullivan and a complement of men. They had taken towns along the West Cork coast.

8. Collins' notes – diary. 20 Aug. 1922, M.P. P7a/62,

9. Fionán Lynch to Bill Stapelton, 1950. Stapelton interview with author 8/5/1977; also. Fionán Lynch in RTÉ interview.

10. *Ibid.*

11. Collins' personal notebook, 20 Aug. 1922, held at time of interview by Collins' nephew, Michael Collins.

12. O'Duffy always signed himself as Owen O'Duffy, but the Irish term is used in many writings.

13. Commander-in-Chief wire To Confidence, 20 Aug. 1922, M.P. P7/B/70/55.

14. Collins' personal notebook, 20 Aug. 1922.

15. *Ibid*. He asked that new form should "be here early Tuesday".

16. John C. Byrne's notes – copy of Collins' diary. Telephone conversation with author 14/8/1978.

17. Ernest Blythe interview with author 9/1/1974.

18. Michael Brennan interview with author 29/11/1973.

19. Commander-in-Chief wire To Confidence, sent 9 pm Recd. Portobello 9.40, 20 Aug. 1922, M.P. P7/B/54.

20. Commander-in-Chief wire To Confidence, 20 Aug. 1922, M.P. P7/B/70/55.

21. Collins to P. Gov. encl. "extract from General O'Duffy despatch". 28 July 1922, M.P. P7/B/38/5.

22. Collins' notes, M.P. P7/B/70/50.

23. C. in C. cipher 4.10 pm. Limerick. Reed. Portobello, 6.15 pm 21 Aug. 1922, M.P. P7/B/70/53.

24. Collins' personal notebook, 20 Aug. 1922, held by Collins' nephew, Michael Collins (at time of research); See also M.P. 20 Aug. 1922, P7a/62.

25. This is in accordance with time details in Collins' notebook, 20 Aug. 1922.

26. On his return journey the following day he was ambushed at Killarney, again between Castleisland and Abbeyfeale and there was a third ambush at Currans.

27. Collins' personal notebook, 20 Aug. 1922.

28. *Ibid.*

29. Calton Younger, *Ireland's Civil War* p.429.

30. Emmet Dalton interview with author 20/3/1974.

Chapter 4

1. Emmet Dalton interview with author 20/3/1974.

2. Letters from Diarmuid Brennan to Dr. Gerald Ahern, dated 1st November 1970, 13th November 1970 and 18 January 1971, in Dr. Gerald Ahern's possession.

3. Commander-in-Chief wire To Confidence, 21 Aug. 1922, M.P. P/7/B/70/52; Mulcahy's response – "these places were under the control of the Royal Engineer Dept. Home Affairs, sending a representative by boat today" – M.P. P7/B/70/50. (The response did not arrive until after Collins' death.)

4. Commander-in-Chief wire To Confidence, 21 Aug. 1922, M.P. P7/B/70/37. Mulcahy wanted confirmation when Collins would like to begin "reconnoitre" and "an understanding that plane will have necessary protection if it lands in Fermoy" – M.P. P7/B/70/34. (Message arrived the day Collins was in West Cork.)

5. Collins' notes – diary, 21 Aug. 1922, at time of interview held by Collins' nephew, Michael Collins.

6. *Ibid.*

7. See *Irish Independent*, 16 August, 1922.

8. Dr. D.J. Ahern interview with author 13/6/1974. "Tom was a great friend of mine, we discussed this many times," he said. See also: Cosgrave to Collins, 17 July 1922, M.P. P7/B/ 29/223; Collins to P. Gov. 16 July 1922, M.P. P7/B/ 29/ 224.

9. During the Republican occupation of Cork the *Cork Examiner* was taken over, with Frank Gallagher using space in it for anti-Treaty propaganda. There were appeals to the pro-Treaty forces to join them; each issue bore an editorial note stating that the items appearing under "Republican News" were outside the Editor's control. From 9 August to 13 August, there was no issue of the *Cork Examiner* printed; when it was in circulation again, the newspaper had a more pro-Treaty stance. *Cork Examiner:* August 8 1922 – Issue No.21604; August 9 1922 – Issue No. 21605; August 13 1922 – Issue No. 21606.

10. Collins' notes-diary, 21 Aug. 1922, at time of interview, held by Collins' nephew, Michael Collins.

11. Emmet Dalton interview with author 2/4/1974.

12. Collins' notes – diary, 21 Aug. 1922.

13. *Ibid.*

14. Emmet Dalton interview with author 2/4/1974.

15. Desmond Fitzgerald to Commander-in-Chief, to Acting Chairman, to M. for Finance, 28 July, 1922, M.P. P7a/50.

16. Emmet Dalton interview with author 2/4/1974. When he parted with this information, it was almost in a whisper. Having told the story, he added, "Maybe I shouldn't have told you, as I never told that to anybody."

17. This is Joe Brennan from Bandon, whose signature subsequently graced the Irish £1 notes. See also Letter from Acting Chairman, Irish Provisional Government, to Collins: "I have reported to Major General Dalton that the following officials have been sent to Cork: Mr. Joseph Brennan – Ministry of Finance, Treasury; Mr James Lysaght-Local Government, Inspector; Mr T.J. Byrne-Architect, Chief Housing Inspector; Mr M. O' Dwyer – Civil Engineer, (Road, Bridges, etc.); D. Kelly – Medical Inspector, Messrs.

NOTES

Gilligan & Duffy Petrol; Mr. Maurice Jones – Post Office Equipment." 14 Aug. 1922, M.P. P7/B/20/6.

18. Collins' personal notebook, 21 Aug. 1922, held at time of interview, by Collins' nephew, Michael Collins. See also Collins' note, Monday 21 Aug. 1922. M.P. P7/B/20/6.

19. Collins' notes – diary, 21 August 1922. *The Cork Examiner*, 14 Aug. 1922, reported: "The havoc done at the Cork Telephone Exchange is of a far reaching character. All the lines are unworkable. The fact that there are some miles of poles down must necessarily impede the work." See also Collins' note, Mon. 21 Aug. 1922, M.P. P7a/62.

20. Emmet Dalton interview with author 2/4/1974.

21. A.J.S. Brady, *The Briar of Life*, p.104, 202–205.

22. See Florrie O'Donoghue Papers NLI MS 31,243; O'Malley, notebooks P17b/95.

23. Dalton would not disclose details of location or the name of priest. "We recovered the money, that is sufficient information," he said. Emmet Dalton interview with author 2/4/1974.

Chapter 5

1. The Earl of Longford and Thomas P. O'Neill, *Eamon de Valera*, p. 198.

2. Dómhnall Mac Giolla Phóil, interview with author 23/5/1988.

3. Peter Golden, *Impressions of Ireland*, pp. 52–56.

4. *Ibid*.

5. Liam Lynch in letter to his brother Tom, 28 March, 1920. Lynch private family papers; See *Liam Lynch: The Real Chief*, by Meda Ryan. Pub: Mercier Press.

6. Liam Deasy interview with author 19/9/1973.

7. De Valera wasn't sure if it could be called a meeting as "there were officers meeting all over the country" and he wasn't sure of the "extent of their authority".

8. Paddy O'Sullivan and Dónal O'Callaghan were in charge of security outside the house while the meeting was in progress. Interview with author 25/11/1973.

9. Dan Sando O'Donovan interview with author 24/11/ 1973.

10. Paddy O'Sullivan interview with author 25/11/1973; Riobárd Langford interview with author, 9/12/1973; Riobárd Langford, who was attached to the Municipal School, formulated the press, operated the machinery, and had the paper organised weeks before Childers arrived in West Cork. His brother Dick Langford also helped with the printing press. The secretary was Lena Corcoran; Ned Galvin letter to author, 28/1/1975.

11. Maggie Sheehan interview with author 28/9/1975.

12. Riobárd Langford interview with author 9/12/1973.

13. Liam Deasy interview with author 19/9/1973.

14. *Ibid.* Deasy in the course of this interview said that at this time he, like Lynch, harboured the hope that should armaments, which were being organized through American sources, arrive, the scene would be totally changed.

15. Maggie Sheehan interview with author 28/9/1975.

16. Liam Deasy interview with author 19/9/1973.

Chapter 6

1. Collins' notebook, 22 Aug. 1922, held by Collins' nephew, Michael Collins. See also Collins' notes, 22 Aug. 1922, M.P. P7a/62.

2. Emmet Dalton interview with author 2/4/1974.

3. Kate O'Mahony interview with author 11/91976. Her daughter Eileen was with her at time of interview.

4. Timmy Kelleher, interview with author 15/4/1974.

5. Known as Denny "The Dane" because there were many families of Longs in the district. His grandfather was a hedge-schoolmaster just beyond Béal na Bláth cross.

6. Timmy Kelleher interview with author 19/4/1974.

7. Newspaper cutting, 23 Aug. 1922, M.P. P7/B/70/27. Details to author from John L. O'Sullivan, 31/7/1974. John L. O'Sullivan, Seán Hales, Maurice Collins, Con Slattery and a section of pro-Treaty forces were involved in this operation.

NOTES

8. Following the Munster plantation, when hundreds of families were moved from England to the fertile lands in the area, the town drew up a charter in 1613. One of its first acts was to pass a by-law, "That no Roman Catholics be permitted to reside in the town."

9. Timmy Kelleher interview with author 19/4/1974.

Chapter 7

1. Pake Sheehan interview with author 20/4/1974.

2. Liam Deasy interview with author 9/9/1973.

3. Lord Longford & Thomas P. O'Neill, *Eamon de Valera*, p. 199.

4. Bill Powell interview with author, 30/3/1974.

5. *Ibid.*

6. During the War of Independence, one of the tactics of the Flying Columns was: avoid confrontation if unprepared, but if an opportunity arises where an ambush can be successfully laid, then do so; surprise the enemy.

7. Sonny O'Neill had been based in Macroom and Bandon after Cork City was taken over by the National Army in early August 1922, and was called to the IRA Brigade headquarters staff meeting. (Bureau of Military History)

8. Jackie Murray interview with author 30/3/1974. Foleys' house was always a 'safe house' for Republicans, just like Murrays'.

9. Jim Kearney interview with author 11/7/1973, Jim Kearney wrote,13/4 1991: "To become an engineer required special training over quite a period."

10. Liam Deasy interview with author, 19/9/1973. Tom Hales has said, "approximately 40 men formed the ambushing party," in a statement to his brother, Seán Hales – "Report of the Ambush at Béal na Bláth 22nd August 1922; by Tom Hales."

11. Jim Kearney interview with author 11/ 7/1973 and 31/7/1974. His information corroborated by that of Liam Deasy, 19/9/1973.

12. Siobhán Creedon interview with author 27/3/1979. (After the Civil War Siobhán Creedon married Seamus Lankford who was responsible for setting up the Republican printing press. Riobárd Langford

was in Moneygave on 21st and 22, August when de Valera called before going on to Béal na mBáth.)

13. Siobhán Creedon interview with author 27/3/1979.

14. *Ibid.*

Chapter 8

1. Emmet Dalton interview with author 2/4/1974.

2. *Ibid.* During the War of Independence, Tom Hales and Pat Harte were captured by the Essex Regiment, their nails were pulled off and they were then dragged behind a lorry for some miles. Harte was so badly affected that his mind snapped and he died a few years later.

3. Emmet Dalton, *Freeman's Journal*, 22/8/1923.

4. Maurice Collins interview with author; also Emmet Dalton interview with author 2/4/1974.

5. James Cahalane interview with author 19/1/1974.

6. This source is private, as the names of the men consulted by Collins are withheld.

7. See Meda Ryan, *The Tom Barry Story*, p. 73.

8. The first Battalion of British Essex Regiment under the command of Major A.E. Percival was drafted into Bandon in January 1920.

9. Michael O'Brien interview with author 8/12/1973.

10. Kathy Hayes interview with author 16/4/1976.

11. Terry Courtney, Charlie O'Shea, Nelius Connolly.

12. Emmet Dalton interview with author 2/4/1974. Collins was about to step into the car when Tim Burke came up to him, and appealed to Collins to try to stop the war which was "tearing families apart."

13. Edith Somerville also had a few words with Jim Woulfe. Woulfe's parents worked for the Somervilles; Jim was born and reared in a house on the estate. (Somerville & Ross.)

Chapter 9

1. Michael O'Brien interview with author 15/12/1973. (O'Brien, Collins' cousin.).

2. *Ibid.*

3. *Ibid.*

4. *Ibid.*

5. *Ibid.*

6. Jerh. Collins interview with author 16/12/1973.

Chapter 10

1. Jerh. Collins interview with author 16/12/1973.

2. Emmet Dalton interview with author 2/4/1974.

3. John L. O'Sullivan interview with author 31/7/1974; See also Calton Younger, *Ireland's Civil War*, p. 427.

4. John. L. O'Sullivan interview with author, 31/7/1974.

5. *Ibid.*

6. *Ibid.*

7. Mulcahy to O'Duffy, 31 August 1922, M.P.

P/B/70/58. The reference to the Lancia is in Dalton to Collins, 14 August 1922. M.P. P7/B/70/58.

8. Con Slattery interview with author 16/1/1975. (Slattery was with Sean Hales' pro-Treaty forces on that day.)

9. John L. O'Sullivan interview with author 31/7/1974.

10. Piarais Béaslaí, *Michael Collins and the Making of a New Ireland*, p. 420.

11. Later Fr. T.F. Duggan was appointed Archdeacon of Cork; he went to Peru on the missions in his later years and died 6 months later.

12. Professor Lucy Duggan, interview with author 10/7/1974.

13. Collins to Cosgrave, 5 Aug. 1922, M.P. P7/B/29/87 to P7/B/29/100.

14. Emmet Dalton interview with author 2/4/1974.

15. *Ibid.* On that very day the *Independent* reported: "Rumours concerning peace overtures are still afloat, but they are discountenanced in trustworthy quarters. Citizens generally feel that the hour of

∽ NOTES ∽

compromise has long since struck, and that there can be no peace until the military operations are successfully and completely ended. It is indeed idle talk of peace when the wholesale destruction of property continues daily ..."

16. Emmet Dalton interview with author 2/4/1974.

17. Jim Woulfe interview with author 29/3/1974.

18. The author interviewed the following, many of whom participated in the ambush, also others who were "runners" for the ambush but not actually participants during the ambush. While others were Republicans who later learned of Sonny Neill having said that he "dropped one man".

Jim Kearney: 12/5/1973, 11/7/1973, 24/2/1974, 10/3/1974, 31/3/1974, 19/4/1974, 12/5/1974, 7/6/1974, 14/6/1974, 27/6/1974, 14/6/1974, 27/6/1974, 10/7/1974, 14/9/1974, 1/12/1974, 28/12/1974, 31/3/1975, 2/7/1975, 9/3/1975, 2/7/1975, 13/2/1976.

Timmy Sullivan: 18/8/1973, 16/2/1974, 31/2/1974, 11/3/ 1974, 29/3/1974, 20/4/1974, 12/5/1974, 13/6/1974, 18/1/1975.
Tom Kelleher: 11/11/1973, 16/2/1974, 17/3/1974,

19/4/1974. (Kelleher has given conflicting stories to the Press on occasions. See below Chapter 15, for his reasons.)

Liam Deasy: 5/12/1973, 9/1/1974, 7/2/1974.

Jim Woulfe: 9/3/1974, 29/3/1974, 22/4/1974, 19/5/1974, 20/7/1974, 22/9/1974.

Bill Powell: 8/12/1973, 10/7/1974, 14/9/1974, 15/3/1975, 2/5/1976.

Emmet Dalton: 2/4/1974, 4/4/1974, 20/4/1974. (Also details from responses to the author's questionnaire plus details from his private notes).

Pat Buttimer: 17/3/1974, 6/6/1974.

Seán Hyde: 13/7/1974, 20/7/1974. Not there during the ambush, but was there earlier that day for the Divisional Meeting. He had set up roadblocks in the Ballincolling area. He took de Valera away, following the decision to set up an ambush. Later he learned of Sonny Neill's participation and action in the ambush.

Con Murphy: 4/9/1974.

∽ NOTES ∽

Dan O'Callaghan: 25/4/1975.

Con Michael Murphy: 13/9/1974.

Patrick Mahony: 9/7/1975.

Charlie Foley: 16/11/1974, 7/6/1975, 4/10/1975, 23/5/ 1976 (not a participant)

Jack Murray: 27/7/1974, 29/11/1974, 9/7/1975 (not a participant)

Tom Murray: 29/11/1974, 9/7/1975 (not a participant)

Charlie Foley: 16/11/1974, 7/6/1975, 4/10/1975, 23/5/ 1976 (not a participant)

Patrick Desmond: 9/7/1975 (not a participant)

Reps. John McPeak, 21/5/1976; also Ray Smith and Jim Nicoll in *Irish Independent*, 18–21, May 1971.

Jim Hurley: Statement and notes dated, 1948. *Freeman's Journal*: 22 August, 1923.

Emmet Dalton's responses to author's questionnaires.

Calton Younger, *Ireland's Civil War* pp. 434 – 438.

Eoin Neeson, *The Life and Death Of Michael Collins*, pp.112–113.

Also other writings and reports.

Author's letter to *Cork Examiner* 23/19/1989, responding to previous letter to that newspaper, stating from her two interviews that Sonny O'Neill's sister Mary (O'Neill) Walsh told her that Sonny accepted the role he took and that he had fired the shot the killed Collins at Béal na mBláth. "He and his brothers" were "all strong Republicans".

19. Commandant Peter Young, letter to author 10 March 1988 – details from Military Archives.

20. Seán O'Connell, RTÉ Archives.

Chapter 11

1. Emmet Dalton interview with author 4/4/1974, and response to questionnaire. Further details given by

Dalton in interviews and in responses to author's questionnaires, also his 1923 article in *Freeman's Journal*.

2. Tom Kelleher interview with author 20/10/1973.

3. Liam Deasy interview with author 19/9/1973.

4. Jim Kearney interview with author 11/9/1973 and 24/2/ 1974.

5. Seán O'Connell, RTÉ archives.

6. Emmet Dalton, *Freeman's Journal*, 22/8/1923.

7. Emmet Dalton interview with author 4/4/1974.

8. Bill Powell interview with author 30/11/1973.

9. *Ibid.*

10. *Ibid.*

11. Other writings have mentioned Crookstown instead of Cloughduv. This may have been because the convoy intended to travel through Crookstown in the morning, and in the night-time confusion they were unaware of their location.

12. Bill Powell interview with author 30/3/1974.

13. Jim Carmody interview with author 10/6/1974.

14. *Ibid.*

15. Emmet Dalton document written by him, his own private collection – viewed, 4/4/1974.

16. Emmet Dalton interview with author 4/4/1974.

17. *Ibid.* Over the years questions have been asked as to whether the Last Rites of the Catholic Church had been administered to the Michael Collins. Dalton said he did not discuss this event over the years; the abortive event at Cloughduv overshadowed, for him, this moment at Victoria Cross. (He says he decided "not to give interviews" over the years, also in a letter to author he said that due to my "persistence" he would respond.)

18. D.V. Horgan interview with author 21/4/1982.

19. Dr. Leo Ahern had been a house-surgeon in the Mercy Hospital. When the troops landed in Cork, Dr. Leo Ahern commandeered Shanakiel Hospital on behalf of the Provisional Government. He went to Dr.

Dunden, under whom he worked in the Mercy Hospital and made arrangements that the seriously injured pro-Treaty army men would be treated at the Mercy Hospital, and Shanakiel would be a type of convalescence home for minor injuries – "what the army would call a casualty clearing station".

20. Jim Woulfe interview with author 9/3/1974; Also Diarmuid Brennan's correspondence letter 9/12/1970, 1/10/1971, in Dr. Gerald Ahern's collection, 'the dead man in the tender in which the corpse was conveyed'.

21. Emmet Dalton interview with author 4/4/1974. At Portobello Barracks when Richard Mulcahy, Chief of Staff, received the news of Michael Collins' death at 1.15 am. on 23 August, he wrote a notice for the army and the people: Stand Calmly by Your Posts. Bend bravely and undaunted to your work. Let no cruel act of reprisal blemish your bright honour. Every dark hour that Michael Collins met since 1916 seemed to steel that bright strength of his and temper his gay bravery. You are left each inheritors of that strength, and of that bravery. To each of you falls his unfinished work. No darkness in the hour – no loss of comrades will daunt you at it, Ireland! The Army serves – strengthened by its sorrow. *Irish Independent*, 23 August 1922.

22. Emmet Dalton interview with author 4/4/1974.

23. *Ibid.*

Chapter 12

1. Mrs Duggan, interview with author 27/7/t975. Mrs Duggan, Warrenscourt, and her husband Con Duggan were owners of Shanakiel Hospital. They still had the crucifix in their home as a memento, on date of interview. Also, Diarmuid Brennan's correspondence to Dr. Gerald Ahern, given to author to view and use.

2. Dr. Leo Ahern interview with author 18/5/1976. Dr. Leo Ahern said they had "a difficult journey" to Dublin as they had to make several detours due to road obstructions; also, his correspondence and Diarmuid Brennan's correspondence with Dr. Gerald Ahern.

3. Fr. Joe Ahern interview with author 4/9/1976. Some years later Fr. Joe Ahern was appointed canon in Aherla.

4. Dr. Gerald Ahern interview with author 24/4/1976 (brother of Dr. Leo Ahern); also correspondence to author. Dr Gerald lived for some time in Cork and

asked me to call anytime when passing, but just to let him know.

5. Letter from Hazel P. Smyth to author 15/1/1975. "The reason it was brought from Cork by boat was that the railways were disrupted at the time owing to the political situation ... the *Classic* was employed only intermittently on the Liverpool/Cork run from June 1921 to 1924, when it remained in the company for seven years."

6. Dalton wire to General Staff 9 am on 23/8/1922. M.P. P7/B/70/39.

7. Later Fr. Joseph Scannell was appointed Dean of Cork.

8. Ernest Blythe interview with author 9/1/1974.

9. Oliver St. John Gogarty, *As I Was Going Down Sackville Street*, p.183.

10. Ulick O'Connor, *Oliver St. John Gogarty*, p 205. According to O'Connor, during the early part of 1922, "Gogarty and Collins would drive out for tea" on evenings to W.T. Cosgrave's house at Beechpark. Here for a short period they would forget the problems of public life, and according to Cosgrave, "Collins would roar with laughter at Gogarty's

sallies, particularly when Gogarty said something more than usually irreverent that caused a shadow to flit across the face of the Vice President" – p. 202.

11. Ernest Blythe interview with author 9/1/1974.

12. Oliver St. John Gogarty, *As I Was Going Down Sackville Street*, p.183.

13. Ernest Blythe interview with author 9/1/1974.

14. Sir John Lavery, *The Life of a Painter*, pp. 216, 217.

15. Elizabeth, Countess of Fingall, *Seventy Years Young*, p. 408.

16. *Ibid*. 409.

17. Sir John Lavery, *The Life of a Painter*, p. 217.

18. *Ibid*.

19. Emmet Dalton interview with author 20/4/1974.

20. Daily newspapers. See also M.P. P7a/64. (Canon Seán Piggott remembers the large numbers of priests in black – not in soutanes. He said many Irish priests returned home from around the world to the funeral.)

21. Griffith's death only preceded Collins' by ten days.

Chapter 13

1. The author interviewed the following for details of what happened directly after the ambush, some of whom were not ambush participants: Jim Kearney, op. cit.; Timmy Sullivan, op. cit.; Bill Powell, op. cit.; Liam Deasy, op. cit.; Tom Kelleher, op. cit.; Seán Hyde, op. cit.; Pake Sheehan, op. cit.; Jim Doyle, 7/12/1974; Tom Barry, op. cit. – already cited; Con Murphy, op. cit.; Michael Murphy, op. cit.; Mary O'Neill Walsh, (Sonny O'Neill's sister. She confirmed to author that Sonny fired the fatal shot that killed Collins, and that Sonny was very forthcoming in telling her. "It was well known," she said.) 16/6/1974, also with Jim Kearney present 25/6/1974; Ned Galvin, 15/2/1974; Tom Taylor, 2/7/1975; Denis Lordan 7/7/1974; Jackie Murray, op. cit.; Tom Murray, op. cit.; Charlie Foley, op. cit.

2. Bill Powell interview with author 14/9/1974.

3. Liam Deasy interview with author 19/9/1973.

4. *Ibid.*

5. On the 24 August 1922, Tom Crofts sent a report to Liam Lynch, Chief of Staff, in which he found that six participants were engaged and that three extra "managed to get back ... the firing was terrific ... I have since learned that Ml. Collins was shot dead during the engagement." There is exaggeration and distortion in parts of this report, which was not seen by the public until 2005. [The author has not seen any account of Sonny Neill's "I dropped one man" in Liam Lynch's private papers. However, the author has knowledge that Liam Lynch was informed rather quickly of Sonny Neill's participation in the ambush by verbal dispatch.) For Crofts report: See, Michael Collins, p. 410, by Peter Hart.]

Chapter 14

1. Liam Lynch's original letter to Liam Deasy 28 August 1922, Military Archives, Cathal Brugha Barracks, Lot 4/3. Liam Lynch to Liam Deasy, Deasy private papers, 28 August 1922. See also M.P. P7a/81, and Eoin Neeson, *The Sunday Review*, 11 January 1959.

2. *Ibid.*

3. *Ibid.*

4. Collins memo, 10 Aug. 1922, M.P. P7/B/2.

∽ NOTES ∽

5. Frank Aiken to Richard Mulcahy, 27 Aug. 1922, M.P. P7a/178. Frank Aiken appealed to Mulcahy "to stop the struggle" and said he would "die in order to prove" his own sincerity and that of "the men opposed to you".

6. Piaras Béaslaí, *Michael Collins*, p. 436.

7. Jim Kearney interview with author 19/4/1974.

8. Timmy Sullivan interview with author 22/6/1974.

9. Emmet Dalton interview with author 20/4/1974; also Dalton's correspondence to author; See also Eoin Neeson, pp. 112–121.

10. Sometime after Collins' death a wooden cross was stuck into the soil beside the area where it was believed he fell. Later a local committee painted a cement stone with a black cross on it. This stone was erected at a part of the road which was reasonably wide, not where the cross initially was, but further down at the opposite side of the road from where Collins fell, and quite a distance north. (From the author's interviews with Jim Kearney & Timmy Sullivan, it was placed where they found the cap on the following morning.) It was beside this stone that the present monument was erected. Here an annual

commemoration ceremony is held as near as possible to 22 August.

11. Collins to O'Duffy, 17 Aug. 1922, M.P. P7/B/21/8.

12. Collins has a note in his diary, "To speak Capt. C. – unprepared escort." Wednesday, 23, August, 1922. Obviously, he intended taking the matter up with Captain Coghlan on his return to Portobello Barracks, M.P. P7a/62.

13. Emmet Dalton interview with author 20/4/1974.

14. Ernest Blythe interview with author 20/3/1974.

15. Jim Woulfe interview with author 9/3/1974.

16. Dr. Leo Ahern interview with author 20/5/1976. (I spent a considerable amount of time questioning Dr. Leo Ahern at his London flat.)

17. Dr. Michael Riordan details 7/3/1974.

18. Dr. Christy Kelly at his London home, a long interview with author 14/1/1974.

19. Dr. Gerald Ahern interview with author 29/4/1976, also many letters author received from Dr. Gerald

Ahern who wrote, 'I will help you clarify any questions you have'. He lived in Cork and, as this was near for me, we became good friends. Later he moved to London.

20. A representative of the late Dr. Cagney, 16/1/1976 (name withheld by request.)

21. Dr. Leo Ahern "remembers it quite clearly".

22. Dr. Leo Ahern interview with author 20/5/1976. Dr. Leo Ahern says he has no recollection of any great discussion with Dr. Gogarty who "had to get on with his task," while he (Dr. Leo) had to attend to other "pressing business in connection with the funeral".

23. Ulick O'Connor, *Oliver St. John Gogarty*, p.206.

24. Dr. Gerald Ahern interview with author 2/5/1976; we spent a considerable amount of time discussing these events.

25. Emmet Dalton, interview with Cathal O'Shannon, RTÉ documentary.

26. Ray Smith & Jim Nicoll, *The Irish Independent*, 20 May, 1971.

27. Oliver Snoddy letter to the author 9/4/1974

28. Oliver Snoddy letter to the author 21/5/1974

29. Brother Allen interview with author 3/4/1976.
30.
31. Edward C. Smith was an agent for a business firm in Cork, and was a past pupil of O'Connell School, Dublin, and close friend of Brother Allen.

32. Each house in a parish took and still takes a turn to have "The Stations".

33. Oliver Snoddy letter to the author 9/4/1974; also author interview with Nell O'Sullivan.

34. The author has a statement made by Tom Hales to his brother Major General Seán Hales: " ... The Column had pulled out of position and only a few men of a rearguard party were there when the car came in sight. They knew they had killed an officer of very high rank with one of the last shots fired but they had no idea who that officer was." Dated 22 August 1922.

35. Liam Deasy interview with author 19/9/1973. "We regretted the type of bullet used. These were picked up after ambushes during the Tan War," he said. Deasy

said that Sonny Neill personally described the event to the IRA's Chief Intelligence Officer, Seán Dowling, when he journeyed to West Cork in September 1922. This information was confirmed by Seamus O'Donovan, G.H.Q. – interview with author 5/6/1975.

36. Tom Barry interview with author 17/4/1976. Following his escape from Maryborough prison in Sept. 1922, Barry got full details of Collins' death. He told me, "Sonny Neill got Collins ..." The following also gave this information to the author: Jim Kearney, 31/3/1974; Timmy Sullivan, 12/5/1974; Tom Kelleher, 6/6/1974; Bill Powell, 15/3/1975; 29/11/1974; Denis Lordan, 7/7/1974; Seán Hyde 13/7/1974; Con Murphy 9/9/1974; Pat Buttimer, 6/6/1974; Dan Cahalane, 7/9/1977; 29/3/1975; Jim Doyle 18/4/1976; Mrs. Mary (Mollie) O'Neill Walsh (Sonny O'Neill's sister), 16/6/1974 – also with Jim Kearney present, on a second occasion. 24/6/1974.

Postscript

1. Tom Barry interview with author 10/4/1976; See also Tom Barry, *Guerilla Days in Ireland*; also Meda Ryan, *Tom Barry: IRA Freedom Fighter*; Pub: Mercier Press.

2. Emmet Dalton interview with author 20/3/1974.

3. *Ibid.*

4. Liam Lynch letter to his brother Tom, 27 October 1922. Lynch private family papers.

5. Free State Order, 7 October 1922:
   "If prisoners are taken they must not be released until they are incapable of further harm. If executions are necessary they must be carried out with no fear of the chimera of popular reaction."

6. Lord Longford and Thomas P. O'Neill, *Eamon de Valera*. p.201.

7. Liam Lynch letter to his brother Tom, 28 October 1922 – Liam Lynch private family papers.

8. Ernest Blythe interview with author 20/30/1974.

9. General Order, 30 November 1922. P7a/83, M.P. (Lynch wrote to the Provisional Government on 27 November: "As your Parliament and Army Headquarters well know, we on our side have at all times adhered to the recognised rules of warfare. In the early days of this war we took hundreds of your forces prisoner but accorded them all the right of

prisoners of war and, over and above, treated them as fellow countrymen and former comrades ... But the prisoners you have taken have been treated barbarously, and when helpless you have tortured, wounded and murdered them ...")

10. Richard Mulcahy signed the following order, 7 December, 1922: "You are hereby notified that being a person taken in arms against the Government, you will be executed at 8 am on Friday, 8 December, as a reprisal for the assassination of Brigadier Seán Hales T.D. in Dublin, on 7 December, on his way to a meeting of Dáil Éireann and as a solemn warning to those associated with you and who are engaged in a conspiracy of assassination against the representatives of the Irish people.
Richard Mulcahy, General Chief of Staff."

Bibliography

Primary Sources

Manuscript Sources University College Dublin, Archives
Ernest Blythe Papers
Richard Mulcahy Papers
Miscellaneous material

Trinity College, Dublin, Records Office,
Erskine Childers Papers

National Library of Ireland
Michael Collins Papers
Jim Kearney's Béal na Bláth Statement
Joseph McGarrity Papers
Kathleen MacKenna Napoli Papers
Manuscripts

Public Records
Records of the Ministry and Cabinet of Dáil Éireann in the State Paper Office, Dublin
Colonial Office Papers, Public Record Office, London

British Library Board Newspaper Library
Jim Kearney's Béal na Bláth Statement

Private Manuscripts
General Michael Collins, Note Books, held at time of interview by Michael Collins, nephew of General Michael Collins
Liam Lynch Papers
Jim Kearney Papers & Letters
Dr. Gerald Ahern Papers & letters.
Diarmuid Brennan's letters and documents.
Dr. Ned Barret Papers
Bill Hales Papers
Seán Hales Notes
Tom Hales Memoir & Hales Papers
D.V. Horgan Papers
Jim Hurley Statement & Notes
Author's Collection

Military Archives
Material received from Commandant Peter Young, Cathal Brugha Barracks, Dublin.
Jim Kearney's Béal na Bláth Statement

BBC Archives
Cork Public Museum, Archives
University College Dublin Archives
RTÉ Archives

BIBLIOGRAPHY

Newspapers & Periodicals

The Irish Times; The Irish Independent; The Freeman's Journal; The Irish Examiner; The Evening Echo; The Sunday Express; The Sunday Times; The Daily Sketch; The Daily Mail; The Sunday Review; The Sunday Independent; The Sunday Press; The Clare Champion; Clare County Express; The Limerick Leader; The Southern Star; The Nenagh Guardian; The Capuchin Annual; The Irish Political Review; An Phoblacht; An tÓglagh; The West Cork News; History Ireland.

Oral Testimony

My reliance has been on the many people who gave unselfishly of their time, some of whom allowed themselves to be quizzed rather vigorously on their observations of events at, and participation in and surrounding the Béal na mBláth ambush; their contribution has been essential. Their names are cited in the Acknowledgements and Notes.

Secondary Sources

Andrews, C.S. *Dublin Made Me.* Cork & Dublin: The Mercier Press, 1979

Barry, Tom. *Guerilla Days In Ireland,* Dublin: *Irish Press, 1949.*

Barry, Tom. *The Reality of the Anglo-Irish War, 1920-21, in West Cork: Refutations, Corrections and Comment on Liam Deasy "Towards Ireland Free".* Tralee, 1974.

Béaslaí, Piaras. *Michael Collins and the Making of a New Ireland,* Dublin: The Phoenix Publishing Co. 1926.

Bell, J. Bowyer. *The Secret Army.* Dublin: Poolbeg, 1989.

Bennet, George. *The History of Bandon*. Cork: Frances Guy, 1869.

Bennett, Richard. *The Black and Tans*. London: New English Library, 1970.

Borgonovo, John. *Florence and Josephine O'Donoghue's War of Independence: A Destiny that Shapes Our Ends*, Dublin 2006.

Boyce, D.G. *Nationalism in Ireland*. London, 1982.

Bowman, John. *De Valera and the Ulster Question*. 1917-73. Oxford: Oxford University Press, 1982.

Brady, A. J. S. *The Briar of Life* (undated)

Breen, Dan. *My Fight For Irish Freedom*. Tralee: Anvil Books Ltd, 1964, 1982.

Brennan, Michael. *The War in Clare. 1911-1921*. Dublin 1980.

Butler, Ewan. *Barry's Flying Column*. London: Burns & Oates, 1961.

Brinton, Crane. *The Anatomy of Revolution*. London 1953.

Collins, Michael. *The Path To Freedom*. Cork & Dublin: The Mercier Press, 1968.

Coogan, Tim Pat. *Ireland Since the Rising*, London: Pall Mall, 1966.

Coogan, Tim Pat. *The I.R.A*. London: Fontana, 1971.

Coogan, Tim Pat. *Michael Collins: A Biography*, London, 1990.

Coogan, Tim Pat, *The Twelve Apostles*, London: Head of Zeus, 2016.

Connell Jnr., Joseph E.A. *Michael Collins: Dublin 1916–22*, Dublin: Wordwell Ltd., 2017.

BIBLIOGRAPHY

Connell Jnr., Joseph E.A. *Dublin in Rebellion: A Directory 1913 – 1923*: Dublin : The Lilliput Press: 2006 & 2009.

Cronin, Seán. *The McGarrity Papers,* Tralee: Anvil Books, 1972.

Crozier, Brigadier General F.P. *Ireland Forever.* London: Cape, 1932.

Curran, J. M. *The Birth of the Irish Free State.* 1921-1923, U.S.A.: Alabama 1980.

Deasy, Liam. *Towards Ireland Free.* Cork & Dublin: The Mercier Press, 1979.

Deasy, Liam. *Brother Against Brother.* Cork & Dublin: The Mercier Press, 1982.

Doherty, Gabriel & Keogh, Dermot. *De Valera's Irelands,* Cork: Mercier Press 2003.

Dwyer, T. Ryle. *Eamon de Valera*, Dublin: Gill & Macmillan, 1980.

Dwyer, T. Ryle. *Michael Collins and the Treaty: His Differences with de Valera.* Cork & Dublin: The Mercier Press, 1981.

Dwyer, T. Ryle. *Michael Collins and the Civil War*, Cork: Mercier Press, 2012.

Farrell, Michael. *Northern Ireland,* The Orange State. London 1975.

Feehan, John M. *The Shooting of Michael Collins – Murder or Accident?* Dublin & Cork: Mercier Press, 1981.

Feehan, John M. *The Shooting of Michael Collins* (with extra chapter "Did Sonny O'Neill shoot Michael Collins?") Cork: Royal Carbery Books, 1991.

Ferriter, Diarmaid. *Ambiguous Republic: Ireland in the 1917s,* London, 2012.

Ferriter, Diarmaid. *A Nation Not a Rabble: The Irish Revolution, 1913–1923*. London, 2015.

Ferriter, Diarmaid, *Between Two Hells: The Irish Civil War*. Profile Books, London 2021.

Fingall, Elizabeth, Countess. *Seventy Years Young*. London: Collins, 1937.

Forester, Margery. *Michael Collins: The Lost Leader*. London: Sidgwick & Jackson, 1971.

Gaughan, J.A. *Austin Stack: Portrait of a Separatist*. Dublin 1977.

Gogarty, Oliver St. John. *As I Was Going Down Sackville Street*: Rich & Cowen, London, 1937.

Greaves, C.D. *Liam Mellows and the Irish Revolution:* London: Lawrence & Wishart, 1971.

Hanley, Brian, *The IRA:1926-1936*. Four Courts Press Ltd., Dublin, 2002.

Hanley, Brian, *The IRA: A Documentary History, 1916–2005*: Dublin, 2010.

Hart, Peter. *Mick: The Real Michael Collins*, London and Oxford: Macmillian, 2005.

Hopkinson, Michael. *Green Against Green*. Dublin: Gill & Macmillan, 1988.

Kee, Robert. *Ourselves Alone (Green Flag)*. Vol. 3. London: Quartet Books, 1976.

Lankford, Siobhán, *The Hope and the Sadness*: Cork, 1980.

Lavery, Sir John, *The Life of a Painter*, London: Cassell, 1940.

Lawlor, Sheila. *Britain and Ireland, 1914-23*, Dublin: Gill & Macmillan, 1983.

Longford, Earl of, and O'Neill, Thomas P. *Éamon de Valera*. Dublin: Gill & Macmillan, 1970.

Lyons, F.S. *Ireland Since the Famine*. London: Collins/Fontana, 1973.

Macardle, Dorothy. *The Irish Republic.* London: Corgi, 1968.

Macready, General Sir Nevil. *Annals of an Active Life*. London: Hutchinson, 1942.

MacDowall, Vincent, *Michael Collins and the Irish Republican Brotherhood*: Dublin 1997.

MacEoin, Uinseann, Ed. *Survivors*. Argenta Publications, Dublin 1980.

Morrison, George. *The Irish Civil War: An Illustrated History*, Dublin 1981.

Murphy, Brian, P. *Patrick Pearse and the Lost Republican Ideal*, Dublin: James Duffy & Company, 1991.

Murphy, Brian P. *The Origins & Organization of British Propaganda in Ireland 1920*, Cork: Aubane Historical Society & Spin Watch, 2006.

Murphy, Gerald. *The Great Cover-Up: the Truth about the Death of Michael Collins*: The Collins Press, Cork, 2018.

Murphy, John A. *Ireland in the Twentieth Century*. Dublin: Gill & Macmillan, 1975.

Neeson, Eoin. *The Civil War 1922-1923*. Dublin: Poolbeg, 1989.

Neeson, Eoin. *The Life & Death of Michael Collins*. Cork & Dublin: The Mercier Press, 1968.

Neligan, Dave. *The Spy in the Castle*. London: MacGibbon

& Kee, 1968.

O'Broin, Leon. *Michael Collins*. Dublin: Gill & Macmillan, 1980.

O'Broin, Leon, Ed. *In Great Haste: The Letters of Michael Collins and Kitty Kiernan*. Dublin: Gill & Macmillan, 1983.

Ó Braoin, Pádraig, *Michael Ó Coileáin*, Cork, 1985.

O'Connor, Batt, *With Michael Collins in the Fight for Irish Independence*. London: Peter Davis, 1929.

O'Connor, Ulick. *A Terrible Beauty is Born*. London: Hamish Hamilton, 1975.

O'Connor, Ulick. *Oliver St. John Gogarty*. London: Granada, 1981.

O'Donoghue, Florence. *No Other Law*. Dublin: The Irish Press Ltd., 1956.

O'Halloran, Clare. *Partition and the Limits of Irish Nationalism*. Dublin: Gill & Macmillan, 1987.

O'Hegarty, P.S. *The Victory of Sinn Féin*. Dublin: Talbot Press, 1924.

O'Mahony, Edward. *Michael Collins, His Life and Times*. Online, 1996.

O'Malley, Ernie. *On Another Man's Wound*. Tralee: Anvil Books, 1972.

O'Malley, Ernie. *The Singing Flame*. Tralee: Anvil Books, 1978.

O'Malley, Ernie. *The Men Will Talk to Me: West Cork Interviews*: Cork: Mercier Press, 2015.

Ó Ruaric, Pádraig Óg, *Truce: Murder Myth and The Last Days of The Irish War Of Independence*, Cork: Mercier Press 2016.

Pakenham, Frank. *Peace by Ordeal.* London: Sidgwick & Jackson, 1972.

Ryan, Desmond. *Seán Treacy and the Third Tipperary Brigade, I.RA.* Tralee 1945.

Ryan, Meda. *The Tom Barry Story.* Cork & Dublin: Mercier Press, 1982.

Ryan, Meda. *Liam Lynch: The Real Chief.* Cork & Dublin: Mercier Press, 1986.

Ryan, Meda. *The Day Michael Collins Was Shot*, Poolbeg Press, Dublin, 1989.

Ryan, Meda, *Michael Collins and the Women Who Spied for Ireland*, Cork: Mercier Press, 1996 & 2006.

Ryan, Meda. *Tom Barry: IRA Freedom Fighter*, Cork: Mercier Press, 2003, & 2006.

Ryan, Meda, *Liam Lynch: The Real Chief.* Mercier Press, 2012.

Ryan, Meda. *Thomas Kent: 16 Lives:* Dublin, The O'Brien Press, 2016.

Shakespeare, Sir Geoffery. *Let Candles Be Brought In.* London: MacDonald, 1949.

Sigerson, S.M., *The Assassination of Michael Collins*, Amazon.com, 2014.

Talbot, Hayden. *Michael Collins' Own Story.* London: Hutchinson, 1923.

Taylor, Rex. *Michael Collins: The Big Fellow.* London: Four Square, 1961.

Taylor, Rex. *Assassination.* London:1961.

Twohig, Patrick J. *The Dark Secret of Bealnablath.* Cork: Tower Books, 1991.

White, Gerry and O'Shea, Brendan. *Baptised In Blood*, Cork: Mercier Press, 2005.

Younger, Calton. *Ireland's Civil War*. London: Muller Ltd, 1968, Fontana Books, 1970.

INDEX

A

Ahern, Dr. Gerald, xxi, xxii, xxx, 37, 41, 71, 84, 157, 190-1, 206, 322n19
Ahern, Fr. Joe, 157,159
Ahern, Dr. Leo, 41, 153-7, 163, 189-93, 314n19
Aherne, Bill, 27
Aiken, Frank, 178, 321n5
Allen, Brother William, 195-8
Amalgamated National Aid Association and Volunteer Dependants' Fund, 9
    ambushes, 10, 13, 94, 105-6, 176, 178, 211, 226
    army split, 20-1
Ashe, Thomas, 9

B

Banim, Mr., 198
banks, 35, 72-75
Barrett, Dick, 259
Barrett, Ned, 94
Barrie, Sir James, 4
Barry, Billy, 227, 240-247
Barry, Tom, 13, 20, 22, 92, 110-11, 135, 207, 217, 226-7, 234, 238, 255
Béal na mBláth
    ambush 128-147
    barricade, 100, 177
    death of Collins, 142
    Collins' cap, 40-3, 145, 158, 175, 188, 194-9, 220, 222, 224
    mines, 100, 75, 77, 95-8, 126
    planned, 95-105
    Republican dispersal, 125
    Republican meeting planned, 83-85
    ricochet theory, 187
    theories, discussion of, 183-188
    traitor theory, 181
Bernard, Fr. Denis, 197
Birkenhead, Lord, 18, 277n14, 288n5
Black and Tans, xviii, 185
Bloody Sunday 1920, 195
Blythe, Ernest, 25, 29, 64, 160-1, 167, 182, 206, 260
Boland, Harry, 35-36
Breen, Dan, 51-2, 64

Brennan, Diarmuid, xxii, xxx, xxxi, 71, 84
Brennan, Joseph, 74
Brennan, Michael, 64
Brien, Dinny, 140, 144, 169-71, 188
Broy, Ned, 9, 44
Brugha, Cathal, 16, 195, 201, 277
Buttimer, Pat, 127, 172, 220, 222

C

Cagney, Dr. Patrick, 190, 196
Dan Cahalane, 226
Cahalane, James, 108-9
Cairo Gang, 11
Callaghan, John, 101-4, 127-137, 140, 143, 170-5, 180, 188, 203, 211, 226
Carmody, Jim, 151
Childers, Erskine, 36, 75, 82-3, 85, 258
Churchill, Winston, 16-7, 20, 28-9, 34, 117, 168
Civic Guards, 31, 65, 71, 75
Civil War
  begins 29
  casualties, 256
  executions and reprisals, 259
  ends 261
Clancy, Peadar, 195
Clarke, Joseph I. C. , 275n3
Clarke, Tom, 6
Clune, Conor, 195
Coakley, Fr. Jeremiah, 197-8
Coghlan, Captain, 182, 322n12
Collins, Hannah, 201
Collins, Jeremiah, 113, 117
Collins, Johnny, 3, 110, 113, 115, 117-8, 165, 166
Collins, Kathy, 3
Collins, Maurice, 108, 120-2
Collins, Michael
  sporting prowess, 1, 2
  childhood, 1-2, 113-7
  begins work in London, 2
  IR membership, 3
  Easter Rising, 6
  interned in Frongoch, 8
  released, 8
  arrest, jumps bail, 10
  Supreme Council IRB, 9
  Sinn Fèin seat, 10
  War of Independence, 10
  intelligence network, 10
  Cairo Gang assassinations, 11
  Treaty negotiations, 15-17
  Northern Ireland, 21, 29, 34, 44, 47, 118
  Four Courts, 20, 23-5, 27-8

INDEX

Wilson assassination, 24
Commander in Chief, 31-2,
personality, 45-6
Griffith's death, 49
illness, 55-57
ambushed Dublin, 56-7
begins inspection tour of country, 47
Cork banks inspected, 72-3
Macroom, 58-9
leaves Cork, 87
Bandon, 92-3, 119
Clonakilty, 108
Skibbereen, 111
Rosscarbery, 109
Sam's Cross, 113-7
Béal na mBláth, 128-147
See also Béal na mBláth death, 141-2
unregistered, xxviii, xxxiv, 41
cap of, 40-3, 145, 158, 175, 188, 194-9, 220-4
revolver of, 43, 145, 196
post-mortem, 156
body taken to Dublin, 159
Cobh lights in honour of, 159
North Wall reception, 160-1
embalming, 161-2
Death mask, 162
lying-in-state, 165-6
funeral, 166-8
theories concerning death, 183-8
bullet used and wound, 175, 176, 188, 191
Collins, Michael (cousin), 78
Collins, Patrick, 6
Collins-Powell, Mary, 37-8, 68
Collins-Powell, Seán, 68
Comyn, Mr., 252
Conlon, Peadar, 76, 88
Conlon, Peter, 60
Conroy, Captain, 59, 60, 89, 90, 149, 154
Conscription, 5, 10
Cooney, Thomas, 60, 153, 244
Coote, Wally, 60, 145
Coppinger, Lieutenant, 76
Corbett, Archdeacon, 66-7
Corcoran, Patrick, 78
Corry, M.B., 60, 87, 138, 180
Cosgrave, W.T., 25, 31, 33, 50, 56, 71, 74, 123, 167-8, 194, 198, 229, 256, 258, 317n10
Craig, Gardner & Co., 6
Creedon (Lankford), Siobhán, 104-5, 304n12
Crofts, Tom, 101, 174, 236-7, 246, 270, 272-3, 320n5
Crosbie, Tom, 72

Crowley, Dinny, 95
Crowley, Jim, 272
Crowley, John, 1-2
Cullen, Tom, 24
Cumann na rnBan, 6, 103, 111, 241-2
Cumann na nGaedhael, 262
Customs and Excise funds, 71, 73

D

Dáil Éireann, 15, 18-20, 56, 75-6, 96, 123, 168, 256-9, 262, 277, 327
Treaty debate, 15-6
postponement proposed, 123
Dalton, Charlie, 150
Dalton, Emmet, 17, 27, 34-8, 43, 48, 52-3, 67-78, 86-9, 94, 106-8, 112-3, 119, 1214, 128, 134, 136-8, 141-56, 158-160, 166, 179-182, 186, 192, 194, 197, 256
Daly, Liam, 93, 198
Davies, Crompton Llewylen, 4
Davies, Moira O'Connor, 4
de Valera, Éamon,
Béal na mBláth, 79-85, 96-98
Mallow, 104-5
Republican President, 257
Unconditional surrender, 261
Civil War ends, 261
turns to political means, 262
de Valera, Sinéad, 12
Deasy, Liam, 13-4, 80-3, 95, 97, 99, 100-4, 122, 127, 137, 143, 170-4, 177, 180, 200-21, 228, 231-7, 260
Dempsey, Pat, 227, 243
Dolan, Joe, 23, 60, 65, 69, 86, 138, 144, 167, 192, 233
Donoghue, Mike, 139
Donoghue, Seán, 240
Dowling, Séan, 324n34
Dublin Castle, 9, 11, 233
Duggan, Fr. T.F., 123, 228
Duggan, Prof Lucy, 123
Dunne, Reginald, 23-9, 50

E

Easter Rising 1916, 6, 8
Ennis, Tom, 99, 186, 240, 256

F

Farrell, Tim, 246
Fingall, Elizabeth Countess of, 54, 56, 162
FitzGerald, Desmond, 73, 161
Flood, Commdt., 66
Flynn, Jimmy, 96, 98

Fogarty, Dr., 165, 167
Foley, Charles, 246
Foley, Charlie, 125, 129, 216
Foley, Tom, 100, 125, 129, 175, 214, 215, 216
Forbes, Matron, 156
Forester, Margery, 23
Fortune, Jimmy 'Wiggy', 60, 183-4
Four Courts occupation, 20, 23-30
   shelling of, 29
Free State Army
   See National Army

G

Gaelic Athletic Association (GAA), 2
Gaelic League, 3
Galvin, Ned, 85
general election 1922, 10
   Gogarty, Oliver St. John, 160-2, 190-1, 317n10
Golden, Peter, 79, 80
Gough, Peter, 60, 153, 244
Grey, Jim, 227, 243
Griffith, Arthur, 15, 19, 24-5, 39, 49, 50-51, 63, 80-1, 168, 264, 287n127
   Treaty, 15
   President, 19
   Wilson assassination, 24
   death, 49

H

Hales, Bill, 3
Hales, Bob, 3
Hales, Dónal, 13, 14, 229
Hales, Madge, 14, 229, 277n17
Hales, Seán, 8, 36, 42-3, 61, 94, 119, 120-2, 198, 200, 206, 226, 229
   shot, 259
Hales, Tom, 13, 41-3, 97-106, 126-9, 147, 173-4, 195-6, 202, 206, 214, 216, 222-3, 229, 272
Hannigan, Commdt. General, 51
Hayes, Kathy, 111
Hayes, Michael, 46
Hayes, Mr., 51
Healy, Captain T. 253
Healy, Tim, 24
Hegarty, Diarmuid, 63
Hogan, William, 71, 75
Holland, Dan, 127, 172, 236-7, 242
Houlihan, Bill, 260-1
Hurley, Jim, 126, 129-30, 137-8, 143, 173, 203, 211, 225, 237
Hyde, Seán, 83, 88, 95, 271, 310

I

Irish Free State
declared, 259
Irish Republican Army (IRA)
See Irregulars
Irish Republican Brotherhood
(IRB), 3, 6, 9, 10, 14, 21-6, 109

K

Kavanagh, Joe, 11
Kavanagh, Seán, 161
Kearney, Jim, 41, 99, 100-4, 127-8, 130, 140, 143-4, 169-75, 179-80, 186, 188, 195-7, 202-231
Kearney, Pete, 127, 137, 139-147, 172, 180, 211, 236-7
Kelleher, Timmy, xxiii, 88-94
Kelleher, Tom, 126, 128-30, 137-8, 143, 148, 173, 203, 209-10, 212, 219-28, 236-7, 243, 247, 250
Kelly, Dr. Christy, xxxi, xxxiii, 156-8, 190-1, 196
Kelly, Thomas, 47
Kennedy, Jerry, 247
Kieran, Kitty, 12, 16, 35, 163-4, 168

L

Langford, Dick, 83, 301n10
Langford, Riobárd, 82-5, 301n10
Lavery, Lady Hazel, 4, 17-8, 50-1, 54-7, 162, 168, 288n5
Lavery, Sir John, 4, 17, 50, 56-7, 162, 164
Legion of Irish Ex-Servicemen, 34
Leigh Doyle family, 55
Lloyd George, David, 4, 15, 17, 27-8, 106
Long, Dinny "The Dane", 91, 95, 100
Long's pub, 90-1, 95, 97, 100, 125-7, 174, 216, 270-1
Lordan, John, 100, 127-9, 147, 171-2, 272
Lynch, Fionán, 31, 58, 60, 61, 181
Lynch, Liam, 14, 29, 22, 29, 44, 80, 83, 85, 95, 104, 172, 174, 177, 206, 228-9, 256-8, 260-1
Lyons, Denis, 1, 109
Lyons, Private, 59

M

Mac Diarmada, Seán, 6
McCarthy, Fr. Dick, 64
McCarthy, Jerh., 3, 112
McDonnell, Mr ., 25
Mac Eoin, Seán, 14
McGarrity, Joe, 258
McGarry, Seán, 200
McGowen, Jimmy, 61

McGrath, Joe, 6, 9, 30-1, 53, 56, 59, 61, 181-2, 264
McKee, Dick, 195
McKelvey, Joseph, 22, 195, 259
McKenna, Joseph, 193-4
McKenna, Kathleen Napoli, 16
MacNamara, James, 11
McPeak, Frank, 252
McPeak, Jock, 60, 87, 129-137, 140, 184-7, 193, 227, 240-254
Macready, General, 28, 168
Maguire, Sam, 3, 9, 23, 26, 275n2
Maryborough prison, 47, 253-4
Mellows, Liam, 22, 259
Moylan, Seán, 14, 22
Moynihan, Jamie, 246-7
Mulcahy, Richard, 30, 32-3, 46-8, 55, 63, 65, 77, 167, 178, 228, 255-6, 259
Mulqueen, Anna, 240-244
Murphy, Con, 171
Murphy, Jerh., 90
Murphy, Michael, 82
Murphy, Tim, 149
Murphy, Fr. Timothy, 149, 172
Murray, Bill, 85, 95, 97, 139, 169, 171-4, 195, 197
Murray, Jackie, 99
Murray, Jim, 41, 173, 195, 197
Murray, Pat, 197
Murray, Tom, 99

N

National Army, 20, 33, 45,49, 70, 80, 132, 160, 202, 233, 240, 242, 244, 248, 250, 252, 255
Neill, Denis 'Sonny', 98-9, 140-1, 143, 169-75, 188-9, 192, 199, 200, 216, 221, 223, 231-236
Neligan, David, 11,13, 206

O

Ó Muirthile, Seán, 135
O'Brien, Fr., 113
O'Brien, Jerh.'The Leaguer', 100, 126
O'Brien, Michael, 110-8
O'Brien, Nancy, 10
O'Connell, J. J. (Ginger), 28
O'Connell, John, 107-8
O'Connell, Seán (Paddy), 130, 142, 144-9, 153-4, 180
O'Connor, Rory, 20, 22-3, 28, 259
O'Connor, Ulick, 27, 191
O'Donoghue, Florence, 77, 88, 123, 156, 236
O'Donovan, Anne Lehane, 111

O'Donovan, Dan 'Sando', 82
O'Donovan Rossa, Jeremiah, 3, 109
O'Driscoll, Margaret Collins, 2
O'Driscoll, Patrick, 168
O'Duffy, Eoin, 14, 32, 33, 48, 51-3, 63-6, 181
O'Friel, Frank, 78, 154
O'Galvin, Seán, 172, 237
O'Higgins, Kevin, 55, 167, 264
O' Kane, John, 18
O'Keeffe, Dan, 67
O'Leary, James, 79
O'Mahony, Tom, 123
Ó Máille, Pádraic, 259
O'Reilly, Joe, 57-9, 163-4, 167
O'Riordan, Dr. Michael, 156
O'Shannon, Cathal, 192
O'Sullivan, Gearóid, 135
O'Sullivan, General, 252
O'Sullivan, John Joe, 198-9
O'Sullivan, John L, 21, 90,91-2
O'Sullivan, Joseph, 23-9, 50, 119, 122
O'Sullivan, Nell, 198
O'Sullivan, Paddy, 82
O'Sullivan, Tadhg, 100,171-2, 174, 272
O'Sullivan, Ted, 246

P

Pearse, Pádraig, 81

Pelly, Mr, 109
Percival, Major A. E., 110-1, 223
Piggott, Fr. Sean, 163, 167
Plunkett, Sir Horace, 54, 56, 59
Plunkett, Joseph, 6
Portlaoise Barracks, 47, 62, 253
Powell, Bill, 81, 97, 211,127, 129, 147,171-2
Powell, Patrick, 71
Power, Albert, 161
Prout, J. T., 52
Provisional Government, 168

Q

Quinn, M, 60, 87, 91, 138, 147

R

Riordan, Dr. Michael, 156, 190
Robertson, John, 251
Roche, Dr., Abp. Cloyne, 66-7
Russell, Pilot Commandant, 50, 72
Ryan, Jerry, 65
Ryan-Hervey, Peter, 73

S

Scannell, Fr. Joseph, 159
Shaw, G.B., 4, 54, 56, 201
Shaw, Mrs G.B., 162

Sheehan, Maggie, 83, 85
Sheehan, Pake, 82
Sheehy, Jack, 93
Sliabh na mBan, xxxii, 60-1, 67, 76, 87, 131, 154, 180, 185-7, 196, 227, 240-2, 247-9
Smith, Edward C., 196
Smith, John J., 65, 86, 91, 93, 124, 126,128,132, 144-8, 193
Snoddy, Oliver, 194-6
Somerville, Edith, 112
Squad, The, 11, 165
Stack, Austin, 16
Stapleton. Captain, 50
Sullivan, Joe, 84
Sullivan, John, L, 36, 119, 122
Sullivan, John (2), 198, 199
Sullivan, Joseph, 23-9, 50
Sullivan, Mick, 247
Sullivan, Captain Tadhg, 84-3
Sullivan, Tadhg, 100, 112, 172, 174, 242
Sullivan, Timmy, 41, 99, 100, 104, 127-31, 133, 137, 140-3, 169-75, 179, 180, 186, 188, 195, 207, 211, 216, 226-9, 261-215, 77, 150
Sullivans, Gurranreagh, 83
Sweeney, Joe, 59

T

Thornton, Frank, 64
Tobin, Acting Major-General, 36
Traynor, Oscar, 30
Treaty negotiations, 15-9
truce, 14, 15
Twomey, May, 103, 240-3

W

Walsh, Batt, 272
Walsh, Paddy, 272
Walsh, Mary O'Neill Walsh, 232
War of Independence, 10, 21, 44-5, 52, 70, 83, 88, 92, 109, 135, 138, 160, 164, 171, 175-6, 202, 223, 230, 232, 235-6, 259
Waters, Tom, 62
White, Anne, 172
Wilson, Sir Henry
  assassination, 23-8, 50, 62
Winter, Colonel Sir Arthur, 11
Woulfe, Jim, xxiii, 60-1, 87, 89, 112, 131-3, 136, 138, 144, 147, 154, 183-4
Woods, Richard, 83, 85
World War I, 232

Y

Young, Peter, 198

If you enjoyed this book from Poolbeg why not visit our website

WWW.POOLBEG.COM

and get another book delivered straight to your home or to a friend's home.
<u>All books despatched within 24 hours.</u>

FREE SHIPPING on orders over €15 in Rep. of Ireland*

Why not join our mailing list at www.poolbeg.com and get some fantastic offers, competitions, author interviews, new releases and much more?

POOLBEG ON SOCIAL MEDIA

- @PoolbegBooks
- poolbegbooks
- www.facebook.com/poolbegpress

*Free shipping on Ireland on orders over €15 and Europe on orders over €65.